SOCIO-HISTORICAL EXAMINATION OF RELIGION AND MINISTRY:
A JOURNAL OF THE GLOBAL CENTER FOR RELIGIOUS RESEARCH

VOL. 5, NO. 1
SUMMER 2023

I0105813

SHERM

Copyright © 2023

www.shermjournal.org

ISSN 2637-7519 (print)
ISSN 2637-7500 (online)
ISBN 978-1-959281-12-2 (print)
ISBN 978-1-959281-13-9 (eBook)

GCRR Press
1312 17th Street Suite 549
Denver, CO 80202
www.gcrr.org

Printed copies of this issue are available for purchase on the GCRR website at: www.gcrr.org/products

General Editor:
Darren M. Slade, PhD

Editorial Advisory Board:
Abimbola A. Adelakun, PhD
Abbas Aghdassi, PhD
Gbenga Emmanuel Afolayan, MA
Peter Antoci, PhD
Robert Gregory Cavin, PhD
Mike Clawson, PhD
Sandra Cohen, MaHL
Carlos Colombetti, PhD
Jack David Eller, PhD
Evan Fales, PhD
Anthony Gill, PhD
Ken Howard, MDiv, MEd
Mark A. Moore, PhD
Josfin Raj S.B, MDiv, ThM
Elisa Robyn, PhD

Typesetter/Copyeditor:
Kimberly Dell
Christian Farren

Socio-Historical Examination of Religion and Ministry (SHERM Journal) is a biannual (not-for-profit) peer-reviewed academic journal that publishes the latest social-scientific, historiographic, and ecclesiastic research on religious institutions and their ministerial practices. SHERM is dedicated to the critical and scholarly inquiry of historical and contemporary religious phenomena, both from within particular religious traditions and across cultural boundaries, so as to inform the broader socio-historical analysis of religion and its related fields of study.

The purpose of SHERM Journal is to provide a scholarly medium for the social-scientific study of religion where specialists can publish advanced studies on religious trends, theologies, rituals, philosophies, socio-political influences, or experimental and applied ministry research in the hopes of generating enthusiasm for the vocational and academic study of religion while fostering collegiality among religion specialists. Its mission is to provide academics, professionals, and nonspecialists with critical reflections and evidence-based insights into the socio-historical study of religion and, where appropriate, its implications for ministry and expressions of religiosity.

TABLE OF CONTENTS

VOL. 5, NO. 1
SUMMER 2023

TABLE OF CONTENTS
-CONTINUED-

VOL. 5, NO. 1
SUMMER 2023

Percentage of U.S. Adults Suffering from Religious Trauma: A Sociological Study

Darren M. Slade,
Global Center for Religious Research

Adrianna Smell,
Case Western Reserve University

Elizabeth Wilson,
Somatic Trauma Therapist

Rebekah Drumsta,
The Vashti Initiative

Abstract: *This sociological study aimed to ascertain the percentage of adults living in the United States who have experienced religious trauma (RT) and what percentage presently suffer from RT symptoms now. After compiling data from 1,581 adults living in the United States, this study concludes it is likely that around one-third (27–33%) of U.S. adults (conservatively) have experienced religious trauma at some point in their life. That number increases to 37% if those suffering from any three of the six major RT symptoms are included. It is also likely that around 10–15% of U.S. adults currently suffer from religious trauma if only the most conservative numbers are highlighted. Nonetheless, since 37% of the respondents personally know people who potentially suffer from RT, and 90% of those respondents know between one and ten people who likely suffer from RT, then it could be argued that as many as one-in-five (20%) U.S. adults presently suffer from major religious trauma symptoms.*

Keywords: Religious Trauma, Adverse Religious Experiences, Spiritual Abuse, Religious Abuse, Religious Trauma Syndrome

Introduction

L eading into the twenty-first century, physician Martin Rossman noticed a disturbing trend among his patients: many were suffering from the lifelong consequences of being raised in a toxic religious environment. He wrote, "A great number of people I see in my medical practice have been traumatized rather than uplifted by their early religious training. I think that

Socio-Historical Examination of Religion and Ministry
Volume 5, Issue 1, Summer 2023   shermjournal.org
© Darren M. Slade; Adrianna Smell; Elizabeth Wilson; Rebekah Drumsta
Permissions: editor@shermjournal.org
ISSN 2637–7519 (print), ISSN 2637–7500 (online)
https://doi.org/10.33929/sherm.2023.vol5.no1.01 (article)

GLOBAL
CENTER for
GCRR RELIGIOUS
RESEARCH
ACADEMIC INSTITUTE

harmful religious training may be one of the great unrecognized causes of mental and physical illness in our culture."[1] Although at the time he did not have a psychological or medical term for what he was witnessing, Rossman's experiential assessment (and prediction) about the pervasiveness of what is now understood to be religious trauma would turn out to be quite accurate. After compiling data from 1,581 adults living in the United States (U.S.), this study confirmed what Rossman and thousands of other practitioners have observed for decades: religious trauma is, in fact, a society-wide phenomenon and spiritual abuse is a chronic problem within religious communities.[2]

Study Rationale and Research Question

One problem is that the label "religious trauma" (RT) has remained ambiguously defined in much of the peer-reviewed literature, making it difficult for clinicians to identify and treat patients presenting with RT symptoms.[3] To make things more complicated, the literature simply assumes that so-called "religious trauma" exists with little or no supporting empirical data. Indeed, most discussions on religious trauma have relied on qualitative research that focuses almost solely on individual experiences through case-studies and interviews. Thus, this article intends to correct the gap in quantitative knowledge by presenting findings from the most exhaustive sociological study on religious trauma to date, which was funded and carried out by the Global Center for Religious Research (GCRR). The purpose of this study was to discover if RT was a society-wide occurrence or simply an affliction that only a few disaffiliated religionists have mentioned in therapy.

The research question for the study is as follows: "What percentage of adults living in the United States have experienced religious trauma at some point in their life and what percentage currently suffer from religious trauma symptoms?" The hypothesis is that about 15–20% of the adult population have suffered from RT while about 5–10% currently suffer from RT symptoms. Before summarizing the study's collection and analysis methodology, it is important first to define the terms used in the study.

---

[1] Rossman, *Guided Imagery for Self-Healing*, 200–1.

[2] Despite the reckless (and uninformed) claim by Brad Wilcox and Riley Peterson that "few people suffer trauma from religion in childhood" (Wilcox and Peterson, "Perspective: Don't Believe the Headlines").

[3] This article will use the term "religious trauma" and the abbreviation "RT" interchangeably as a simple method to variegate both the language and grammar of the essay.

Defining Religious Trauma

With the exception of a few vague or improvised characterizations today, most references to the term "religious trauma" in popular literature have received no official or clinically-justifiable definition, and the references often appear only in relation to religious fundamentalism.[4] However, a psychological use of the term "religious trauma" has existed since at least 1952, as illustrated in Theodore Hoffman's book review of *The Man Outside* by Wolfgang Borchert. Here, Hoffman described the protagonist character, Beckmann (from Borchert's play, *Draußen vor der Tür*), who appears to suffer from post-traumatic stress disorder and wants to commit suicide. Instrumental to his play is the quest for healing when confronted with religion-induced despair and failed religious expectations. Hoffman's review states,

> The style used to present the action brilliantly illuminates the central question of Beckmann's right to suicide, but with it comes a hazy religious trauma to which the play probably owes its success in Germany. Borchert's constant preoccupation with exclusion, with being denied the world inside the door, leads him to metaphysical violence. God is reviled for His impotence, and indeed appears in the play as a feeble old man....The play ends in rhetorical nihilism, with Beckmann challenging God to exist.[5]

Though not intending to be a psychological commentary, Hoffman neatly characterized what would later be labeled "religious trauma" among clinicians.[6] Only recently, from the 1990s onward, have specialists started using the term as a clinical descriptor for the powerful psychological complications that have

---

[4] Cf. Fox, "Adverse Religious Experiences and LGBTQ+ Adults," 10–11. The term "religious fundamentalism" is loosely defined here as a diverse and ever-changing federation of cobelligerents within different religious traditions that display militancy, sectarianism, and dogmatic absolutism as their most distinctive characteristics (See Slade, *The Logic of Intersubjectivity*, 13, 41–70).

[5] Hoffman, book review of *The Man Outside*, 22.

[6] From the 1960s through the 1980s (with sporadic instances in the 1990s and early 2000s), the phrase "religious trauma" was mostly used in relation to the overarching social, political, and economic upheaval that occurred from European contact with Islam and the violence of the Protestant Reformation (see for example, Oldfield, *The Problem of Tolerance and Social Existence*, 33). The term was likewise used as a substitute for people's life-altering religious conversion experiences or a more general societal religious fervor (see for example, Noon, "Frederic Dan Huntington," 85 and Boylan, "The Role of Conversion in Nineteenth-Century Sunday Schools," 43, 45).

damaging, stress-related effects on people's mental and physical health. For instance, clinical psychologist, Paul Foxman, wrote in 1996,

> Paradoxically, I find that some anxiety patients who were raised with religion have difficulty attaining spirituality and coming to terms with God. It appears that some religious background experiences, such as harsh discipline in religious school, boring church services, empty religious rituals, and moral teachings based on fear and threat, are traumatic for children….As a result, spiritual awakening in adulthood can be hindered, and some people may require healing from religious trauma before a spiritual attitude or personal relationship with God is possible.[7]

Likewise, David Derezotes, Director of the Bridge Training Clinic and Chair of Practice and Mental Health, wrote in 2000,

> Underidentification reactions occur when the worker so dislikes what he sees in the client that the worker cannot feel empathy for the client or accept the client's spiritual path. Often, this reaction is associated with spiritual and religious trauma in the worker's own past. There are many social workers who are quite angry at adults in their family or church who were spiritually abusive or neglectful. These adults may have used religion to rationalize physical or sexual abuse, they may have tried to stop their children from developing their own spiritual beliefs, or they may have taught their children to feel toxic shame about themselves or unnecessary fear of the world.[8]

In 1992, one of the first attempts to provide an actual definition for RT research appeared in the work of Annie Imbens and Ineke Jonker, who succinctly explained that it is "the negative consequences of an oppressive religious ideology" where religious and theological symbols, texts, and rituals can activate someone's trauma responses. They defined it further,

> A *religious trauma* is the interpretation of all relational experiences on the basis of fear of and anger toward a God by whom one feels rejected,

---

[7] Foxman, *Dancing with Fear*, 363. At this point in the literature, the term "religious trauma" also appears to be used as a synonym for general cognitive dissonance or religious uncomfortability, desecration, and sacrilege (see for example, Idema III, *Freud, Religion, and the Roaring Twenties*, 93 and US Senate, *Native American Grave and Burial Protection Act*, 402).

[8] Derezotes, *Advanced Generalist Social Work Practice*, 133.

deceived, and punished; one also feels this anger toward a church community by which one feels cast out, threatened, and deceived. One may experience the community as an obstacle on the road to God.[9]

By the early 2000s, it became apparent to many clinicians that a psychological form of religious trauma not only existed, but it needed to be discerned in clients as a potential mental health factor. In 2003, Deana Morrow recognized that oppressive religious doctrines can and do cause psychological damage to lesbian women, including generating lifelong feelings of guilt, shame, low self-esteem, "internalized homophobia," depression, and suicidal ideations.[10] In 2005, Maureen Kitchur included the term "religious trauma" as part of a list of EMDR questions to help identify developmental interruptive experiences.[11] In a subsequent volume, Martha Jacobi identified alienation, guilt, anger, grief, and shame as lasting effects of "religiously based trauma" that arise from a religion's failure to provide support for and/or a violation of someone's emotional, physical, or financial boundaries.[12]

It was not until 2011 when Marlene Winell first coined the expression "religious trauma syndrome" in the magazine, *Cognitive Behaviour Therapy Today*, that psychologists as a whole had a change in perspective, linking abusive religious environments to a mental health disorder.[13] According to Winell, "Religious Trauma Syndrome is the condition experienced by people who are struggling with leaving an authoritarian, dogmatic religion and coping with the damage of indoctrination."[14] Winell's work has been instrumental in bringing international awareness to the study of RT. However, because of recent advances in the mental health sciences, many clinicians and researchers now believe the term "syndrome" is an outdated tag line that can be more detrimental than helpful. This move away from the term "syndrome" is for the simple reason that it manufactures arbitrary parameters on people's lived experiences, thereby excluding them from treatment options or alienating them with feelings of being diseased or abnormal. As such, the common misuse of "syndrome" has become problematic for many academics and practitioners because trauma occurs on an individualized spectrum and does not consistently present with the same cluster

---

[9] Imbens and Jonker, *Christianity and Incest*, 166; italics in original.
[10] Morrow, "Cast into the Wilderness," 119–20.
[11] Kitchur, "The Strategic Developmental Model for EMDR," 20.
[12] Jacobi, "Using EMDR with Religious and Spiritually Attuned Clients," esp. 474–90.
[13] Winell, "Religious Trauma Syndrome," 16–18.
[14] Winell, "Religious Trauma Syndrome," https://www.journeyfree.org/rts/.

of symptoms, as would be required for a bona fide "syndrome" diagnosis.[15] Indeed, it is best to recognize trauma as something that happens *to* a person, which then causes a disruption to their central nervous system, as opposed to something commonly associated with genetic abnormalities or diseases.

Recognizing that RT is nothing more than a standard clinical understanding of *trauma*,[16] except that it derives from within a religious context, Alyson Stone rightly expanded on Winell's work to acknowledge that RT often occurs outside of authoritarian, restrictive, and dogmatic fundamentalism. Stone provided a preliminary definition in 2013, which would later serve as a basis for the fuller definition created by the North American Committee on Religious Trauma Research (NACRTR), a subdivision within GCRR. Stone characterized this mental health problem as "pervasive psychological damage resulting from religious messages, beliefs, and experiences."[17]

Years later, in 2020, Michelle Panchuk characterized RT as "putative experiences of the divine being, religious practice, religious dogma, or religious community that transform an individual in a way that diminishes their capacity for participation in religious life."[18] Building on her work, Cheryl Johnston defined the term as "a spectrum of conditions resulting from a traumatic experience perceived by the survivor to be caused by religious practices, religious communities, religious teachings, symbols, and/or the divine being to the extent that the survivor's ability to participate in religious life" has been disrupted.[19] As a result of these experiences, a person's sense of religious self or worldview is devastated, from which deconversion then ensues.[20] While greatly enhancing the clinical understanding of religious trauma, the problem with these definitions is that they focus too much on a person's inability to participate in a faith community or to develop some sense of spirituality. Nonetheless, deconversion (or a lack of religiosity) are not characteristic of

---

[15] See Powell, "Religious Trauma Syndrome."

[16] Maria Root helpfully characterizes the standard clinical understanding of "trauma" as "a destruction of basic organizing principles by which we come to know self, others and the environment; traumas wound deeply in a way that challenges the meaning of life" (Root, "Reconstructing the Impact of Trauma on Personality," 229). For a historical and psychological overview of what "trauma" is and how it can be caused, see Petersen, *Religious Trauma*, 9–21 and Karris, *The Diabolical Trinity*, 3–8.

[17] Stone, "Thou Shalt Not," 324.

[18] Panchuk, "Distorting Concepts, Obscured Experiences," 608. Elsewhere, Panchuk illustratively described religious trauma as "people who have come to God asking for bread, but who seem to have received stones and serpents in its place" (Panchuk, "The Shattered Spiritual Self," 506).

[19] Johnston, "The Predictive Relationship of Religious Trauma," 10–11.

[20] Cockayne, Efird, and Warman, "Shattered Faith," 120–21.

everyone suffering from RT, and many people still find therapeutic healing from within a faith-based community.[21] Indeed, the sometimes-positive benefits of religiosity or spirituality on mental health is why it is important for the academic study of religious trauma to be as neutral as possible, as opposed to being overtly anti- or pro-religion. Furthermore, Winell, Panchu, and Johnston appear to exclude the possibility for someone to suffer from RT despite having no direct contact with a religious institution. Countless examples exist of non-religiously-affiliated persons suffering from secondary and vicarious trauma simply for witnessing the injury caused by some religionists.[22]

Thus, when considering the shortcomings of previous definitions, as well as the need to integrate direct, indirect, and insidious forms of trauma,[23] the North American Committee on Religious Trauma Research publicly issued a more clinically-justifiable definition on November 8, 2020:

> Religious trauma results from an event, series of events, relationships, or circumstances within or connected to religious beliefs, practices, or structures that is experienced by an individual as overwhelming or disruptive and has lasting adverse effects on a person's physical, mental, social, emotional, or spiritual well-being.[24]

This definition has since been adopted by other researchers and practitioners, including (among others) Alex Fox, Rebekah Drumsta, Tas Kronby, Carmen Rumbaut, the Satya Wellness Collective, and advisory board members for the Center for Congregational Ethics.[25] It is this definition from NACRTR that was

---

[21] Petersen, *Religious Trauma*, 5. See also, the relevant literature review in Bryant-Davis et al., "Religiosity, Spirituality, and Trauma Recovery," 306–14 and Koch and Edstrom, "Development of the Spiritual Harm and Abuse Scale," 476–506.

[22] Gubi and Jacobs, "Exploring the Impact on Counsellors," 191–204.

[23] For details, see Root, "Reconstructing the Impact of Trauma," 229–65.

[24] With deepest appreciation, this definition of religious trauma was thoughtfully and carefully created in partnership with the following trauma experts and researchers: Laura Anderson, LP, LMFT; Kathryn Keller, PHD, LPC-S; Brian Peck, LCSW; Alyson M. Stone, PhD, CGP; Suandria Hall, LPCC, Life Coach; Elizabeth Wilson, LPC, LAC; and Maggie Parker.

[25] Fox, "Adverse Religious Experiences and LGBTQ+ Adults," 10–11; Drumsta, "Spiritual Abuse and Seven Other Terms Defined"; Kronby, "Religious Trauma & Autism"; Rumbaut, "Healing Religious Trauma Through Art"; Satya Wellness Collective, "Religious Trauma Counseling"; Center for Congregational Ethics, "The Right, The Good."

employed in GCRR's sociological survey, which also acted as a foundation for other related terms.[26]

Defining Related Terms

Because of the overlap in characteristics and definitions, Megan Thomas's 2023 study used the terms "religious abuse," "religious trauma," and "religious trauma syndrome" interchangeably throughout her text.[27] Nevertheless, it is important to make a distinction between religious *trauma* and other terms that are frequently used in the literature, such as everyday religious *stressors*, moral injury, and religious or spiritual *abuse*, the latter of which is a source of (but not equivalent to) later religious trauma.[28]

For the purposes of this study, terms such as religious abuse[29] and spiritual abuse[30] fall under the umbrella term of "**Adverse Religious Experiences**" (AREs), which was defined in this study as:

Any experience of a religious belief, practice, or structure that undermines an individual's sense of safety or autonomy and/or negatively impacts their physical, social, emotional, relational, sexual, or psychological well-being.[31]

In other words, AREs are the incidents that can (and often do) *cause* religious trauma, but AREs are not the same as religious trauma itself. Moreover, the study defines "**RT participants**" as those who self-identify as having had religious trauma at some point in their life (based on GCRR's definition above).

Finally, "**RT symptoms**" are the six major lasting adverse effects on a person's well-being, generally as a direct result of AREs. The six manifestations

---

[26] A slight variation of GCRR's definition also appears on the Religious Trauma Institute's website, which adopted over 67% of GCRR's exact verbiage, changing only the first fifteen words (Religious Trauma Institute, "What is Religious Trauma?").

[27] Thomas, "Church Hurt," 13.

[28] Oakley, Kinmond, and Humphreys, "Spiritual Abuse in Christian Faith Settings," 144–54.

[29] For a definition of "religious abuse," see Swindle, "A Twisting of the Sacred," 18 and Koch and Edstrom, "Development of the Spiritual Harm and Abuse Scale," 477.

[30] For an overview of what constitutes "spiritual abuse," see Koch and Edstrom, "Development of the Spiritual Harm and Abuse Scale," 476–506, as well as Oakley, Kinmond, and Humphreys, "Spiritual Abuse in Christian Faith Settings" 144–54.

[31] The one distinction between this definition and others is its incorporation of a person's *sexual* well-being. Cf. Religious Trauma Institute, "Adverse Religious Experiences Survey" and Slade, "Adverse Religious Experiences (AREs) vs. Religious Trauma (RT)."

are: anxiety, stress, fear, depression, shame, and nightmares. While these six are not an exhaustive list, they do encompass the majority of what clinicians and patients have identified as chronic problems associated with religious trauma, such as interpersonal, emotional, and cognitive difficulties, as well as symptoms concomitant with Post Traumatic Stress Disorder (PTSD) and Complex-PTSD.[32] Moreover, based on anecdotal discussions with clinicians and members of the NACRTR, these specific symptoms are also the easiest for patients to self-identify as experiencing for themselves, as opposed to other symptoms like hyper-vigilance, dissociation, and decreased self-worth.

Research Question and Methodology

GCRR partnered with Springtide Research Institute's Custom Research Division in order to develop a comprehensive sociological survey designed to explore if and how religious trauma is happening among American adults.[33] This sociological survey used a combination of existing and original, customized questions to gather data relating to RT, including experiences that cause the trauma and the types of contexts in which the trauma occurs. In addition to general well-being measures and contextual variables, sociology experts at Springtide focused specifically on comparative measures by incorporating numerous questions from the "Survey of Adverse Religious Experiences" study conducted in 2020 by the Religious Trauma Institute.[34]

Dimensions of RT variables included symptoms of an anxiety disorder, clinical depression, and PTSD as a direct result of religion. Likewise, religious trauma experiences and religious trauma context variables included circumstances such as internal conflict with congregational leadership and feelings of alienation or fear. Additionally, the study assessed experiences with AREs, general emotional wellness, the use of coping mechanisms, and demographic characteristics.

---

[32] Koch and Edstrom, "Development of the Spiritual Harm and Abuse Scale," 477–48; Jones, Power, and Jones, "Religious Trauma and Moral Injury," 115040; Petersen, *Religious Trauma*, 4–5; Stone, "Thou Shalt Not," 323–37; Karris, *The Diabolical Trinity*, 15–17, 51–59.

[33] As an independent research institute, GCRR implemented its own in-house institutional review board (IRB) to ensure the research practices and survey questions follow standard ethical and federal regulations for the protection of human subjects. This in-house IRB met monthly throughout the second-half of 2020 and then again in early 2022 under NACRTR leadership, which (in addition to the names listed in n24 above) also included Gill Harvey, DPsych; Janyne McConnaughey, PhD; and Rebekah Drumsta, MA, CPLC.

[34] Religious Trauma Institute, "Adverse Religious Experiences Survey."

The data was collected using Alchemer panel services, formerly known as SurveyGizmo.[35] The survey was launched on 24 August 2021 and closed on 7 September 2021. A total of 1,669 completed responses were collected through this panel.[36] As a result, this sample is large enough to be generalizable for the total U.S. adult population. Although findings discussing the nuances of religious trauma experienced by specific groups (e.g., RT respondents currently suffering from RT symptoms and the demographics of RT respondents) are directional as opposed to representational since the study cannot guarantee these more nuanced groups are representative of the entire U.S. population. The only screening criteria was geographic location where survey participants were required to be living in the United States. During both the data collection and analysis phase, GCRR specialists employed stringent parameters on what would qualify as RT in order to ensure that the final numbers would not be an exaggeration of real-world factuality. The result is that this study's conclusions are purposely conservative in order to avoid unrestrained sensationalism.

Results

The survey was launched in August 2021 with 1,581 participants ranging from 18–100 years old and with a demographic makeup that is representative of the total U.S. adult population. For example, 51% of the respondents identified as white, 25% as black, and 10% as Hispanic or Latino. Likewise, 81% of participants identified as heterosexual and roughly 16% as non-heterosexual (*Figure 1*).

---

[35] Springtide only works with suppliers with a proven track record of high data quality. Respondents who are either reported as providing a careless session, or fail an automated attention/competency check in the survey are reported back to the suppliers. Suppliers with a low-quality score are subsequently removed from their network. ReCAPTCHAs, red herrings, and survey timers are all automated methods they use on the survey level to catch respondents who rush their session.

[36] After data collection, using IBM SPSS Statistics 28.0, GCRR removed all respondents who were under the age of 18 (n=88). Hence, this report's conclusions are based on a total of 1,581 survey responses.

Figure 1

"What is your age?"		
	FREQUENCY	PERCENT (%)
18–29	412	26.1
30–49	603	38.1
50–69	428	27.1
70–99	137	8.7
100+	1	0.1
TOTAL	1,581	100.00

"Which race do you most identify with?"		
	FREQUENCY	PERCENT (%)
WHITE	799	50.5
BLACK	393	24.9
HISPANIC or LATINO	158	10.0
ASIAN	123	7.8
AMERICAN INDIAN or ALASKA NATIVE	36	2.3
NATIVE HAWAIIAN or PACIFIC ISLANDER	12	0.8
OTHER	60	3.8
TOTAL	1,581	100.00

"Which gender do you most identify with?"		
	FREQUENCY	PERCENT (%)
FEMALE or TRANSGENDER FEMALE	730	46.2
MALE or TRANSGENDER MALE	709	44.8
NON-BINARY	142	9.0
TOTAL	1,581	100.00

"What is your sexual orientation?"		
	FREQUENCY	PERCENT (%)
HETEROSEXUAL	1,277	80.8
BISEXUAL	112	7.1
HOMOSEXUAL	45	2.8
ASEXUAL	32	2.0
LESBIAN	28	1.8
PANSEXUAL	18	1.1
QUEER	8	0.5
SAME-GENDER LOVING	6	0.4
OTHER	9	0.6
QUESTIONING or UNSURE	10	0.6
PREFER NOT TO SAY	36	2.3
TOTAL	1,581	100.00

When provided with the NACRTR definition of religious trauma, a total of 438 respondents (27.7%) self-identified as having experienced RT at some point in their life (*Figure 2*).

Figure 2

"Do you believe you have experienced religious trauma (based on the definition above)?"		
	FREQUENCY	PERCENT (%)
YES	438	27.7
NO	1,143	72.3
TOTAL	1,581	100.00

Of those who self-identified as having experienced religious trauma, about one-half (52%) were young adults (between 18 and 34), with another 23% of RT participants being between 35 and 44. Moreover, RT participants identified primarily as White (44%) or Black (31%), followed by Hispanic or Latino

(11%) and Asian (8%). The sexual orientation of most RT participants was heterosexual (70%) and bisexual (12%).[37]

Almost two-thirds of respondents believe that people suffer from religious trauma (65.1%). Over one-third of the total respondents (37.3%) stated that they personally know someone who likely suffers from RT, wherein two-thirds (66.4%) of that 37% claimed to know between one and four people, and one-third (33.5%) indicated they know five or more people who potentially suffer from RT (*Figure 3*).

Figure 3

"Do you think people suffer from religious trauma (based on the definition above)?"		
	FREQUENCY	PERCENT (%)
YES	1,029	65.1
NO	522	34.9
TOTAL	1,581	100.0

"Do you know people who potentially suffer from religious trauma (based on the definition above)?"		
	FREQUENCY	PERCENT (%)
YES	590	37.3
NO	991	62.7
TOTAL	1,581	100.0

---

[37] Note that because of the directional nature of this study, it would be incorrect to infer from this statement alone that a significant percentage of the LGBTQ+ community do not suffer from religious trauma. See the "Limitations and Future Research" section below for details.

"How many people do you think you know who potentially suffer from religious trauma (based on the definition above)?"		
NO. OF PEOPLE	FREQUENCY	PERCENT (%)
1	111	18.8
2	111	18.8
3	100	16.9
4	70	11.9
5	58	9.8
6	29	4.9
7	12	2.0
8	11	1.9
9	3	0.5
10	25	4.2
11+	60	10.2
TOTAL	590	100.0

Interestingly, twenty of the 'yes' respondents indicated that they know 100 or more people who potentially suffer from RT.

The survey also examined six major symptoms associated with trauma and their correlation to religious contexts. Of the 1,581 participants, 17% and 16% suffer from anxiety and stress (respectively) specifically because of religion. Moreover, 15% are negatively impacted by fear and depression due to religion, whereas 13% suffer from religion-induced shame and more than one-in-ten suffer from religion-induced nightmares (*Figure 4*).

Figure 4

"To what extent do the following negatively impact your life because of religion?"		
	FREQUENCY	PERCENT (%)
ANXIETY		
Quite a bit	149	9.4
Very much so	115	7.3
TOTAL	264	16.7
STRESS		
Quite a bit	151	9.6
Very much so	99	6.3
TOTAL	276	14.9
FEAR		
Quite a bit	150	9.5
Very much so	86	5.4
TOTAL	236	14.9
DEPRESSION		
Quite a bit	126	8.0
Very much so	103	6.5
TOTAL	229	14.5
SHAME		
Quite a bit	127	8.0
Very much so	90	5.7
TOTAL	217	13.7
NIGHTMARES		
Quite a bit	101	6.4
Very much so	82	5.2
TOTAL	183	11.6

These six symptoms are reasonable when considering that nearly 22% (341) of respondents do not think they live up to the expectations of their religion and almost 13% (202) have been accused of this very thing by others. Additionally, 11% and 12% of participants feel at least one of the six symptoms because religious leaders or religious family members (respectively) do not accept them for who they are. Almost one-in-ten (9.2%) experience trauma symptoms because they have to hide their true selves in religious settings (*Figure 5*).

Figure 5

"I feel shame, fear, stress, anxiety, etc. because religious leaders have not accepted me for who I am / have tried to change who I am."		
	FREQUENCY	PERCENT (%)
UNCHECKED	1,400	88.6
CHECKED	181	11.4
TOTAL	1,581	100.00

"I feel shame, fear, stress, anxiety, etc. because religious family members have not accepted me for who I am / have tried to change who I am."		
	FREQUENCY	PERCENT (%)
UNCHECKED	1,391	88.0
CHECKED	190	12.0
TOTAL	1,581	100.00

"I feel shame, fear, stress, anxiety, etc. because I feel like I have to hide who I truly am in religious settings."		
	FREQUENCY	PERCENT (%)
UNCHECKED	1,536	90.8
CHECKED	145	9.2
TOTAL	1,581	100.00

These adverse religious experiences seemingly lead to religious trauma, as 66.0% of those who disclosed facing an ARE also self-identified as having experienced RT. Of the 438 people who self-identified as having experienced RT, 53 (12.1%) reported suffering from all six symptoms (*Figure 6*).

Figure 6

Number of Participants who self-identified as having experienced RT and currently suffer from:			
	Any 3 out of 6 RT Symptoms	Any 4 out of 6 RT Symptoms	Any 5 out of 6 RT Symptoms	All Six RT Symptoms
Percent (%)	29.9	22.6	17.8	12.1
No. (out of 438)	131	99	78	53

Related to the topic of symptoms is the rationale behind tabulating those who suffer from any three or more of the six major symptoms, as opposed to constructing a hierarchy of indicators where, for example, nightmares might be listed as more severe than shame. The NACRTR decided that a hierarchy of severity is person-relative and, thus, would be artificially imposed on people's lived experiences. For one RT sufferer, feelings of depression may be more inimical to their daily living than experiencing nightmares. For another sufferer, their nightmares may be so intense that this particular symptom overshadows all others. The point is that trauma survivors experience the intensity of their symptoms differently, making it unnecessarily restrictive to require that someone suffer from "worse" symptoms in order to be considered a RT sufferer.

Finally, participants who categorize themselves as having experienced religious trauma typically had:

- a high school diploma (25%),
- some college (27%),
- a bachelor or graduate degree (39%).

Likewise, just over one-fifth (21%) of those who self-identified as having had RT have been convicted of a crime. Generally, the RT participants were:

- married or in a domestic partnership (42%)
- single, never married (40%),
- divorced or separated (14%).

Almost two-thirds of RT participants (65%) said they were at least financially stable if not living comfortably and had a household income that they described as average or higher (66%) relative to others.

Significantly, there were some participants who contradicted themselves by indicating that they currently suffer from three or more trauma symptoms specifically due to religion, but they did *not* self-identify as having experienced RT at some point in the past. In other words, because these participants currently suffer from multiple RT symptoms simultaneously, these respondents should have marked 'yes' when asked, "Do you believe you have experienced religious trauma" (*Figure 7*).

Figure 7

Number of Participants who did *not* self-identify as having experienced RT but currently suffer from:				
	Any 3 out of 6 RT Symptoms	Any 4 out of 6 RT Symptoms	Any 5 out of 6 RT Symptoms	6 out of 6 RT Symptoms
Percent (%)	9.2	5.2	3.9	1.9
No. (out of 1,143)	105	59	45	22

Forty-five out of the 1,143 'no' respondents (3.94%) said they currently suffer from five out of the six major symptoms of RT because of religion. Moreover, fifty-nine 'no' respondents (5.16%) suffer from four of the six symptoms because of religion. Of the total 1,581 participants, 14.9% currently suffer from three of the six RT symptoms, and 10% suffer from four of the six (*Figure 8*).

Figure 8

People Who Currently Suffer from Religious Trauma Symptoms				
	Any 3 out of 6 RT Symptoms	Any 4 out of 6 RT Symptoms	Any 5 out of 6 RT Symptoms	6 out of 6 RT Symptoms
Percent (%)	14.9	10.0	7.8	4.7
No. (out of 1,581)	236	158	123	75

In summation, the following rounded data are of particular importance:

1. 28% self-identify as having experienced RT at some point in their life;
2. Of those who say they do not suffer from RT, 5.2% currently suffer from four of the six major RT symptoms;
3. Of the total sample (n=1,581), 15% say they currently suffer from at least three of the six RT symptoms;
4. Of the total sample (n=1,581), 37.3% say they personally know someone who likely suffers from RT;
5. Of those who personally know someone, 90% claimed to know between one and ten people who likely suffer from RT;
6. Of those who disclosed having had an ARE, 66% also self-identified as having experienced RT;

When accounting for those six data points, it is likely that around one-third (27–33%) of U.S. adults (conservatively) have experienced religious trauma at some point in their life (based on the definition above*).* That number increases to 37% if those suffering from any *three* of the six major RT symptoms are included. It is also likely that around 10–15% of U.S. adults currently suffer from religious trauma if only the most conservative numbers are highlighted. Nonetheless, since 37% of the respondents personally know people who potentially suffer from RT, and 90% of those respondents know between one and ten people who likely suffer from RT, then it could be argued that as many as one-in-five (20%) U.S. adults presently suffer from major religious trauma symptoms.[38]

Discussion

Overall, the number of religious trauma survivors and sufferers found in this study correlates well with a recent spiritual abuse survey by Daniel Koch and Leihua Edstrom where one-half of their 3,222 respondents were told that they risked eternal damnation at least once or twice if they ever left their particular religious group. Likewise, four-in-ten had been pressured into forgiving an abuser while the abuse was still ongoing, and 71% reported that young children were being taught graphic portrayals of Hell, Satan, or demons at least once or twice, with 34% reporting that these developmentally-inappropriate descriptions were being taught very often. Moreover, 56% reported observing religious leadership protect, as well as aggrandize, abusers within their congregation at least once or twice. Over one-half (52%) reported having been the target of intentional victim-blaming for their own abuse. One-half of all the respondents have occasionally witnessed their religious leader publicly shame other congregants; 54% reported being the victim of similar public shaming (14% reported being publicly shamed often or all the time by religious leaders or other congregants). Finally, 65% of their respondents reported occasionally "being made to feel shame over naturally occurring sexual desires (not actions)" while 22% reported being made to feel shame all the time.[39] Seeing as how GCRR's study found that 66% of those with an ARE also self-identified as having experienced religious trauma, it becomes more

---

[38] For data outputs, visit: https://www.gcrr.org/religioustrauma.

[39] Koch and Edstrom, "Development of the Spiritual Harm and Abuse Scale," 476–506. Cf. other studies with similar results in Nobakht and Dale, "The Importance of Religious/Ritual Abuse," 3575–88 and Oakley and Kinmond, "Developing Safeguarding Policy and Practice for Spiritual Abuse," 87–95.

evident that RT is likely an even greater chronic problem for many religious institutions than what is recognized by clinicians and other religionists.

Perhaps the most unique factor with GCRR's study is the number of respondents (as many as 11%) who did not identify as having experienced religious trauma despite currently suffering from multiple RT symptoms. There are a number of reasonable explanations for this discrepancy, including a general reluctance to admit being a trauma sufferer, a misconception about trauma, or simple human error when selecting survey answers.

For many people, there may be an inherent stigma around the notion of suffering from RT and the scapegoating that can accompany it. Those admitting to religious trauma may also feel the added pressure of needing to protect their religious community and avoid being seen as a dissident or apostate.[40] Indeed, there is a tendency for many religious communities to disparage mental health services.[41] In the Koch and Edstrom survey, 50% of the respondents said they had been deterred from seeking medication or other mental health treatment at least once or twice.[42] As Paula Swindle neatly summaries,

> This potential for victim blaming also may contribute to a pressure for the victim to keep the abuse secret. There may be added pressure to protect the church family from losing a beloved leader or protecting the very public image of a church leader when the leader is the abuser. Knowing the scandal it could cause and the scrutiny the victim is likely to experience may act as a deterrent to exposing the abuse. The fear of ostracism from an important community also may contribute to the secrecy.[43]

Moreover, the word "trauma" is often only associated with maximally acute and sometimes rare adverse occurrences, such as wartime combat and sexual assault. In this case, some people may assume that they need to have PTSD or have survived a major life-and-death situation in order to qualify as having been traumatized.[44] Because some religious environments frequently do not prioritize mental health, often expressing criticism or skepticism about the subject matter entirely, some individuals may have learned to dissociate from their emotions

---

[40] Swindle, "A Twisting of the Sacred," 10–11, 46–51.
[41] Lehmann, "Christianity and Mental Illness Stigma," 1–24; Mathison, "Mental Health Stigma in Religious Communities."
[42] Koch and Edstrom, "Development of the Spiritual Harm and Abuse Scale," 484, 489.
[43] Swindle, "A Twisting of the Sacred," 48–49.
[44] Cf. Petersen, *Religious Trauma*, 9–21.

in order to follow spiritual expectations.[45] As a result, it is reasonable to conclude that some respondents may actually suffer from religious trauma without realizing it themselves.

Limitations and Future Research

It is important to recognize that the individual demographic groups identified in GCRR's survey are directional as opposed to representational. As such, the survey as a whole (with its 1,581 participants) is an accurate representation of the total U.S. adult population. However, the survey cannot be used to identify the percentage of religious trauma sufferers within individual demographics because GCRR did not ensure the study had census matches with race, gender, region, etc. Therefore, cross-tabulations with those variables are not generalizable. For example, of the total participants, only eighteen self-identified as pansexual. This is far too small a sample size and cannot be construed as representing adult pansexuals living in the United States. Thus, readers cannot discern percentage numbers for these more nuanced segments of the population, but they can use this survey to extrapolate for the entire U.S. as a whole. Future research should focus specifically on more differentiated segments in order to determine the percentage of RT sufferers within those demographic groupings.

Furthermore, the idea that around one-third of the U.S. adult population *has* experienced religious trauma at some point in their life, while only as little as one-in-ten *currently* suffer from it, should not be viewed as a discrepancy in the survey results or participant self-reporting. Instead, it is important to recognize that not all survivors who have experienced the lasting adverse effects of trauma continue to do so throughout their entire lifetime. This fact is due to a number of possibilities that might involve the person receiving professional therapeutic treatment or having developed the necessary coping skills to relieve the symptoms themselves. What was not studied in this survey and should, therefore, be a focus of future research is the duration that people had to endure religious trauma before recovering from most or all of its symptoms.

Another component to consider is sexual dysfunction and its potential correlation to religious trauma as an additional RT symptom. Since both sexual shame and sexual suppression are known to occur within religious belief systems, it is likely that many religious trauma sufferers will also present with

---

[45] Cf. Dorahy and Lewis, "The Relationship Between Dissociation and Religiosity," 315–22.

some type of sexual dysfunction, such as an inability to reach orgasm, physical pain during sex, a feeling of being abnormal, flawed, or immoral for engaging in sex acts, and an overall denial of sexual urges and desires. These types of symptoms can not only disturb a person's core identity, but they can also cause a lifelong disruption of meaningful interpersonal relationships.[46] Thus, it is important for future research to explore sexual dysfunction as a potential major symptom of religious trauma.

Conclusion

The purpose of this study was to discover if religious trauma was a society-wide phenomenon or simply an affliction of only a small few. As predicted by numerous clinicians, the survey found that religious trauma is a chronic problem within the U.S. adult population. In fact, NACRTR's original hypothesis under-estimated the total numbers by as much as 10–15%. After compiling data from 1,581 adults living in the United States, this sociological study found that it is likely around one-third (27–33%) of U.S. adults (conservatively) have experienced religious trauma at some point in their life (based on the definition above). That number increases to 37% if those suffering from any *three* of the six major RT symptoms are included. It is also likely that around 10–15% of U.S. adults currently suffer from religious trauma if only the most conservative numbers are highlighted. Nonetheless, since 37% of the respondents personally know people who potentially suffer from RT, and 90% of those respondents know between one and ten people who likely suffer from RT, then it could be argued that as many as one-in-five (20%) U.S. adults presently suffer from major religious trauma symptoms.

BIBLIOGRAPHY

Boylan, Anne M. "The Role of Conversion in Nineteenth-Century Sunday Schools." *American Studies* 20, no. 1 (1979): 35–48.

Bryant-Davis, Thema, Monica U. Ellis, Elizabeth Burke-Maynard, Nathan Moon, Pamela A. Counts, and Gera Anderson. "Religiosity, Spirituality, and Trauma Recovery in the Lives of Children and Adolescents." *Professional Psychology: Research and Practice* 43, no. 4 (2012): 306–14. doi.org/10.1037/a0029282.

---

[46] Cf. Crocker, "Persevering Faith," 26 and Fox, "Adverse Religious Experiences and LGBTQ+ Adults," 142–49.

Center for Congregational Ethics. "The Right, The Good." Facebook, May 19, 2021. https://tinyurl.com/5d72847v.

Cockayne, Joshua, David Efird, and Jack Warman. "Shattered Faith: The Social Epistemology of Deconversion by Spiritually Violent Religious Trauma." In *Voices From the Edge: Centring Marginalized Perspectives in Analytic Theology*, edited by Michelle Panchuk and Michael Rea, 119–40. New York, NY: Oxford University Press, 2020.

Crocker, Seth C. "Persevering Faith: A Qualitative Exploration of Religious Trauma and Spiritual Resilience in Sexual Minority Christians." Doctoral diss., Regent University, 2021.

Derezotes, David S. *Advanced Generalist Social Work Practice*. Thousand Oaks, CA: SAGE Publications, 2000.

Dorahy, Martin J., and Christopher Alan Lewis. "The Relationship Between Dissociation and Religiosity: An Empirical Evaluation of Schumaker's Theory." *Journal for the Scientific Study of Religion* 40, no. 2 (2001): 315–22. https://doi.org/10.1111/0021-8294.00058.

Drumsta, Rebekah. "Spiritual Abuse and Seven Other Terms Defined." Accessed February 16, 2023. https://tinyurl.com/yck4t5zw.

Fox, Alex. "Adverse Religious Experiences and LGBTQ+ Adults." Doctoral diss., Antioch University New England, 2022.

Foxman, Paul. *Dancing With Fear: Overcoming Anxiety in a World of Stress and Uncertainty*. Lanham, MD: Rowman and Littlefield, 1996.

Gubi, Peter Madsen, and Rachel Jacobs. "Exploring the Impact on Counsellors of Working With Spiritually Abused Clients." *Mental Health, Religion & Culture* 12, no. 2 (2009): 191–204. doi.org/10.1080/13674670802441509.

Hoffman, Theodore. Book Review of *The Man Outside* by Wolfgang Borchert. *New Republic* 126, no. 26 (June 30, 1952): 21–22.

Idema III, Henry. *Freud, Religion, and the Roaring Twenties*. Savage, MD: Rowman and Littlefield, 1990.

Imbens, Annie, and Ineke Jonker. *Christianity and Incest*. Translated by Patricia McVay. Minneapolis, MN: Fortress Press, 1992.

Jacobi, Martha S. "Using EMDR with Religious and Spiritually Attuned Clients." In *EMDR Solutions II: For Depression, Eating Disorders, Performance, and More*, edited by Robin Shapiro, 472–94. New York, NY: W. W. Norton, 2009.

Johnston, Cheryl Lynn. "The Predictive Relationship of Religious Trauma and Spiritual Abuse on Meaning-making, Trust, and Depression." Doctoral diss., Northcentral University, 2021.

Jones, Timothy W., Jennifer Power, and Tiffany M. Jones. "Religious Trauma and Moral Injury From LGBTQA+ Conversion Practices." *Social Science & Medicine*, 2022, 115040. doi.org/10.1016/j.socscimed.2022.115040.

Karris, Mark Gregory. *The Diabolical Trinity: Healing Religious Trauma From a Wrathful God, Tormenting Hell, and a Sinful Self*. Grasmere, ID: SacraSage Press, 2023.

Kitchur, Maureen. "The Strategic Developmental Model for EMDR." In *EMDR Solutions: Pathways to Healing*, edited by Robin Shapiro, 8–56. New York, NY: W. W. Norton, 2005.

Koch, Daniel, and Leihua Edstrom. "Development of the Spiritual Harm and Abuse Scale." *Journal for the Scientific Study of Religion* 61, no. 2 (2022): 476–506.

Kronby, Tas. "Religious Trauma & Autism." Learn From Autistics, February 7, 2023. https://tinyurl.com/yvyp7mb5.

Lehmann, Curtis S. "Christianity and Mental Illness Stigma: Critical and Constructive Perspectives on Blame and Social Distancing." *Journal of Religion & Spirituality in Social Work: Social Thought*, 2021, 1–24. https://doi.org/10.1080/15426432.2021.1971593.

Mathison, Lily Amelia. "Mental Health Stigma in Religious Communities: Development of a Quantitative Measure." Master's thesis, Iowa State University, 2016.

Morrow, Deana F. "Cast into the Wilderness: The Impact of Institutionalized Religion on Lesbians." In *Trauma, Stress, and Resilience Among Sexual Minority Women: Rising Like the Phoenix*, edited by Kimberly F. Balsam, 109–20. Binghamton, NY: Harrington Park Press, 2003.

Nobakht, Habib Niyaraq, and Karl Yngvar Dale. "The Importance of Religious/Ritual Abuse as a Traumatic Predictor of Dissociation." *Journal of Interpersonal Violence* 33, no. 23 (August 4, 2017): 3575–88. https://doi.org/10.1177/0886260517723747.

Noon, Rozanne Miller. "Frederic Dan Huntington, First Bishop of Central New York, His Role in Religion and Reform in the Nineteenth Century." Doctoral diss., University of California, 1971.

Oakley, Lisa Ruth, and Kathryn Susan Kinmond. "Developing Safeguarding Policy and Practice for Spiritual Abuse." *Journal of Adult Protection* 16, no. 2 (2014): 87–95. https://doi.org/10.1108/jap-07–2013-0033.

Oakley, Lisa, Kathryn Kinmond, and Justin Humphreys. "Spiritual Abuse in Christian Faith Settings: Definition, Policy and Practice Guidance." *Journal of Adult Protection* 20, no. 3/4 (2018): 144–54. https://doi.org/10.1108/jap-03–2018-0005.

Oldfield, John J. *The Problem of Tolerance and Social Existence in the Writings of Félicité Lamennais, 1809–1831.* Leiden: Brill, 1973.

Panchuk, Michelle. "Distorting Concepts, Obscured Experiences: Hermeneutical Injustice in Religious Trauma and Spiritual Violence." *Hypatia* 35, no. 4 (2020): 607–25.

———. "The Shattered Spiritual Self: A Philosophical Exploration of Religious Trauma." *Res Philosophica* 95, no. 3 (2018): 505–30.

Petersen, Brooke N. *Religious Trauma: Queer Stories in Estrangement and Return.* Lanham, MD: Lexington Books, 2022.

Powell, Alisha. "Religious Trauma Syndrome: Examples, Symptoms, & 7 Ways to Cope." Choosing Therapy, November 25, 2022. choosingtherapy.com/religious-trauma-syndrome/.

Religious Trauma Institute. "Adverse Religious Experiences Survey." 2020. https://tinyurl.com/266k4hfd.

———. "What is Religious Trauma?" 2022. https://tinyurl.com/4prkv5zy.

Root, Maria P. P. "Reconstructing the Impact of Trauma on Personality." In *Personality and Psychopathology: Feminist Reapproaisals*, edited by Laura S. Brown and Mary Ballou, 229–65. New York, NY: Guilford Press, 1992.

Rossman, Martin L. *Guided Imagery for Self-Healing: An Essential Resource for Anyone Seeking Wellness.* 2nd ed. Tiburon, CA: H J Kramer Incorporated, 2000.

Rumbaut, Carmen. "Healing Religious Trauma Through Art." Medium, April 18, 2022. https://tinyurl.com/23ukyt9v.

Satya Wellness Collective. "Religious Trauma Counseling." Accessed February 16, 2023. https://www.satyawellnesscollective.com/religious-trauma-counseling.

Slade, Darren M. "Adverse Religious Experiences (AREs) vs. Religious Trauma (RT): An Important Distinction." Global Center for Religious Research, August 8, 2022. https://www.gcrr.org/post/adversereligiousexperiences.

———. *The Logic of Intersubjectivity: Brian McLaren's Philosophy of Christian Religion*. Eugene, OR: Wipf and Stock, 2020.

Stone, Alyson M. "Thou Shalt Not: Treating Religious Trauma and Spiritual Harm With Combined Therapy." *Eastern Group Psychotherapy Society* 37, no. 4 (2013): 323–37.

Swindle, Paula J. "A Twisting of the Sacred: The Lived Experience of Religious Abuse." Doctoral diss., University of North Carolina at Greensboro, 2017.

Thomas, Megan S. "Church Hurt: A Therapeutic Approach for Treating Religious Trauma and Spiritual Bypass." Psychology Doctoral Specialization Projects, Eastern Kentucky University, 2023.

US Senate, One Hundred First Congress, Second Session. *Native American Grave and Burial Protection Act (repatriation); Native American Repatriation of Cultural Patrimony Act; and Heard Museum Report*. Hearing Before the Select Committee on Indian Affairs S. 1021 and S. 1980. Adopted May 14, 1990.

Wilcox, Brad, and Riley Peterson. "Perspective: Don't Believe the Headlines. Few People Suffer Trauma From Religion in Childhood." Deseret News, August 1, 2022. https://tinyurl.com/mr97rkh4.

Winell, Marlene. "Religious Trauma Syndrome." Journey Free. Accessed February 11, 2023. https://www.journeyfree.org/rts/.

———. "Religious Trauma Syndrome: It's Time To Recognize It (Part I)." *Cognitive Behaviour Therapy Today* 39, no. 3 (2011): 16–18.

ABOUT THE AUTHORS

Darren M. Slade (PhD) earned his doctorate in theology and church history from the Rawlings School of Divinity (Virginia). He is an adjunct professor of ancient history and comparative religion at the Rocky Mountain College of Art and Design. In addition to his philosophical work, *The Logic of Intersubjectivity*, Dr. Slade specializes in the socio-political development of religious belief systems that include ancient Near-Eastern, Church, and Islamic history, as well as Second-Temple hermeneutical practices, the intersection of religion and science-fiction, and misotheism. He is also the Director of the North American Committee on Religious Trauma Research (NACRTR). Darren currently serves as President of the Global Center for Religious Research.

Adrianna Smell (MA) earned her graduate degree in applied sociology from the University of Northern Colorado (UNCO). She is currently pursuing a PhD in Sociology with specializations in research methods and social inequality from Case Western Reserve University (CWRU). Since 2019, Adrianna has worked as an associate researcher at Springtide Research Institute. She has also worked as a research assistant in the Sociology Department at CWRU, the Prevention Research Center for Healthy Neighborhoods at CWRU, and the Social Research Lab at UNCO.

Elizabeth Wilson (LPC, LAC) is a. Licensed Professional Counselor and Licensed Addiction Counselor at Reflective Wellness: Mind & Body. She has experience working in private practice, residential settings, and in the community with populations of all ages that suffer from mental illness, trauma, substance abuse and behavioral issues. She has been a somatic trauma specialist since 2017.

Rebekah Drumsta (MA, CPLC) is a board member of The Vashti Initiative, a non-profit with the goal to empower and assist those transitioning out of religious and spiritual abuse. She is also the Chief Operating Officer of NPE Friends Fellowship, an international non-profit organization that assists individuals and their families who have received unexpected results from at-home DNA tests. Rebekah is a Certified Professional Life Coach and holds an undergraduate degree in Urban Ministry and Family Crisis (with a Christian Counseling minor), as well as a graduate degree in Religious Education. She has made appearances on and consulted with BBC, NBC, ABC, and a variety of other platforms such as podcasts and film projects. To learn more about her work, visit RebekahDrumsta.com.

MORE FROM THE AUTHORS

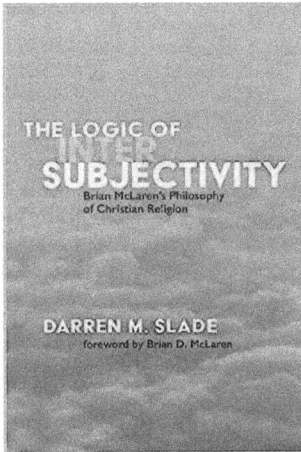

*The Logic of
Intersubjectivity*
Wipf & Stock, 2020

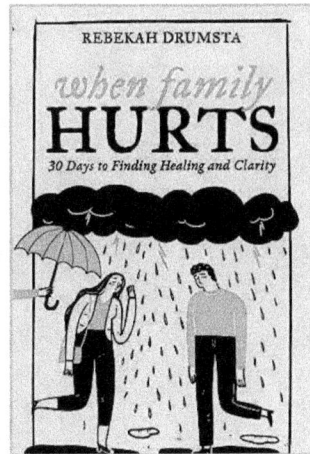

When Family Hurts
Clay Bridges Press, 2021

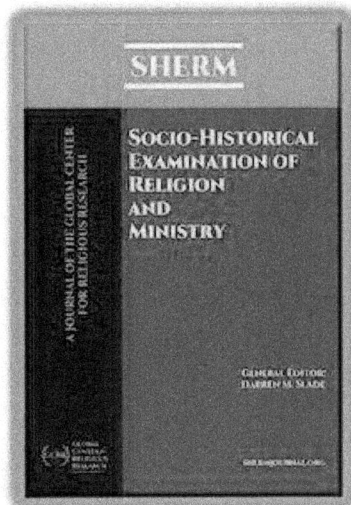

I WENT THROUGH FIVE MENTAL HEALTH PROFESSIONALS

FOR THE FIRST TIME, SOMEONE WAS ABLE TO IDENTIFY WHAT WAS REALLY GOING ON in the depths of my mind and nervous system and how to actually help me.

I was raised from birth to believe I am a sinner and that the only way to achieve fulfillment and joy in this life and the next is to follow the doctrines of my faith.

I was taught you're either all in or all out, so when I found that my questioning led to an inability to be all in, I couldn't see any other way but to leave behind everything.

This led to a very long and lonely period of rebuilding my entire worldview from scratch, while trying to pretend to my family that everything was fine because I didn't want them to worry about my eternal salvation.

before finally finding one who was educated on the causes, manifestations and treatment options for Religious Trauma. When I first heard of Religious Trauma, I imagined extreme situations like physical violation or radical cult indoctrination.

But I soon came to realize that it very closely describes my experience, and it explains the numerous trauma responses I carry with me, including chronic mental health issues and physical health issues related to an overwhelmed nervous system.

I always regarded my faith as very positive – I felt loved, secure and safe. It was a source of strength in my life. But what my therapist helped me realize is that my crippling emotional and mental health challenges actually stem from my own seemingly innocent faith upbringing and the religious teachings of my faith that had taken a foothold deep in my psyche and created a toxic environment of fear and shame.

RELIGIOUS TRAUMA

CERTIFICATION TRAINING
AND RESOURCES FOR
TRAUMA SUFFERERS

Become an advanced trauma-informed practitioner today!

info@gcrr.org

www.gcrr.org/RT

SHERM 5/1 (2023): 30–42

More on the Relevance of Personhood and Mindedness: The Euthanasia Debate

David Kyle Johnson,
King's College (PA)

Abstract: *In my first paper for SHERM, I argued that "fetus personhood" is irrelevant to the abortion debate. In this paper, I will argue that personhood is irrelevant to the euthanasia debate as well. Even though a terminally ill patient is a person, ending their life can still be moral. Because personhood (and mindedness) is only instrumentally valuable as means to attaining the good life, if a terminal illness has now made that impossible, it is permissible (when both the doctor and patient agree) for the doctor to help the patient end their life. Thus, euthanasia should be legal.*

Keywords: Euthanasia, Active Euthanasia, Daniel Callahan, Don Marquis, Intrinsic Value of Life

Introduction

In my first article for SHERM, "The Relevance (and Irrelevance) of Questions of Personhood (and Mindedness) to the Abortion Debate," I argued that "person" should be defined in terms of sentience (the capability of perceiving and feeling), sapience (intelligence), and self-awareness (consciousness of one's own feelings and intelligence).[1] I called any being that is sentient, sapient, and self-aware "fully-minded" and defined "personhood" as such: "a being is a person *if and only if* it is the kind of being that is typically fully-minded."[2] This, it turns out, was a bit short-sighted. I should have said that "a being is a person if and only if it is (a) fully-minded or (b) the kind of being that is typically fully-minded." The latter allows for non-fully-minded persons (e.g., those with mental deficiencies) to still be persons, which they clearly are. The former would allow for new kinds of persons to emerge. For example, the

---

[1] Johnson, "The Relevance (and Irrelevance) of Questions of Personhood (and Mindedness) to the Abortion Debate," 121–53.

[2] Johnson, "The Relevance (and Irrelevance) of Questions of Personhood (and Mindedness) to the Abortion Debate,"128.

Socio-Historical Examination of Religion and Ministry
Volume 5, Issue 1, Summer 2023 shermjournal.org
© David Kyle Johnson
Permissions: editor@shermjournal.org
ISSN 2637-7519 (print), ISSN 2637-7500 (online)
https://doi.org/10.33929/sherm.2023.vol5.no1.02 (article)

pig Okja, in the Netflix film *Okja*, is clearly a person even though pigs are not typically considered fully-minded. In the same way, if a non-human primate is one day fully-minded, it would be a person, even if its species is not typically fully-minded. Although this oversight did not affect the validity or cogency of the argument I presented in my original article, it is a mistake worth correcting (which I hope I have now done).

In my first article, I also articulated what science has revealed about mindedness and what is responsible for it. It turns out that mindedness has nothing to do with the soul—the concept of a separable immaterial substance that dates back to the ancient Greeks. Indeed, philosophers generally agree that philosophical objections to the idea that souls exist have no answer, and neuroscience has shown that every bit of one's mentality is produced by one's brain. In essence, the concept that humans have souls, for a lack of a better term, has been philosophically and scientifically "debunked."[3] Minds are the products of functioning brains, and when one's brain ceases to function, one's mind ceases to exist. We are not the "luminous beings" Yoda suggested we are in *The Empire Strikes Back*.

It was the purpose of my first article to explore the relevance of these philosophical and scientific discoveries to the debate about the morality and legality of abortion. But, as one might guess, these discoveries are relevant to far more than that, and are especially relevant to religious issues surrounding death. In this article, I shall explore how they are related to the issue of euthanasia. In a subsequent paper, I will explore how they are related to issues surrounding the afterlife.

Personhood, Mindedness, and Euthanasia

Euthanasia is the act of prematurely ending someone's life, at their request, when they have a terminal illness so that they can avoid its painful final stages. This basically comes in two forms. There is assisted suicide, in which a doctor will hook a patient up to a machine that will administer a lethal dose of a drug that will kill the patient painlessly, and then let the patient "push the button" themselves. (This is what the recently developed Swiss "Sacro

---

[3] For a short explanation of why scientists and philosophers do not believe in souls, see Johnson, "Do Souls Exist?" 61–75. For a much longer, more thorough, and better explanation, see, Musolino, "The Soul Fallacy: What Science Shows We Gain From Letting Go of the Soul."

Machine" allows.)[4] Then, there is active euthanasia, in which a doctor pushes the button for them, at their request, because the patient is unable to do so. For simplicity, I will be referring to both activities with one term, "euthanasia." I assume that the permissibility or impermissibility of both activities goes hand in hand. Both are different than passive euthanasia, where a doctor removes a patient from life support if it is clear that they do not wish (or would not wish) to be on it; as I shall discuss briefly below, that is already legal, and widely considered moral.

Unlike with abortion, the being that would be killed by an act of euthanasia is fully-minded and unquestionably a person, so there is no debate about personhood among those who disagree about euthanasia. Instead, the euthanasia debate centers around the question of whether a doctor assisting a person in ending their life early upon request for the purpose of avoiding a painful death is morally permissible. Importantly, an assumption made by both sides is that, even though the morality and legality of euthanasia are technically separate questions, if it is morally permissible, it should be legal—and if it is never morally permissible, it should be illegal.

The Primary Objections

The arguments against euthanasia usually focus on two claims: (1) allowing doctors to prematurely end a patient's life to deal with a terminal illness will lead to doctors treating non-terminal conditions (like old-age, mental illness, or depression) in this way; (2) regardless of the goal, euthanasia is the killing of a person, and that is always wrong (except in certain extenuating circumstances, such as self-defense or in war, that do not apply in cases of euthanasia). Let us consider each argument in turn.

The first claim is a slippery slope argument that, although it does not concern issues of personhood and mindedness, should still be addressed. Slippery slope arguments are usually fallacious. Even if some first step is in the direction of some undesirable outcome, that fact provides no reason to think that outcome will be reached. To think it will be, one must also establish that the first step is on a slope and that the slope is slippery (e.g., that the first step will lead to a chain reaction that ends in disaster). Without such an argument, for all we know, the "slope" might instead be a level plane or even a difficult uphill climb. When I step outside my office, I am one step closer to Florida, and the top of Mount Everest, but that does not mean I will end up in either location.

---

[4] See O'Dea, "Sarco suicide capsule hopes to enter Switzerland."

In other words, the burden of proof is on the one making the claim that the slope is slippery.[5] And when it comes to euthanasia, not only do we *not have evidence* that the slope is slippery, we *have direct evidence* that it is not. That is not to say that some, like J. Peirra, have not tried to suggest it is slippery—that legalizing euthanasia will lead to "euthanasia creep" (doctors using euthanasia to treat a wider and wider variety of non-terminal conditions).[6] But his argument has been "debunked" (i.e., revealed to have been filled with unsupported statements and misinterpreted evidence).[7] In reality, while euthanasia in the case of terminal illness does become more common after it is legalized (as one would expect for most things after they are legalized), in countries where euthanasia has already been legal for years, such as the Netherlands, Colombia, Belgium, and Luxembourg, euthanasia creep has not occurred.[8]

More relevant to our topic of personhood and mindedness is the second objection: regardless of the goal, euthanasia is the killing of a *person*, and killing a person is always wrong (unless it is to save the life of another person, as in self-defense or war). But something we learned from the abortion debate in my last article (perhaps ironically from the "pro-life" side of the debate) reveals the weakness in this argument against euthanasia. Recall that Don Marquis argued that what makes the act of murder morally wrong is not the mere fact that it is the killing of a person; instead, it is the fact that the act has prevented the occurrence of future minded experiences that otherwise would have taken place—experiences that the person in question would have wanted to have.[9] This is why we react to the premature death of children and the death of the elderly differently. A bus accident that kills fifty elderly people is tragic, but not as tragic as one that kills fifty children. The former had the chance to experience most of their lives; the latter did not—the latter had more future experiences robbed from them.

According to Marquis, this means that abortion is morally problematic regardless of whether a fetus is a person. Since (even if a fetus is not currently a person), a fetus would have future experiences if left alone, and aborting it

---

[5] For more on this fallacy, see Muniz entry "Slippery Slope" in Arp, Barbone, and Bruce's *Bad Arguments: 100 of the Most Important Fallacies in Western Philosophy*, 385–7.

[6] Pereira, "Legalizing Euthanasia or Assisted Suicide: The Illusion of Safeguards and Controls," 38-45.

[7] Downie, (et al.) "Pereira's Attack on Legalizing Euthanasia or Assisted Suicide: Smoke and Mirrors," 133–8.

[8] Symons, "When It Comes to Euthanasia, Not All Slippery Slope Arguments Are 'Bullshit.'"

[9] Marquis, "Why Abortion is Immoral," 183–202.

would rob it of them, abortion cannot simply be dismissed as a morally neutral action. In my last article, I argued that the rights of the mother outweigh the rights of the fetus, even if it is a person with (as Marquis puts it) a "future like ours." So Marquis' argument is not sufficient to establish his anti-abortion thesis. But it does take the teeth out of objections to euthanasia based on the mere idea "that killing a person is always wrong." If what makes killing wrong is the fact that it prevents the occurrence of future experiences, namely experiences that the person in question would have wanted to have, then one cannot base their objection to euthanasia merely on the fact that it is an act of killing. Not only does a terminally ill patient not have many future experiences left, but the ones they have left are not the kind of experiences they want to have. The key element that makes killing wrong—the person having a future like ours—is absent in cases of euthanasia.

To put it another way: a person's merely being alive is not intrinsically valuable. Not even being a person is intrinsically valuable. What is intrinsically valuable is the experiences one has as a person: one's mindedness. Being alive, being a person, is instrumentally valuable as the means by which one is minded and has worthwhile experiences. So, if a person's future worthwhile experiences have already been robbed from them by a terminal illness, their "being alive" is no longer valuable. Consequently, if one helps such a person end their life, they are not harming them by robbing them of something valuable. Indeed, one is helping them avoid something that is not valuable, something they want most to avoid: a painful death.

The fact that merely being alive is not intrinsically valuable is bolstered by common intuitions and laws about passive euthanasia, where a patient beyond hope of recovery is taken off life support. When the patient's wishes to not live on life support have been made clear, it is legal to take them off life support and generally considered morally acceptable to do so. The same is true with DNR (do not resuscitate) orders. A paramedic is doing nothing wrong if they do not save the life of someone with a DNR, even if they could. Why? Because merely being alive is not intrinsically valuable.

The Role of Consent and Evaluation

From such intuitions and laws, it would seem to be a straight line to the conclusion that euthanasia is morally permissible. If "they didn't want to live like that" is reason enough to allow someone to die, then "they don't want to live like that" should be reason enough to help someone die. Co-director of the Yale-Hastings Program in Ethics and Health Policy Daniel Callahan would likely disagree, however. In his article, "When Self Determination Runs Amok," he points out that a patient no longer wanting to live is not reason enough to morally justify helping them die.[10] A teenage boy, for example, may want to die after his longtime girlfriend dies, but that would not morally justify helping him commit suicide. Unless someone really would be better off not experiencing the future that is ahead of them, euthanasia would not be justified. Callahan also points out that a doctor determining that a patient's future days will be not worth living is not enough to justify euthanasia either; even if the doctor knows that a patient's well-being would be secured by euthanasia, if the patient does not request it, the doctor should not perform it.

But as an argument that euthanasia is never justified (and thus should be illegal), Callahan's objections fall short. Indeed, they merely reveal the roles that patient consent *and* a doctor's evaluation play when euthanasia is justified: neither is sufficient, and both are necessary. If in the face of the last throes of a painful terminal illness, a patient decides they would rather not suffer and requests euthanasia, and the doctor's evaluation of their prognosis aligns with that determination, then it is morally justified—despite the fact that it involves the active killing of a person. Their painful terminal illness is an extenuating circumstance and the patient's right of self-determination to secure their own well-being makes euthanasia morally permissible. But if either patient consent or the doctor's agreement with the patient's assessment is missing, it is not.

Of course, if made legal, safeguards would need to be put in place to make sure that patients are of sound mind when they make the request, and that doctors' evaluations of their patient's prognosis is sound—and such safeguards have already been effective where euthanasia is legal.[11] They will not be flawless, of course. No system is perfect. But denying someone euthanasia when they want and need it seems just as morally problematic as administering it when, beyond all odds, they would have recovered. No one should be forced to live though a painful terminal illness against their wishes. If you would be willing to suffer through the final stages of a terminal illness on the off chance of the discovery of a miracle cure, you should have that right; but you should not have the right to legally force the same decision on others.

---

[10] Callahan, "When Self-Determination Runs Amuck," 409–415.
[11] Brock, "Voluntary Active Euthanasia," 10–22.

The Soldier Analogy
and the Hippocratic Oath

To drive the point home, consider an analogy. Suppose the last two soldiers of an army are on a battlefield; one's arms are injured and the other's legs. The latter cannot walk, and the former cannot carry the latter off the battlefield. But they both know that remaining guarantees that they will be captured by the enemy, tortured for weeks, and then killed. The latter insists the former flee, knowing that staying to protect him is futile, but asks his friend for one final favor: "Kill me now, so that I can avoid weeks of suffering before being killed at our enemy's hands." Would the former do something wrong by granting the request? Obviously not. Indeed, one might argue that he is morally obligated to grant it. His friend has nothing ahead of him but pain and misery; the part of his life that was worth living is over. Given the circumstance, killing him is the only way to save him.

The analogy to euthanasia is obvious of course, but one might object that the analogy does not hold because the job of a soldier is different than the job of a doctor; the former is to kill his enemy and protect his own, the latter takes an oath to heal and do no harm. But there are two things to say in response to this objection. First, if a doctor's only role was that of a healer, a doctor could not even prescribe pain medication in the case of a painful terminal illness. Since it will do nothing to heal the patient, it would be outside their designated role. But, of course, we think treating pain is well within a doctor's purview. Since sometimes euthanasia is the only way to treat pain in the case of terminal illness, it would seem that administering euthanasia is also within a doctor's purview. In short, given how they function in society, it seems that we think a doctor's role goes beyond merely "healing" and extends to "helping us cope with illness." Since, for some painful terminal illnesses, the only way to cope with them is an early death, the role we have given doctors seems to imply that they should be permitted to administer euthanasia (when the aforementioned necessary conditions are met).

Second, the argument that "euthanasia violates the Hippocratic Oath to do no harm" is problematic in many ways. For one, as we have seen, ending a patient's life in the face of a painful terminal illness is not doing harm because it is not robbing the patient of meaningful future experiences. Second, the fact that it would violate a doctor's oath does not mean that administering euthanasia would be immoral. If you make a promise (say, to pick up a friend from the airport), but a more important matter comes up (say, your wife goes into labor), it is not wrong to break that promise. Likewise, if ending someone's life in the face of a terminal illness is the right thing to do, then a doctor should do it, regardless of a promise they made in medical school, or what others think their "role as a doctor" must be. Indeed, if euthanasia in the case of terminal illness is something a doctor should be able to do, their oath should be revised to reflect that. This might seem revolutionary, but the Hippocratic Oath has actually been revised many times.[12]

To solidify this conclusion, suppose the soldiers mentioned above had taken an oath to never kill a fellow soldier after they finished bootcamp. Should this prevent the former soldier from granting his friend's request? Of course not. The moral obligation to help his friend outweighs the moral obligation to "keep his promises" or "honor his oaths." Indeed, the former soldier likely realizes that whoever wrote that oath neglected to take into consideration the possibility of situations like the one in which he has found himself. The Hippocratic Oath seems to be short-sighted in the same way.

Of course, the problem created by the Hippocratic Oath could also be solved by hospitals creating new positions for physicians whose only job would be to, when requested, determine whether euthanasia is warranted and administer it accordingly. Such physicians would simply take a different oath. Indeed, given the expertise needed, and the strain such requests would put on ordinary doctors, this may be a good suggestion anyway. In any event, however, it seems that the argument that active euthanasia, when both the patient requests it and the doctor recommends it, is morally justified, and thus should be legal.

Conclusion

In my first paper for SHERM, I discussed the relevance of issues surrounding personhood and mindedness to the issue of abortion, arguing that the issue of "fetus personhood" is irrelevant to the abortion debate. Even if a fetus is a person, abortion can still be moral. In a way, in this paper, I have argued that personhood is irrelevant to the euthanasia debate as well. Even though a terminally ill patient is a person, ending their life can still be moral. Because personhood (and mindedness) is only instrumentally valuable as means to attaining the good life, if a terminal illness has now made that impossible, it is permissible (when both the doctor and patient agree) for the doctor to help the patient end their life. Thus, euthanasia should be legal. In a subsequent

---

[12] Hulkower, "The History of the Hippocratic Oath: Outdated, Inauthentic, and Yet Still Relevant," 41–44.

article, I hope to explore how the issues of personhood and mindedness are relevant to another religious issue: our hope for an afterlife.

BIBLIOGRAPHY

Arp, Robert, Steven Barbone, and Michael Bruce. *Bad Arguments: 100 of the Most Important Fallacies in Western Philosophy*. Hoboken, NJ: Wiley-Blackwell, 2019.

Boahen, Kwabena. "Neuromorphic Microchips." *Scientific American*, Sept. 1, 2006.

Boldrini, Maura. Camille A. Fulmore, Alexandria N. Tartt, Laika R. Simeon, Ina Pavlova, Verica Poposka, Gorazd B. Rosoklija, Aleksandar Stankov, Victoria Arango, Andrew J. Dwork, René Hen, and J. John Mann. "Human Hippocampal Neurogenesis Persists throughout Aging." *Cell Stem Cell* 22, Issue 4 (2018): 589–99.

Bremmer, Jan N. *The Rise and Fall of the Afterlife: the 1995 Read-Tuckwell Lectures at the University of Bristol*. London: Routledge, 2009.

Brock, W., Dan. "Voluntary Active Euthanasia," *The Hastings Center Report* 22, no. 2 (1992): 10–22.

Bynum, Caroline Walker. *The Resurrection of the Body in Western Christianity, 200–1336*. New York Chichester, West Sussex: Columbia University Press, 2019.

Callahan, Daniel. "When Self-Determination Runs Amuck." In Eldon Soifer (Ed). *Ethical Issues Perspectives for Canadians*. 2nd ed. Peterborough, Ontario: Broadview Press Ltd, 1997: 409–15.

Chakraborty, Rajshekhar, Areej R. El-Jawahri, Mark R. Litzow, Karen L Syrjala, Aric D. Parnes, and Shahrukh K. Hashmi. "A Systematic Review of Religious Beliefs about Major End-of-Life Issues in the Five Major World Religions." *Palliative and Supportive Care* 15, no. 5 (2017): 609–22.

Conn, Christopher H. "Human Nature and the Possibility of Life after Death: Why Christian Orthodoxy Requires Compositional Substance Dualism." *Philosophy & Theology* 20, (2008): 129–49.

Copeland, Jack. "The Curious Case of the Chinese Room." *Synthese* 95, no. 2 (1993): 173–86.

Corcoran, Kevin. *Rethinking Human Nature: A Christian Materialist Alternative to the Soul*. Baker Academic, 2006.

Cowell, Alan. "After 350 Years, Vatican Says Galileo Was Right: It Moves." *The New York Times*, Oct. 31, 1992.

Cullmann, Oscar. *Immortality of the Soul or Resurrection of the Dead? The Witness of the New Testament*. Eugine, OR: Wipf & Stock Publishers, 2000.

Downie, J, K. Chambaere, and J.L. Bernheim. "Pereira's Attack on Legalizing Euthanasia or Assisted Suicide: Smoke and Mirrors." *Current Oncology* 19, no. 3 (2012): 133–38.

Hick, John. "The Resurrection of the Person." *Death and Eternal Life*. London: Palgrave Macmillan, (1985): 278–96.

Hulkower, Raphael. "The History of the Hippocratic Oath: Outdated, Inauthentic, and Yet Still Relevant." *Einstein Journal of Biology and Medicine* 25, no. 1 (2016): 41–44.

Gaston, Thomas E. "The Influence of Platonism on the Early Apologists." *Heythrop Journal: A Bimonthly Review of Philosophy and Theology* 50, no. 4 (July 2009): 573–80.

James Giles. "The No-Self Theory: Hume, Buddhism, and Personal Identity" *Philosophy East and West* 43, no. 2 (April 1993): 175–200.

Johnson, David Kyle. "Does Free Will Exist?" *Think* 42, No. 15 (2016).

Johnson, Davide Kyle. "The Relevance (and Irrelevance) of Questions of Personhood (and Mindedness) to the Abortion Debate." *SHERM* 1, no. 2 (2019): 121–53.

Johnson, David Kyle. *The Big Questions of Philosophy*. Chantilly, VA: The Great Courses/The Teaching Company, 2016.

Krulwich, Robert. "Can ET And Christmas Co-Exist?" *NPR*, Dec. 22, 2010.

Kuhn, Robert L. "Would Intelligent Aliens Undermine God?" *Science and Religion Today*. Mar. 18, 2010.

Lycan, William G. "Is Property Dualism Better off than Substance Dualism?" *SpringerLink*, Springer Netherlands, Feb. 12, 2012.

Marquis, Don. "Why Abortion is Immoral," *The Journal of Philosophy* 86, no. 4 (April, 1989): 183–202.

O'Meara, Thomas F. *Vast Universe: Extraterrestrials and Christian Revelation.* Wilmington, DE: Michael Glazier, 2012.

Paine, Thomas. *The Age of Reason: Part the Second. Being an Investigation of True and of Fabulous Theology. Second edition.* Farmington Hills, MI: Gale Ecco, 2010.

Parfit, Derek. "The Psychological View." *Self and Identity: Contemporary Philosophical Issues.* NYC: Macmillan Publishing Company, (1991): 227–66.

Pereira, J. "Legalizing Euthanasia or Assisted Suicide: The Illusion of Safeguards and Controls." *Current Oncology* 18, no. 2 (2011): 38–45.

Schick, Theodore and Lewis Vaughn. *Doing Philosophy 6th Edition.* NYC: McGraw Hill, 2020.

Searle, John. "Minds, Brains, and Programs." *Behavioral and Brain Sciences* 3, (1980): 417–24.

Spalding, Kristy, Ratan D. Bhardwaj, Bruce A. Buchholz, Henrik Druid, and Jonas Frisén. "Retrospective Birth Dating of Cells in Humans." *Cell* 122, Issue 1 (2005): 133–43.

Symons, Xavier. "When It Comes to Euthanasia, Not All Slippery Slope Arguments Are 'Bullshit.'" *The Conversation*, May 21, 2019.

Silva, Lynn A. *The Problem of the Self in Buddhism and Christianity.* London: Palgrave Macmillan, 1979.

Thatcher, Adrian. "Christian and the Concept of a Person." In A. Peacocke and G. Gillette's (eds.) *Persons and Personality.* Oxford: Blackwell, 1987.

Title, Peg. *What If...: Collected Thought Experiments in Philosophy.* London: Pearson/Longman, 2005.

Treier, Danel, Walter A Elwell (eds.) *Evangelical Dictionary of Theology* Grand Rapids, MI: Baker Academic, 2001.

van Inwagen, Peter. "The Possibility of Resurrection" *International Journal for Philosophy of Religion* 9, no. 2 (1978): 114–21.

Vogels, "Review of 'The Garden of Eden and the Hope of Immortality', by James Barr." *Critical Review of Books in Religion* 7 (1994).

Wallenhorst, S D. "The Drake Equation Reexamined." *Quarterly Journal of the Royal Astronomical Society* 22, (1981): 380–87.

ABOUT THE AUTHOR

David Kyle Johnson is professor of philosophy at King's College (Wilkes-Barre, Pennsylvania) who also produces lecture series for The Teaching Company's (aka Wondrium's) The Great Courses. His specializations include metaphysics, logic, philosophy of science, and philosophy of religion, and his "Great Courses" include Sci-Phi: Science Fiction as Philosophy, The Big Questions of Philosophy, and Exploring Metaphysics. Kyle has published in journals such as Sophia, Religious Studies, Think, Philo, Religions, and Science, Religion and Culture. He has also written numerous book chapters, including eleven entries in Bad Arguments: 100 of The Most Important Logical Fallacies in Western Philosophy (Wiley-Blackwell, 2018). He is also the editor-in-chief of The Palgrave Handbook of Popular Culture as Philosophy (Palgrave, forthcoming), and the editor of Black Mirror and Philosophy: Dark Reflections (Wiley-Blackwell, 2019). He maintains two blogs for Psychology Today (Plato on Pop and A Logical Take), and most of his academic work is available for free download on academia.edu.

MORE FROM THE AUTHOR

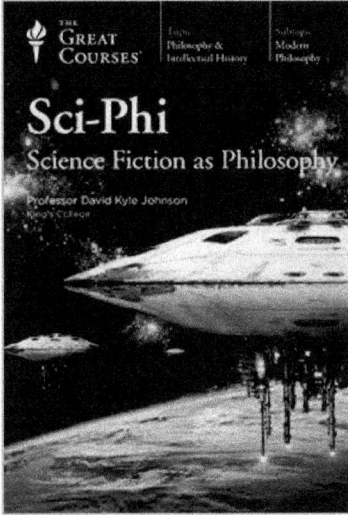

Sci-Phi:
Science Fiction as Philosophy
The Great Courses, 2018

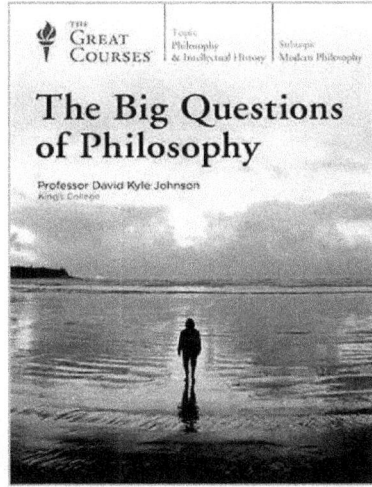

The Big Questions of Philosophy
The Great Courses, 2016

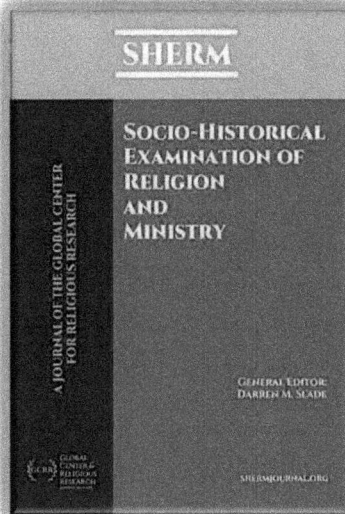

THE AMITYVILLE HORROR

An Inquest into Paranormal Claims

FRANK R. ZINDLER

Frank Zindler's day-by-day investigation of the infamous 28-day "ordeal" is a textbook example of how to investigate claims of demonic possession and other supernatural yarns. It draws upon everything from weather records for the demonic days to court records of a trial in which the Lutzes and the lawyers sued each other for fraud; from polygraph reports to interviews with priests, police, and other Amityville persons mentioned in the original book to the auction inventory of possessions provided by the realtor who sold the house to the Lutzes. Demonstrating extensive plagiarism from the novel The Exorcist, Zindler's deconstruction of Jay Anson's "True Story" is the definitive critique of a hoax that since 1977 has grown into a half-billion-dollar industry that feeds upon public ignorance and superstition.

GCRR PRESS

SHERM 5/1 (2023): 44–67

The Trickster:
A Political Theology for Our Time

Jack David Eller,
Global Center for Religious Research

Abstract: *Political theology has traditionally been dominated by Christian concepts, specifically the concept of a law-giving and order-preserving god. Other political theologies are possible, however, and this essay considers one—the trickster—a culture hero and comic buffoon who delightedly and shamelessly violates and subverts order to inaugurate a new reality of his own making, if not of his own will. The first half of the essay introduces the trickster as a cross-cultural agent of creative destruction, a messenger and civilization-bringer, and a clever fool. The second half explores how the last two centuries of Western social and intellectual history have shifted the ground from under a god of order toward a spirit of flux, transience, paradox, and liminality. The essay concludes that the contemporary post-modern state of permanent liminality is better symbolized and grasped through the mythical lens of the trickster than the biblical god, including and especially contemporary global right-wing populism, whose leading figures reflect the wicked energy and appeal of the trickster impulse.*

Keywords: Liminality, Political Theology, Post-modern, Post-truth, Trickster

---

[T]he characteristics of the trickster capture with a striking completeness the main features of modernity—exchange, production, interaction, growth, destruction, dissolution, substitution, subversion, or new versions—so much so that the trickster could be outright considered as the deity of modernity.[1]

For two millennia, political theology was conducted in the theistic, more specifically the Christian, voice. The enduring concern was the relation between "God and government" or between divine power and temporal leadership and social organization; in practice, as Saul Newman notes, "the problem of political theology is a way of thinking about the foundations and legitimacy of power" in the human kingdom, empire, or state.[2] This project is understandable in a world dominated by Christianity and in search of absolutes

---

[1] Horvath and Szakolczai, *Political Sociology and Anthropology of Evil*, 159–60.
[2] Newman, *Political Theology*, xx.

Socio-Historical Examination of Religion and Ministry
Volume 5, Issue 1, Summer 2023 shermjournal.org
© Jack David Eller
Permissions: editor@shermjournal.org
ISSN 2637-7519 (print), ISSN 2637-7500 (online)
https://doi.org/10.33929/sherm.2023.vol5.no1.03 (article)

of law and authority, a world like the ancient and medieval West. The Christian god, like the Hebrew god before him and the Muslim god after, is a god of law, of truth and fundamentally of order, whose key feature is constancy, stability, or immutability—also the key aspiration of human rulers and their regimes. Institutions, rules, and hierarchies once established should ideally be settled and beyond question.

However, in characterizing political theology as the *"ever-changing relationships* between political community and religious order, between power [or authority: *Herrschaft*] and salvation [*Heil*]"[3] (emphasis added), Jan Assman alerted us to the reality that not only the association between politics and religion but the *qualities of politics and religion* themselves change over time, new religious ideas calling forth new political systems but equally *new political ideas and experiences calling forth new religious concepts.* This perception was greatly advanced by Carl Schmitt, who reoriented political theology away from order and law and toward the violation of order/law, the change, the exception: "Sovereign is he," Schmitt famously wrote, "who decides on the exception."[4]

Accordingly, recent international experience has witnessed a wave of leaders—often identified as right-wing populist, authoritarian, or illiberal—who show indifference if not disdain for established political norms, traditions, institutions, laws, constitutions, or facts themselves. When an American president like George W. Bush utters, "I'm the decider," or like Donald Trump declares, "the one that matters is me. I'm the only one that matters, because when it comes to it, that's what the policy is going to be," we have left the *civitas dei* and entered the *civitas exceptio* or *civitas voluntas/potestas*. On the Weberian (and also Marxian) premise that different religions flourish in different social and political soil, it is thus time for a different political theology, one not constructed on a constant figure like the Judeo-Christian-Islamic god but on a being that personifies change, instability, flux, transgression, creative destruction, and wicked fun. That being is the trickster.

Please Allow Me to Introduce Myself:
The Trickster

Across world religion and folklore, one of the most ubiquitous characters is the trickster, sometimes a demi-god, sometimes a human or an animal (or some combination thereof). In a foundational study, Barbara

---

[3] Quoted in de Vries, "Introduction: Before, Around, and Beyond the Theologico-Political," 25.

[4] Schmitt, *Political Theology*, 5.

Babcock-Abrahams called him (as most tricksters are male) the "expression of ambiguity and paradox, a confusion of all customary categories."[5] She listed sixteen common traits of tricksters cross-culturally, including a disregard for spatial and temporal boundaries, prodigious appetites for food and sex, anomalous qualities of gender and age (both or alternately male and female or young and old), a connection with "crossroads, open public places (especially the marketplace), doorways, and thresholds," and most importantly behavior that is "generally amoral and asocial—aggressive, vindictive, vain, defiant of authority, etc.)."[6]

In a subsequent study, William Hynes distilled the traits of the trickster down to six essential components: "(1) the fundamentally ambiguous and anomalous personality of the trickster. Flowing from this are such other features as (2) deceiver/trick-player, (3) shapeshifter, (4) situation-invertor, (5) messenger/imitator of the gods, and (6) sacred/lewd bricoleur."[7] At the crux of the trickster is anomaly, even sacrilege: "his activities are often outlawish, outlandish, outrageous, out-of-bounds, and out-of-order. No borders are sacrosanct, be they religious, cultural, linguistic, epistemological, or metaphysical. Breaking down division lines, the trickster characteristically moves swiftly and impulsively back and forth across all borders with virtual impunity."[8] Inevitably, his disrespect for boundaries and order extends to truth itself; "lying, cheating, tricking, and deceiving" are all part of his *modus operandi*.[9] He is not even faithful to or stable in his own shape, easily "alter[ing] his shape or bodily appearance in order to facilitate deception."[10] He treats the world around him with the same inconsequence:

No order is too rooted, no taboo too sacred, no god too high, no profanity too scatological that it cannot be broached or inverted. What prevails is toppled, what is bottom becomes top, what is outside turns inside, what is inside turns outside, and on and on in an unending concatenation of contingency.[11]

---

[5] Babcock-Abrahams, "A Tolerated Margin of Mess," 160.
[6] Babcock-Abrahams, "A Tolerated Margin of Mess," 159–60.
[7] Hynes, "Mapping the Characteristics of Mythic Tricksters," 34.
[8] Hynes, "Mapping the Characteristics of Mythic Tricksters," 34.
[9] Hynes, "Mapping the Characteristics of Mythic Tricksters," 35.
[10] Hynes, "Mapping the Characteristics of Mythic Tricksters," 36.
[11] Hynes, "Mapping the Characteristics of Mythic Tricksters," 37.

Paradoxically, the trickster's inattention to consequences is itself highly consequential, and herein lies his greatest meaning and contribution. His antics, often comic, are not perfectly negative or destructive but are often profoundly positive and constructive. Babcock-Abrahams recognized that he is widely identified with creativity,

> often bringing such defining features of culture as fire or basic food, and yet he constantly behaves in the most antisocial manner we can imagine. Although we laugh at him for his troubles and his foolishness and are embarrassed by his promiscuity, his creative cleverness amazes us and keeps alive the possibility of transcending the social restrictions we regularly encounter.[12]

Michael Carroll, locating the trickster as "selfish buffoon" and "culture hero," also stressed that he "is often the agent responsible for creating the conditions that allowed for the development of human civilization," like Prometheus stealing fire from the gods and bestowing its boon on humanity, or in other cases teaching people the skills of language, agriculture, blacksmithing, and so forth.[13]

The trickster is seldom if ever the high god, ultimate creator of the universe. He appears after creation, to upset and re-form the natural and social world. He frequently does not intend to establish a new order, let alone aid others. On these grounds, Harold Scheub ranks him below the creator god but above the culture hero; he "lacks the sublime connection with the gods," although he is sometimes descended from them and serves as an intermediary or messenger between them and mankind.[14] Surely enough, he "disrupts harmony" but then founds a new order, although "it is according to his own whim, his own sense of order."[15] Either way—intentionally or accidentally, beneficently or maliciously—he "is always reinventing the world, testing boundaries, relearning the possibilities"; he is never quite the culture hero or leader, rather he is forever,

> doing things to leaders that we dare not do, saying things that we dare not say. Trickster is amiable at times, brutal at others. He is unpredictable. The friendly spider and the cuddly hare may also be deadly. That is the

---

[12] Babcock-Abrahams, "A Tolerated Margin of Mess," 147.

[13] Carroll, "The Trickster as Selfish-Buffoon and Culture Hero," 106.

[14] Scheub, *Trickster and Hero*, 6.

[15] Scheub, *Trickster and Hero*, 6.

seemingly quirky power of the trickster. He is the clown, who makes one laugh ... but nervously, because, in his stupidity and witless humor, we see ourselves.[16]

In short, society and reality, order and truth, do not bind him, but in crucial ways he binds them. As a rule-breaker, he becomes a rule-maker.

The deep significance of the trickster is that, just as he is protean (an adjective derived from another tricksterish god, Proteus, renowned for his flexibility and mutability, his capacity to take many shapes like the water over which he presided), he demonstrates that the social and physical world is protean too—given form by the creator god to be sure, but nevertheless malleable to the actions of a powerful and willful being. Like the reality that he molds via his "outrageous, obscene, death-dealing, uncaring, ignoble" conduct, he "remains forever an undifferentiated force; he is never tamed, never domesticated, although he may appear to be so at times, usually as a part of a sly plan to gain something for himself."[17] His profane and irreverent ways naturally feel like corruption and immorality from the perspective of the existing order, but "he imposes his own corrupt sense of order on the real world"[18] *just as the original creator god imposed his sense of order on the world in the first place.*

A few brief examples of tricksters across history and culture will illustrate the point. In Western mythology, the preeminent trickster-god is the Greek Hermes, although Prometheus and the Norse god Loki also wear the label. Son of Zeus and younger brother of Apollo, Norman O. Brown called Hermes the Thief (who as a newborn stole cattle from his elder sibling) and "god of the boundary-stone" (the *herm* or stone-heap, situated at doorways, crossroads, hilltops, and other such sites where strangers might intersect, including the marketplace).[19] According to William Doty he was the patron of "craftspersons, cooks, heralds, teachers, and servants" as well as "roads and travelers," and he inhabited the domain of "change, movement, and alteration."[20] Doty considered Hermes, like Prometheus, to be a culture-bringer, not a deity who invents new realities but one who delivers them to humans; akin to his trickster peers, Hermes performed not creations but "corrections and restorations" with the effect "of making the cosmos more habitable for

---

[16] Scheub, *Trickster and Hero*, 7.
[17] Scheub, *Trickster and Hero*, 34.
[18] Scheub, *Trickster and Hero*, 34.
[19] Brown, *Hermes the Thief*, 38.
[20] Doty, "A Lifetime of Trouble-Making," 48.

mankind."[21] Most fascinatingly, Doty noticed a link between Hermes and hermeneutics, the function of establishing and conveying meaning:

> Hermes carries messages from one person or deity to another; he does not always originate them, and he may select or adapt what he alone chooses to present, and when. As the divine messenger, he participates in the formidable creative power of Zeus as its facilitator, as the one who provides for bringing into language what was only potential.[22]

Another famed trickster figure is Eshu or Eshu-Elegba. The Yoruba of West Africa related Eshu-Elegba to a number of diverse but related social spaces—"crossroads, compound entrances, market places, king's palaces, shrines within compounds, and divining sessions."[23] What these threshold places have in common is mystery and liminality. It is easy to see how crossroads, entrances, shrines, and ceremonies are liminal, but from the Yoruba viewpoint the market is also a "marginal world, a place where the unexpected can occur and fortunes can be reversed"; there, as in all these locations, "Order is fragile" due to the "welter and diversity of forces for good and ill, of forces of change and transformation—personal and impersonal—that pervade human experience."[24] At such sites, where the "awareness of the unexpected, of the accidental, and of fate, is heightened," that is "where Eshu must be acknowledged."[25] Based on this account, John Pemberton concluded that Eshu-Elegba was a trickster deity, characterized by caprice, deception, provocation, and potential harm. He may trip you and trick you, but his trickery "must not be seen simply as deceit; it is a power," specifically the power of "secret action" and unpredictable changes of course.[26] Moises Lino e Silva finds Eshu in the Afro-Brazilian religion of Umbanda, where he is "the god of all agreements and disagreements, lord of all paths and crossroads and the master of all order and confusion."[27] Umbanda's Eshu is the vehicle for a "radical sort of transformation of … the very existential order and of the very epistemological basis from which to judge existence."[28] Eshu thus represents and brings

---

[21] Doty, "A Lifetime of Trouble-Making," 55.
[22] Doty, "A Lifetime of Trouble-Making," 62.
[23] Pemberton, "Eshu-Elegba," 22.
[24] Pemberton, "Eshu-Elegba," 25.
[25] Pemberton, "Eshu-Elegba," 25.
[26] Pemberton, "Eshu-Elegba," 26.
[27] Lino e Silva, "Ontological Confusion," 34
[28] Lino e Silva, "Ontological Confusion," 43–4.

confusion but a kind of confusion that devotees understand and value; Lino e Silva makes the pregnant observation that Brazilian evangelical Christians do not appreciate such confusion, deeming it inappropriate, sinful, and literally devilish. We will return to this point shortly.

Traditional and indigenous religions and mythology are replete with trickster figures. Paul Radin's classic 1956 study chronicled the Winnebago (Native American) character Wakdjunkaga, which translates as "the tricky one." Radin branded Wakdjunkaga a fool and breaker of taboos, mentally a child; more importantly, though, he "is at one and the same time creator and destroyer, giver and negator....He possesses no values, moral or social, is at the mercy of his passions and appetites, yet through his actions all values come into being."[29] Throughout Native American and African societies, tricksters star in folktales in the guise of animals such as coyotes, hyenas, birds, snakes, and insects. The Asante (West African) trickster Anansi was depicted as a spider. A typical boundary-crosser and messenger from the gods, Emily Marshall opined that he "existed halfway between the earth and the sky and had the power to restructure both the world of the divine and the human"; although selfish and antisocial, Anansi "brought both wisdom and stories to earth from the realm of Nyame [the high god]" thereby bestowing on humanity "the fundamentals of civilization, wisdom (knowledge) and stories (history)."[30]

We could multiply examples of the trickster, but he is actually only one actor in a cast of religious exceptions. The so-called ritual clown exists in many religions; a human being rather than a god, a ritual clown like the Hopi *tsukskut* or the Yaqui Chapayeka accompanies many otherwise serious religious rituals. The masked Chapayeka, for instance, injects an element of innovation and comedy through his performance, which is sometimes "playful and quite intentionally very funny" and at other times "more straightforward, aloof, or even frightening."[31] And like tricksters, they can cross or erase boundaries, even the boundary between sacred and profane. With their behavioral unpredictability they "do not just represent otherness in the world-outside-the-ritual, they bring it with them"—which does not contradict or subvert the ritual but "is a part of the efficacy and power of the total ritual."[32] The well-known role of shaman likewise achieves its effects—especially healing—by crossing boundaries (e.g. "soul flight" to the spirit realm) and by integrating spirits into his/her body and personality, thus becoming a multiple person capable of seeing

---

[29] Radin, *The Trickster*, ix.
[30] Marshall, "Liminal Anansi: Symbol of Order and Chaos," 31–2.
[31] Keisalo, "A Semiotics of Comedy," 102.
[32] Keisalo, "A Semiotics of Comedy," 115–6.

multiple perspectives (spiritual and human, alive and dead) and living in an ongoing state of flux.

Finally, anthropologists, folklorists, and religious studies scholars have documented entire ritual complexes that seem to challenge and invert social relations, including political hierarchies. Variously named "rituals of rebellion," "rituals of reversal," and "symbolic inversions," they involve violations or exceptions to gender roles and dress, caste exclusions, sexual norms, and political statuses. Of the most interest to us are occasions when the king or other authority is insulted, reviled, abused, or even attacked. During the South African Swazi *Incwala* or *Ncwala* ceremony, participants sang scathing critiques of the king, such as "you have wronged/bend great neck/those and those they hate him, they hate the king. King alas for your fate/King they reject thee/King, they hate thee."[33] When the king emerged from his sanctuary, he appeared in the guise of Silo, the "monster of legends." Nevertheless, the ritual ultimately concluded in the reinstallation of the king and the health of the Swazi people and land.

Clearly, tricksters and tricksterish behaviors are abundant in the world's religions and cultures. Some observers have even claimed to find trickstery in Judeo-Christian scripture. Robert Miller argued that wise king Solomon was a trickster, comparing him to the Lenape (Native American) trickster Wehixamukes, emphasizing that the king was born from an anomalous union (the adultery of David and Bathsheba), had a voracious sexual appetite, founded the genre of wisdom literature, and was regarded as a fool and "man-who-misunderstands."[34] Miller and others have further nominated Abraham, Joseph, Isaac, Esther, and of course the serpent in the garden for the trickster designation, and John Anderson presents an extended case for Jacob. But Anderson grants that Jacob did not act alone and that Yahweh behaved, in that moment and in other moments in the Bible, as a deceiver and a trickster—part of what he calls a "theology of deception" that justifies divine dishonesty "as serving a larger theological purpose: deception employed in the interest of YHWH's fidelity to the covenant and the covenant people."[35] Dean Nicholas too discovered lying and deception liberally distributed through the Pentateuch,[36] and Kathleen Warwick-Smith bluntly dubbed Yahweh a trickster, whose comportment in Genesis and elsewhere "reveals his trickster leanings. He is a liminal figure, a loner, possesses an ambiguous gender identity, is

---

[33] Kuper, *An African Aristocracy*, 204.
[34] Miller, "Solomon the Trickster," 503.
[35] Anderson, *Jacob and the Divine Trickster*, 178.
[36] Nicholas, *The Trickster Revisited*.

devious, and acts with an impetus towards cultural development and progress through an emissary and culture hero, in this story, Eve."[37]

As appealing as it is to haul the biblical god into the trickster tent, lying and deviousness alone do not a trickster make. Warwick-Smith has to confess that relative to prototypical tricksters like Hermes, Eshu, and the rest, "the Hebrew god pales in comparison"; he "is far more serious, far less burlesque, and consequently far less fun."[38] We must concur. The biblical god and the trickster do not operate in the same "modality," to use a term from Babcock-Abrahams: the trickster inhabits "the comic modality ... where violation is generally the precondition for laughter and communitas, and there tends to be an incorporation of the outsider, a leveling of hierarchy, a reversal of statuses." In contrast, she held that Yahweh and the religious and social traditions that flow from him dwell in "the tragic type and pattern. In this modality, the individual who violates the boundaries of what is generally conceived as the social or human structure is punished, and the social order is preserved by the projection of evil onto the victim."[39]

"What is the price we pay," Warwick-Smith sagely asks, "in our Judeo-Christian dominated society with a sanitized deity unable to hold the dualism of light and dark?"[40] Because the Abrahamic god works in only one mode (call it tragedy, seriousness, sobriety, or "truth"), there is no room in him for the other modes that undeniably compose the natural and social world. The monotheistic Yahweh is a monochrome god in a colorful universe. His very (putative) constancy and immutability make him the total anti-trickster (a few tricks and deceptions notwithstanding). He is the rock of ages as the continents drift beneath him, the ground of being in a universe of becoming, the unmoved in a world of motion. But this means that inconstancy, mutability, and all of the other things that he is not become marginalized and demonized as evil, heresy, blasphemy (Ioan-Alexandru Grădinaru labels the trickster the "deity of the blasphemous language"[41]) as evinced by the evangelical horror of confusion recounted by Lino e Silva above. Traces of violation remain in Christian cultures, like the practice of carnival, which in its twelfth-century Roman form was "the principal manifestation and proof of an irreducible popular proclivity for entertainment and hilarity, for the grotesque, for laughter, for parody, and for derision, all of which are tendencies clearly opposed to the austerity and

---

[37] Warwick-Smith, "Yahweh. Trickster," 4.
[38] Warwick-Smith, "Yahweh. Trickster," 1.
[39] Babcock-Abrahams, "A Tolerated Margin of Mess," 153.
[40] Warwick-Smith, "Yahweh. Trickster," 8.
[41] Grădinaru, "The Ways of the Trickster."

rigidity of high culture in general, and to the clerical one in particular."[42] It is little wonder that the Catholic Church "resolutely condemned and sometimes repressed all the practices" associated with the festival, not least masking which acquired satanic meanings but also temporary trickster-like transformations of "boys into girls, men into animals, adults into children, and even Christians into Mohammedans."[43]

Those accustomed to living in a Yahweh-centric society often miss the oppressiveness of a spiritual regime of unrelenting order. However, through the eyes of those encountering it for the first time, we can recapture some of the shock and discomfort. During the 1810s and 1820s an event known as the "Polynesian iconoclasm" unfolded across indigenous Pacific island societies; locals turned away from their traditional religions, even demolished temples and desecrated sacred objects, and embraced Christianity. Missionaries and Western explorers naturally saw this as the triumph of the one true god. What they failed to appreciate is that periodic, indeed annual, overthrowing of religious norms and institutions was part of Polynesian culture: each November, when the constellation Pleiades was rising, social rules were loosened and social distinctions reduced or ignored: on Tahiti,

> people drank large quantities of kava and sang blasphemous cursing songs. Commoners and nobles, men and women, then bathed together in the ocean....Over the next four days, sexual orgies and feasting took place....During this period of revelry the high priest was secluded and blindfolded so that he would not see the violations of sacred restriction.[44]

In the process, temples and artifacts were destroyed. Then a few months later as Pleiades sank below the horizon, order was restored: sacred statues were displayed in "a dramatic performance through which gods were called to sanctify their images and then sent away, leaving only priests and high chiefs as their representatives."[45] Yet there was always uncertainty that traditional rules and authority might be permanently unmade. Then in June 1815 as the stars descended, the Christianized chief Pomare asserted control, instructing local chiefs and priests to dispose of pagan temples and objects, inaugurating a new politics and political theology based on the new god, Jehovah. What he, his followers, and other islanders did not expect, and discovered to their dismay,

---

[42] Testa, *Rituality and Social (Dis)Order*, 21.
[43] Testa, *Rituality and Social (Dis)Order*, 114.
[44] Sissons, *The Polynesian Iconoclasm*, 14.
[45] Sissons, *The Polynesian Iconoclasm*, 17.

was that Jehovah/Yahweh did not brook any further uncertainty or challenge to his order; the cycle of structure and anti-structure was abolished, replaced by stifling spiritual monotony, which drove some islanders to repudiate Christianity.

And Yet It Moves:
The Trickster Nature of Post-Modernity and Politics

The rock of ages has been eroding for a long time. A turning point was Galileo's revelation that the earth is neither central nor static, inspiring his apocryphal and defiant comment (*"e pur si muove"*) after the Church condemned his discovery. Jumping to the modern era, almost two centuries ago Marx warned in the 1848 "Communist Manifesto" that, "All that is solid melts into air, all that is holy is profaned, and man is at last compelled to face with sober senses, his real conditions of life, and his relations with his kind." Hardly a decade later, Darwin taught that variations and change, not ideal types and stasis, were the reality of biological life. Less than thirty years more passed before Nietzsche announced the death of God: in *The Gay Science* (section 125), the message comes from a madman, who queries, without the fixed ground of being, "Whither is [the universe] moving now? Whither are we moving? Away from all suns? Are we not plunging continually? Backward, sideward, forward, in all directions? Is there any up or down? Are we not straying, as through an infinite nothing? Do we not feel the breath of empty space?" Nietzsche emphasized the vertigo, the nausea of gazing into such an abyss, but he got cause and effect backward: the universe was not suddenly moving because Christianity's god was dead, but rather that god was dead to us, was no longer credible, because we suddenly noticed the universe moving.

The injuries to conventional political theology accelerated around the turn of the century, coming from every angle. Einstein's general relativity theory and anthropology's cultural relativism both corroded previous certainties: no longer was there a single absolute point from which to view and judge the world but instead the position (physical or cultural) of the observer shaped the perception of knowledge and truth. Disorientation was evident in the art and literature of the late nineteenth century and only exacerbated by the destruction wrought by World War I. From those ashes artistic/intellectual movements like Dada and surrealism arose. In his 1918 "Dada Manifesto," Tristan Tzara wrote,

There is no ultimate truth … Does anyone think that, by a minute refinement of logic, they have demonstrated the truth and established the correctness of their opinions?…I detest greasy objectivity, and harmony, the science that finds everything in order … I am against systems, the most acceptable system is on principle to have none.[46]

According to Jed Rasula, the potent mix of "irreverence and ingenuity" coursing through Dada (and subsequent styles like surrealism, cubism, etc.) endorsed and embraced "destruction as a creative weapon"; enacting the Nietzschean dictum to give a push to anything that is already falling, and "[r]ealizing there would be no return to normal life after the hostilities [of the war] ceased, the Dadaists assaulted any lingering fantasy of normality," let alone of the pipedream of constancy.[47]

At the same moment that the Great War was ending and Dada was being born, many were celebrating or mourning the reign of absurdity. Echoing Marx, Yeats wrote in his 1920 poem "The Second Coming," "Things fall apart, the center cannot hold, mere anarchy is loosed upon the world." The Second World War only superficially restored sense to the world (a sense of good versus evil, of freedom versus totalitarianism) while threatening all sense—especially the sense of a omnipotent and loving god—with the Holocaust and the atomic bomb. These experiences birthed Sartre's 1943 *Being and Nothingness* and Camus' novels *The Stranger* (1942) and *The Plague* (1947), introducing existentialism with its burden of freedom and its obligation of choice (heresy, *hairesis*, in an earlier age of Church domination).

The human-made (and thus human-changeable) nature of social life was heralded from multiple quarters. Knowledge was a language game (Wittgenstein), social systems were merely regimes of truth (Foucault), and even science, that bastion of facts, lurched from one paradigm to the next (Kuhn). For the social sciences, Peter Berger and Thomas Luckmann's 1966 *The Social Construction of Reality* was the ultimate statement of the social origin of knowledge. But worse was to come, for instance Jean Baudrillard's 1981 *Simulacra and Simulation*, prophesying how simulation does not represent reality but *replaces* reality and "threatens the difference between the 'true' and the 'false,' the 'real' and the 'imaginary.'"[48] The simulation does not "refer to"

---

[46] Tzara, "Dada Manifesto."
[47] Rasula, *Destruction was My Beatrice*, 301.
[48] Baudrillard, *Simulacra and Simulation, 3.*

reality, rather producing "models of a real without origin or reality: a hyperreal" which is sometimes more appealing, if not more convincing, than reality.[49]

Thus we have crossed a line from modernity to post-modernity, from truth to post-truth. Although characterized in different ways by rival scholars, post-modernity stresses the subjective, the superficial, the spontaneous, the unofficial and non-bureaucratic. It doubts progress, let alone truth: in most versions, there is no ultimate reality, no certain truth, no absolute ground or center. Hence, knowledge is "decentered," especially displacing Western and Christian society from the center and "provincializing" it. A culmination of at least two centuries of intellectual and practical effort, post-modernity leaves the individual both saturated with "facts" and claims and saddled with the responsibility to figure it out for herself. Or, in the words of Walter Truett Anderson, in the traditional pre-modern condition there was no choice, for reality was given: "If you choose, you are at least modern. If you know you are choosing, you are postmodern."[50]

Most recently, Zygmunt Bauman expressed the lived quality of late modernity or post-modernity as "liquid." Unlike solids, fluids "cannot easily hold their shape"; "Fluids, so to speak, neither fix space nor bind time…. [They] do not keep to any shape for long and are constantly ready (and prone) to change it."[51] Reiterating the intuitions of Marx and Nietzsche more than a century prior, Bauman argued that we simply "found the pre-modern solids in a fairly advanced state of disintegration," pulverized by economic, political, scientific, artistic, and philosophical forces.[52] And, repeating the lessons of Dada and existentialism, the individual finds herself in,

> an individualized, privatized version of modernity, with the burden of pattern-weaving and the responsibility for failure falling primarily on the individual's shoulders. It is the patterns of dependency and interaction whose turn to be liquefied has now come. They are now malleable to an extent unexperienced by, and unimaginable for, past generations; but like all fluids they do not keep their shape for long.[53]

Indeed, to employ Marx's stronger language, sometimes life and reality feel so volatile that they have morphed from liquid to gas.

---

[49] Baudrillard, *Simulacra and Simulation,* 1.
[50] Anderson, *Reality Isn't What It Used to Be,* 112.
[51] Bauman, *Liquid Modernity,* 2.
[52] Bauman, *Liquid Modernity,* 3.
[53] Bauman, *Liquid Modernity,* 6.

The keywords of post-modernity are heard often enough: discontinuity, flux, transience, hybridity, borderlands, rupture, emergence. One term seized upon by diverse thinkers is *liminality*. Originally developed in ritual studies, liminality (from Latin, *limen*, threshold) denotes the transition from one status to another (child to adult, single to married, profane to sacred) and especially the moment of statuslessness when the person undergoing transformation is "betwixt and between," neither child nor adult, etc. In the formulation of its most renowned advocate, anthropologist Victor Turner, liminality is a temporary state, for neither the individual nor the society can remain in limbo (from Latin, *limbus*, border or edge) for long.[54] But liminality is also powerful and creative: it is a nursery where new types and new forms arise.

What many scholars have diagnosed in the post-modern condition, though, is a situation of *permanent liminality*. One of its most ardent spokesmen, Arpad Szakolczai, defines permanent liminality as what "simply happens when a temporary suspension of, or deviation from, the normal, everyday, taken for granted state of affairs becomes permanent."[55] Elsewhere he adds that life today "involves an infinite period of transition, in which the stable elements of social life, representing not just rigid external constraints on individual freedom, but also the condition of possibility of meaningful life, are one by one liquidated."[56] He and others have opined that permanent liminality is a situation of being frozen on the threshold, but this is not quite right, or at least not quite how most people experience it most of the time. Rather than being stuck in one spot (although, admittedly, some confront it in that way, such as asylum seekers or refugees in camps or holding stations), permanent liminality is encountered as *an indefinite series of thresholds*. Instead of expecting things to remain the same (a thoroughly *pre-modern* mentality) in regards to job and career, lifestyle, institutions and values, or political authorities, or even expecting to change and then settle or abide in a new condition, we have more or less come to anticipate change to be persistent and unending; no sooner than we cross a threshold, personal or collective, and enter a new "room" do we face another threshold and another room, and then another and another *ad infinitum*. A trivial but telling example is the voyage that music fans have made from vinyl records to cassette tapes to compact discs to mp3s to whatever comes next—or the eternal pursuit of the next generation of iPhone.

Where we do align with Szakolczai is in his identification of permanent liminality with the trickster. In various articles and books he invokes the figure

---

[54] Turner, *The Forest of Symbols*.
[55] Szakolczai, "Permanent (Trickster) Liminality," 3.
[56] Szakolczai, "Living Permanent Liminality," 28.

of the trickster, the restless crosser of boundaries; at one point he equates permanent liminality with trickster liminality. And all of this, finally, converges on the political. At virtually the same moment that Dada artists were making and performing their art, and Yeats was suffering the collapse of the center, political scientist Carl Schmitt was reformulating political theology. As noted at the outset of this essay, Schmitt located the heart of political authority not in order but in exception; real power comes not in following the law—that is procedure, not sovereignty—but in unmaking and remaking the law. Law and all its concomitants (institutions, constitutions, etc.) are not stable or settled once and for all; they emerge from the mind—and more importantly, *the will*— of political actors. The key notion for Schmitt is "the decision," which is akin to the miracle in religion; it is the eruption or hierophany of a willing agent into the social order, a second and ongoing creation, never finished, never closed.

Westerners like to believe that the political order, especially the democratic order, sits on some bedrock (i.e. a constitution or an underlying political culture), but even that bedrock is tectonic. After all, some human agents had to write the constitution in the first place, and other human agents can interpret it, amend it, ignore it, or replace it altogether. As long as there is general, usually tacit, consensus on what the rules and procedures are, and a commitment to honor those rules and procedures, political life seems orderly. However, recent experience has demonstrated how truly vulnerable and dependent political order is—and how a condition of permanent political liminality can be fomented in which every aspect of law and political interaction is contestable and contested, is "politicized" in the sense of being made subject to acts of will and battles of will. At the extreme, even the most basic concepts and commitments, like "democracy" itself, are critiqued, questioned, and potentially rejected.

Already a century ago Schmitt wondered whether "the sovereign" in the strong sense actually existed, and we might ponder whether we would want one to exist. But surely there have been, indeed lately there has been a wave of, authoritarian, "populist" parties and executives who show little regard for traditions, institutions, constitutions, or law—or for truth itself. The twentieth century had its share of demagogues and dictators, like Lenin and Stalin, Mussolini and Hitler, and Mao. Ironically, at the moment when communism was imploding and liberal democracy was celebrating its triumph, a new generation of authoritarians was coming to office—Andreas Papandreou (Greece, 1981), Alberto Fujimori (Peru, 1990), Silvio Berlusconi (Italy, 1994), Viktor Orbán (Hungary 1998 and 2010), Recep Tayyip Erdoğan (Turkey, premier 2003, president 2014), Lech Kaczyński (Poland, 2005) and Andrzej

Duda (Poland, 2015), Vladimir Putin (Russia, president 2000, prime minister 2008, president again 2012), and Jair Bolsonaro (Brazil, 2019), not to mention parties such as France's National Front (now National Rally), Germany's *Alternative für Deutschland*, and Holland's People's Party of Freedom waiting to turn popularity into power.

Most if not all of these figures and parties represent some form of "populism" in the sense that they mobilize "the people" (typically conceived in nationalist or ethnic/racial terms) against a putative enemy comprising not only foreigners and migrants but "liberals," other political parties, and the political system itself, which allegedly obstructs the will of the people, embodied in the person of the leader. William Mazzarella calls such populism a political theology, in which the president or premier or prime minister is the sacred nation's salvific agent in whom followers/devotees place complete faith.[57] This level of personalistic leadership and authority is by definition and necessarily anti-institutional, ideally "unmediated" and therefore highly labile and unpredictable. And a consistent script or set of tactics repeats across cases, featuring demonizing the opposition; marginalizing (and if possible dissolving) the legislature; disregarding (and if possible rewriting) the constitution; packing the courts with loyalists; insulting, intimidating, or assuming control over the media; and undermining and discrediting any "experts" and their "facts" that might threaten the regime.

These are recognizable schemes of the postmodern trickster. In fact, Xymen Kurowska and Anatoly Reshetnikov apply the moniker "trickstery" to Putin's Russia, referring to behavior that "produces normatively undecidable situations that exceed the analytical capacities of, for example, the strategic use of norms, norm contestation, and stigma management literatures"; among the tools utilized by Putin and his cronies are "satire, prevarication and ambiguity about the truth,"[58] as well as flat-out lying and denial and allegedly assassination. Masha Gessen goes further, positing a "Putin paradigm" that equally implicates Donald Trump: "Both Trump and Putin use language primarily to communicate not facts or opinions but power: it's not what the words mean that matters but who says them and when. This makes it impossible to negotiate with them and very difficult for journalists to cover them."[59] Noting the natural affinity between the two men (and other strongmen like Kim Jong Un and Xi Jinping), Gessen continues, paraphrasing Marshall McLuhan, "Lying is the message. It's not just that both Putin and Trump lie, it is that they lie in

---

[57] Mazzarella, "Populism as Political Theology."
[58] Kurowska and Reshetnikov, "Trickstery," 232–3.
[59] Gessen, "The Putin Paradigm."

the same way and for the same purpose: blatantly, to assert power over truth itself." Why such inveterate lying? "Tricksters can consolidate their power by purposefully 'magnifying the flux,'" Kurowska and Reshetnikov justifiably reason.[60]

Which brings us finally to Trump the would-be sovereign, who fits Orrin Klapp's profile of the "clever hero," Klapp's term for the trickster:

> He may not be a good man—indeed, he is usually far from being an exemplar of virtue, nor is he outstanding as a servant of his group.
>
> He is supreme for wit, resourcefulness, nimbleness, elusiveness, deceit, impudence, and sense of humor.
>
> He does not meet an opponent head-on but prefers to trick him. He is a specialist in triumphant but sometimes shady transactions which, on the whole, amuse people more than they outrage them.
>
> [He aims to] inflict a loss of prestige on those who oppose him....It is also important that his opponent should be humiliated in some comic way. "Insult to injury" is the motto....Taunting, derision and impudence are an essential part of and a fitting climax to the role.
>
> [He possesses] a mental facility like jiujitsu before which even people of capacity feel discomfited and naïve. Not profundity but a quick shrewdness demonstrated in encounter with others is the mark of a clever hero.[61]

I am not arguing here that Trump is a real trickster; as much as some analysts are eager to crown him the trickster-king of America, he departs from the classic trickster in essential ways—he occupied a seat of power, which tricksters ordinarily do not, and he was stubbornly and ironically consistent in everything from his macho persona to his blue-suit-and-red-tie uniform and his sophomoric name-calling and Twitter rants. Plus, hardly a solo performer, he operates with an entire ecosystem buoying and emboldening him, from the alt-right and Anonymous to QAnon and all manner of lone and organized internet "trolls" (another overlooked but productive mythological character). Morten Axel Pedersen holds that Trump resembles less the trickster and more the wrestler of World Wrestling Entertainment fame (a business with which he was directly associated). Pedersen reckons that Trump, a character in his own pugilistic soap opera, is "both [trickster and wrestler] at the same time...a dual

---

[60] Kurowksa and Reshetnikov, "Trickstery," 249.
[61] Klapp, "The Clever Hero," 21.

or composite figure, who may display both a wrestler and a trickster side depending on the moment and setting."[62] Others have proposed different models for him, from stand-up comedian and carnival barker to reality-television star, ruthless businessman, schoolyard bully, and sociopath. Indeed, the impossibility of classifying him, of restricting him to just one category, may be his most tricksterish quality and also why it has proven "to be so difficult to further destabilize and deflate him" whether with comedy, political criticism, or fact checking.[63]

Whether Trump, Putin, and their ilk constitute a latter-day Loki is less important than how they represent and exploit what Helena Bassil-Morozow calls the "trickster impulse,"[64] which we could summarize as a cavalier, often gleeful, and frequently contemptuous attitude toward established rules and accepted truths in pursuit of the trickster-actor's interests and agendas. The trickster impulse is less authoritarian than epicurean, arguably less Schmittian than Schopenhauerian—the consummate imposition of will on reality. Roland Boer captures the trickster impulse in his study of political myth, which (like all myth?) evinces "the eschatological process characterized by the future perfect—what will have been," the "political possibilities" of such myth-speaking (or, in the Putin/Trump paradigm, *mis*-speaking) being inherently "ambiguous and contradictory, for reaction and subversion operate in a dialectical tension. And so the potential for subversion arises in a sly and cunning manner."[65] As Lewis Hyde aptly put it in the title of his book, the trickster (deity or demagogue) "makes this world"[66]: when he is finished, the world "will have been" as he left it.

Conclusion

"Modernity lost a valuable psychic resource in abandoning its trickster/medial fool myth," Susan Rowland insisted.[67] Of course, tricksters are far from absent on the (post)modern scene; we find them in counter-heroes and anti-heroes from Brer Rabbit and Bart Simpson to the Joker, the latter of whom, as portrayed by Heath Ledger, prides himself as an agent of anarchy and chaos, a subverter of order. In fact, Mary Douglas heralded the joke as an "opportunity

---

[62] Pedersen, "Trump's Two Bodies," 165.
[63] Pedersen, "Trump's Two Bodies," 165.
[64] Bassil-Morozow, "Loki Then and Now."
[65] Boer, *Political Myth*, 26.
[66] Hyde, *Trickster Makes This World*.
[67] Rowland, "Jung, the Trickster Writer," 294.

for realizing that the accepted pattern has no necessity. Its excitement lies in the suggestion that any particular ordering of experience may be arbitrary and subjective," injecting "an exhilarating sense of freedom from form in general."[68]

If popular culture and populist politics remember the trickster, it is scholarship and spirituality in the West that have largely forgotten him, and the project of this essay has been to recover the trickster as just such a psychic and analytical resource. Much of the contemporary world makes more sense through the lens of the trickster than through the lens of rational discourse (and its nemesis, the lie) and of the biblical god. This is certainly the case with post-truth politicians like Putin and Trump, whose unwavering popularity among their base suggests something deeper and more primal, more emotional and mythical, than ordinary politics. It forces us to ponder that politics transcends or escapes rational discourse, sober deliberation, and respect for precedent and law. Instead, we confront the extent to which law and order themselves—their formation, application, enforcement—depend on the participation in, the personification of, law by social actors, not only executives but legislators, police, judges, juries, and the rest. At every point, the political process is susceptible to human will, which echoes the trickster narrative.

Hence, another grander ambition of the essay is to reform political theology on the recognition that a stable god like Yahweh is not the only or best prism for contemplating power, nor is the theology in political theology necessarily about religion per se. Rather, Victoria Kahn encourages us to contemplate political theology as "poiesis," making, formation, creation or re-creation[69]—whether by a monotheistic god, a trickster being, or a contemporary political leader. The function of political theology is, or should be, not so much to settle our political rules and roles, to solve political problems or to legitimate existing political order, as to provide symbolic tools to better understand our political, social, and even physical reality—a reality, we have come to appreciate and can no longer deny, that is defined more by flux than stability, movement than stasis, invention than order. For this end, like the totem for Lévi-Strauss, the trickster is good to think. Thinking through the trickster, we can honor order while seizing the wicked and vertiginous freedom "that promises contemporary creativity parallel to the figure's primordial contributions in the order of things."[70]

---

[68] Douglas, "The Social Control of Cognition," 365.

[69] Kahn, *The Future of Illusion*, 3.

[70] Doty and Hynes, "Historical Overview of Theoretical Issues," 22.

BIBLIOGRAPHY

Anderson, John E. *Jacob and the Divine Trickster: A Theology of Deception and YHWH's Fidelity to the Ancestral Promise in the Jacob Cycle.* Winona Lake, IN: Eisenbrauns, 2011.

Anderson, Walter Truett. *Reality Isn't What It Used to Be: Theatrical Politics, Ready-to-Wear Religion, Global Myths, Primitive Chic, and Other Wonders of the Postmodern World.* San Francisco: Harper & Row, 1990.

Babcock-Abrahams, Barbara. "'A Tolerated Margin of Mess': The Trickster and His Tales Reconsidered." *Journal of the Folklore Institute* 11, no. 3 (March 1975): 147–86.

Bassil-Morozow, Helena. "Loki Then and Now: The Trickster against Civilization." *International Journal of Jungian Studies* 9, no. 2 (2017): 84–96.

Baudrillard, Jean. *Simulacra and Simulation.* Translated by Sheila Faria Glaser. Ann Arbor: University of Michigan Press, 1995 [1981].

Bauman, Zygmunt. *Liquid Modernity.* Cambridge, UK and Malden, MA: Polity Press, 2000.

Boer, Roland. *Political Myth: On the Use and Abuse of Biblical Themes.* Durham, NC: Duke University Press, 2009.

Brown, Norman O. *Hermes the Thief: The Evolution of a Myth.* New York: Vintage Books, 1969 [1947].

Carroll, Michael P. "The Trickster as Selfish-Buffoon and Culture Hero." *Ethos* 12, no. 2 (Summer 1984): 105–31.

de Vries, Hent. "Introduction: Before, Around, and Beyond the Theologico-Political." In *Political Theologies: Public Religions in a Post-Secular World*, edited by Hent de Vries and Lawrence E. Sullivan, 1–88. New York: Fordham University Press, 2006.

Doty, William G. "A Lifetime of Trouble-Making: Hermes as Trickster." In *Mythical Trickster Figures: Contours, Contexts, and Criticisms*, edited by William J. Hynes and William G. Doty, 46–65. Tuscaloosa, AL: The University of Alabama Press, 1993.

Doty, William G. and William J. Hynes "Historical Overview of Theoretical Issues: The Problem of the Trickster." In *Mythical Trickster Figures: Contours, Contexts, and Criticisms*, edited by William J. Hynes and William G. Doty, 13-32. Tuscaloosa, AL: The University of Alabama Press, 1993.

Douglas, Mary. "The Social Control of Cognition: Some Factors in Joke Perception." *Man* 3, no. 3 (1968): 361–76.

Gessen, Masha. "The Putin Paradigm." *New York Review of Books* (December 13, 2016). https://tinyurl.com/6yb4mu5n, accessed November 17, 2021.

Grădinaru, Ioan-Alexandru, "The Ways of the Trickster." https://tinyurl.com/34za359r, accessed December 1, 2021.

Horvath, Agnes and Arpad Szakolczai. *The Political Sociology and Anthropology of Evil: Tricksterology*. London and New York: Routledge, 2021 [2020].

Hyde, Lewis. *Trickster Makes This World: Mischief, Myth, and Art*. New York: Farrar, Straus, and Giroux, 1998.

Hynes, William J. "Mapping the Characteristics of Mythic Tricksters." In *Mythical Trickster Figures: Contours, Contexts, and Criticisms*, edited by William J. Hynes and William G. Doty, 33–45. Tuscaloosa, AL: The University of Alabama Press, 1993.

Kahn, Victoria Ann. *The Future of Illusion: Political Theology and Early Modern Texts*. Chicago and London: The University of Chicago Press, 2014.

Keisalo, Marianna. "A Semiotics of Comedy: Moving Figures and Shifting Grounds of Chapayeka Ritual Clown Performance." *HAU: Journal of Ethnographic Theory* 6, no. 2 (2016): 101–21.

Klapp, Orrin E. "The Clever Hero." *The Journal of American Folklore* 67, no. 263 (1954): 21–34.

Kuper, Hilda. *An African Aristocracy: Rank among the Swazi*. London: Oxford University Press, 1947.

Kurowska, Xymena and Anatoly Reshetnikov. "Trickstery: Pluralising Stigma in International Society." *European Journal of International Relations* 27, no. 1 (2021): 232–57.

Lino e Silva, Moises. "Ontological Confusion: Eshu and the Devil Dance to *The Samba of the Black Madman.*" *Social Dynamics* 41, no. 1 (2015): 34–46.

Marshall, Emily Zobel. "Liminal Anansi: Symbol of Order and Chaos—An Exploration of Anansi's Roots Amongst the Asante of Ghana." *Caribbean Quarterly* 53, no.3 (September 2007): 30–40.

Mazzarella, William. "Populism as Political Theology." Lecture, Columbia University, New York, NY (April 23, 2019). https://tinyurl.com/2r9r3vmd, accessed December 1, 2021.

Miller, Robert D. "Solomon the Trickster." *Biblical Interpretation* 19, no. 4–5 (2011): 496–504.

Newman, Saul. *Political Theology: A Critical Introduction.* Cambridge: Polity Press, 2019.

Nicholas, Dean Andrew. *The Trickster Revisited: Deception as a Motif in the Pentateuch.* New York: Peter Lang, 2009.

Pedersen, Morten Axel. "Trump's Two Bodies: The Trickster-Wrestler as a Political Type." In *The Politics of Joking: Anthropological Engagements*, edited by Jana Kopelent Rehak and Susanna Trnka, 152–67. London and New York, Routledge, 2019.

Pemberton, John. "Eshu-Elegba: The Yoruba Trickster God." *African Arts* 9, no. 1 (1975): 20–7, 66, 70, 90, 92.

Radin, Paul. *The Trickster: A Study in American Indian Mythology.* London: Routledge and Kegan Paul, 1956.

Rasula, Jed. *Destruction was My Beatrice: Dada and the Unmaking of the Twentieth Century.* New York: Basic Books, 2015.

Rowland, Susan. "Jung, the Trickster Writer, or What Literary Research Can Do for the Clinician." *Journal of Analytical Psychology* 51, no. 2 (2006): 285–99.

Scheub, Harold. *Trickster and Hero: Two Characters in the Oral and Written Traditions of the World.* Madison, WI: The University of Wisconsin Press, 2012.

Schmitt, Carl. *Political Theology: Four Chapters on the Concept of Sovereignty.* Translated by George Schwab. Chicago: The University of Chicago Press, 2005 [1934].

Sissons, Jeffrey. *The Polynesian Iconoclasm: Religious Revolution and the Seasonality of Power.* New York and Oxford: Berghahn, 2014.

Szakolczai, Arpad. "Permanent (Trickster) Liminality: The Reasons of the Heart and of the Mind." ESF Exploratory Workshop, Affectivity and Liminality: Conceptualising the Dynamics of Suspended Transition. Brighton, United Kingdom (November 17–19, 2013).

Szakolczai, Arpad. "Living Permanent Liminality: The Recent Transition Experience in Ireland." *Irish Journal of Sociology* 22, no. 1 (2014): 28–50.

Testa, Alessandro. *Rituality and Social (Dis)Order: The Historical Anthropology of Popular Carnival in Europe.* New York and London: Routledge, 2021.

Turner, Victor W. *The Forest of Symbols: Aspects of Ndembu Ritual.* Ithaca, NY and London: Cornell University Press, 1967.

Tzara, Tristan. "Dada Manifesto." https://tinyurl.com/2s3x83rn, accessed January 23, 2023.

Warwick-Smith, Kathleen. "Yahweh. Trickster." Academia. tinyurl.com/5yjfkfyj, accessed November 9, 2021.

ABOUT THE AUTHOR

Jack David Eller is a cultural anthropologist and Director of Global Anthropology of Religion for the Global Center for Religious Research. He has conducted fieldwork on religion and religious change among Australian Aboriginals, and his current areas of specialization include ethnic/religious violence, atheism/secularism, and psychological anthropology. He is the author of numerous articles and books on cultural anthropology, anthropology of religion, religious and ethnic violence, and atheism/secularism.

MORE FROM THE AUTHOR

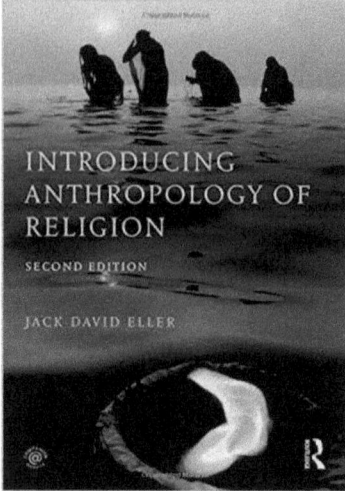

*Introducing Anthropology of
Religion*, 2nd edition
Routledge, 2015

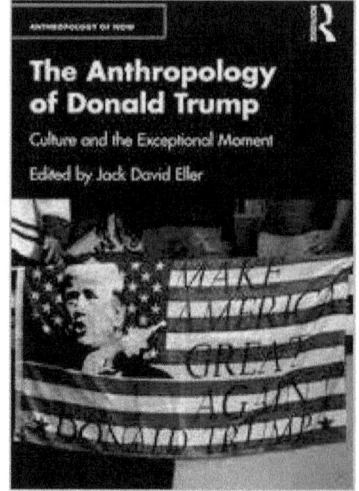

*The Anthropology of
Donald Trump*
Routledge, 2022

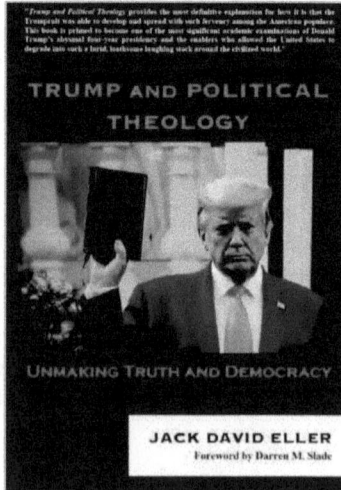

Trump and Political Theology
GCRR Press, 2020

The True Ring Cannot Be Worn:
A Panikkarian Way Out of the Logic of the Three Rings

A Paper Presented at the
International eConference on Interreligious Dialogue

Valerio Marconi,
University of Urbino Carlo Bo

Abstract: *The Parable of the Three Rings is famous in its versions by Boccaccio and Lessing. They share the fundamental idea that only one religion is true but human condition does not let us know which one is the true one. It is an inherently modern idea to stress on the limits of human knowledge while arguing against pure forms of skepticism and relativism. The result of the parable is friendship in both versions, yet the question of truth remains at the center of the conceptual framework underlying the stories. On the contrary, scholars started giving much more relevance to the ethical side of dialogue, so that interpersonal relationship is not just the result of a cognitive process. Personal encounter should be prior to the question of truth. This new approach is challenged by the nature of the relationship with the other. Should it be symmetrical and mutual? Views on dialogue inspired by Lévinas must answer negatively. If we want to keep the relevance of friendship we should rather prefer Buber's idea of dialogue. In our world, despite this, inequalities are such that symmetry and mutuality cannot be the standard condition of dialogue and we must be responsible in advance for the other (in the sense of Lévinasian servitude for the other). A mediation between these two standpoints can be found in Panikkar's notion of inter-in-dependence, as I shall argue. In fact, this notion combines the interdependence present in Buber's I-Thou relationship and the independence or separation stressed by Lévinas in the relation to the other understood in terms of relation between absolute terms.*

Keywords: Responsibility, Mutuality, Dialogue, Interculturality, Religious Diversity

Introduction

S tories can tell us much about a cultural tradition, but they can also open up new argumentative paths. The Parable of the Three Rings is a tale focused on a philosophical question: "Which of the three monotheistic

Socio-Historical Examination of Religion and Ministry
Volume 5, Issue 1, Summer 2023   shermjournal.org
© Valerio Marconi
Permissions: editor@shermjournal.org
ISSN 2637-7519 (print), ISSN 2637-7500 (online)
https://doi.org/10.33929/sherm.2023.vol5.no1.04 (article)

GLOBAL
CENTER *for*
RELIGIOUS
RESEARCH
ACADEMIC INSTITUTE

faiths is the true one?"[1] Its main and most renown variants are by Giovanni Boccaccio and Gotthold Ephraim Lessing; they offer insight into how modernity thought of religious diversity. Yet there is a seemingly older version of the story which suggests a different way of addressing this question.[2] As this paper will try to show, the insight buried inside the text of this version can be translated into the terms of the current debate about interreligious dialogue. Philosophy of interreligious dialogue inspired by Martin Buber and Emmanuel Lévinas is nowadays granting priority to the ethical side of interfaith encounter, rather than to its alethic side. In this perspective, personal encounter should be prior to the question of truth, i.e. interfaith dialogue should be *with* someone rather than *on* something. The result is a change of the terms of the problem: "Which of the monotheistic faiths is the best one?"[3] The turn from Truth to Goodness overcomes every exclusivism, keeps some relevant aspects of the Modern Age mindset towards religious diversity, and is faced with the ethical issue concerning the nature of the relationship with the religious other. The latter issue sounds like this: "Is my responsibility towards the other infinite?" The meaning of the question is whether symmetry should prevail over asymmetry or asymmetry should be prior to mutuality in the relationship; views inspired by Buber are inclined to favor mutuality, while those inspired by Lévinas are committed to asymmetry and infinite responsibility, i.e. who enters the encounter ethically should be responsible for the other's reaction and never try to grasp the other by means of categories. It has been argued that Buber is actually not in conflict with Lévinas concerning the asymmetry of the ethical relationship, but this seems to apply only to the relationship with God through the encounter with the human other.[4] In the specific context of interreligious dialogue, the issue is not the need for keeping God's transcendence intact since it is a matter of whether shared responsibility could be the best option or not. A Christian standpoint should imply a larger amount of responsibility for the Christian side of the encounter, but even a protestant scholar in interreligious dialogue has remarked that both mutuality and responsibility are highly relevant

---

[1] The question comes from Middle Ages, nowadays we should at least include Bahai Faith as a fourth monotheism (cf. Buck, "Bahá'í Contributions," 260–77, 262).

[2] The version is part of a collection titled *Il Novellino*. It was written after 1291, the date ranges between the late thirteenth century and the early fourteenth (cf. Shagrir, *The Parable of the Three Rings and the Idea of Religious Toleration in European Culture*, 89, 107).

[3] Generally put, "Which is the best religion?".

[4] Cf. Kelly, "Reciprocity and the Height of God: A Defence of Buber against Lévinas," 65–73.

in practice.[5] Arguably, a Jewish approach could go in this direction too.[6] Yet this stress on responsibility and even on an infinite one cannot be a common ground for a viable philosophical approach to such a thorny subject matter. The present paper shall try to find a way of combining mutuality and responsibility by relying on Raimon Panikkar's notion of *inter-in-dependence*.

The Logic of the Three Rings

The Parable of the Three Rings is famous in its versions by Boccaccio and Lessing. They share the fundamental idea that only one religion is true but human condition does not let us know which one is the true one.[7] It is an inherently modern idea to stress the limits of human knowledge while arguing against pure forms of skepticism and relativism. What takes place in Boccaccio's and Lessing's tales goes beyond mere tolerance. The result of the parable is friendship in both versions, yet the question of truth remains at the center of the conceptual framework underlying the stories.

Boccaccio

The *Decamerone* ("Ten days") is a book on storytelling as a way to survive. The great plague challenges both knowledge and society.[8] So, it is not surprising that skepticism plays a major role in this collection of tales. The cosmical and social order pictured by Giotto and Dante is broken down into pieces. Out of the ashes of the past, the *lógos* emerges as the only restructuring power: "The redeeming word is universally human *lógos* that crosses divisions and cultures."[9] Here is how such a power works in Boccaccio, according to Roberto Celada Ballanti:

> This is a basis for a new *community of destine* for invocating and co-researching beings. It is characterized by a *concordia discors* [disagreeing

---

[5] Cf. Volf, *Exclusion and Embrace: A Theological Exploration of Identity, Otherness, and Reconciliation*; and Leirvik, "Philosophies of Interreligious Dialogue: Practice in Search of Theory," 16–24.

[6] See Sclafani, "A Jewish Educational Approach to Religious Pluralism."

[7] See Celada Ballanti, *La Parabola dei Tre Anelli: Migrazioni e Metamorfosi di un Racconto tra Oriente e Occidente* for some reflections on the tradition shared by Boccaccio and Lessing, a contextualized analysis of their versions of the parable, and an assessment of their affinities.

[8] Celada Ballanti, *La Parabola dei Tre Anelli*, 1–22.

[9] Celada Ballanti, *La Parabola dei Tre Anelli*, 23. Translation is mine.

agreement] where dialogue is not polemics or apologetics and, if we are unified, we are so because of a shared *lógos*. While nominating the truth, such a *lógos* pushes towards a new acquisition that is always an ulterior unity where diversity is both the starting point and the arrival. This *community of destine* is one of the main gains of the parable of the three rings. Here is—in this little tale—the announcement of a new instance after the break down, of a *religion after the plague*.[10]

The parable already had a tradition lasting some centuries when Boccaccio turned it into a literary masterpiece and granted it a new meaning.[11] It is in the *Decamerone* that the parable assumes its modern form. Boccaccio was the first Christian author to present the Jewish character and the Muslim character as positive ones, showing a degree of open-mindedness and self-criticism that were trackable only in Muslim versions of the story before him.[12] This can be taken as a sign that the question posed by Salahuddin is meant to be read as a truly philosophical question by the audience:

The book was oriented toward an informed, urbane, and secular audience, whose attitudes toward nature, love, Church, society, and so forth run counter to that of dour clergymen. The nascent Italian humanist movement challenged the theological outlook that a person should act only for the sake of his soul's salvation, and opposed the widespread medieval methods of learning, such as scholasticism, which was regarded as an outmoded, rigid system. This skeptical attitude toward religion, and toward religions in general, was in line with a new and flexible philosophical framework that placed questions about the human condition front and center.[13]

This cultural background is enriched by the fact that the tale was previously circulating in a context in which interreligious encounter was taking place throughout Italy under the rule and influence of Frederick II.[14] Furthermore, Boccaccio's version already shows an element that will

---

[10] Celada Ballanti, *La Parabola dei Tre Anelli*, 25.
[11] For a huge reconstruction of this tradition, see Shagrir, *The Parable of the Three Rings and the Idea of Religious Toleration in European Culture*.
[12] Cf. Poorthuis, "The Three Rings. Between Exclusiveness and Tolerance," in *The Three Rings: Textual Studies in the Historical Trialogue of Judaism, Christianity, and Islam*, 257–85, esp. 263–64.
[13] Shagir, *The Parable of the Three Rings*, 97.
[14] Shagir, *The Parable of the Three Rings*, 100–7.

characterize Lessing's fully modern one: "since it is not possible to prefer one religion over the others, the choice between religions is in fact arbitrary and shaped by earthly factors."[15] As Nathan—Lessing's counterpart of Boccaccio's Melchisedech—will claim, religious identity comes from the trust one feels towards relatives.

There are key passages of the tale which help us understand how the modern logic of religious truth works:

> Saladin sent for Melchisedech, and after having received him in an amicable manner, had the Jew sit down beside him. 'You're a worthy man,' said Saladin, 'and many people have told me about your great wisdom and your deep knowledge of the ways of God. Consequently, I would gladly learn from you which of the three laws—the Jewish, the Saracen, or the Christian—you think to be the true one.'[16]

> 'After their father's death, they all claimed the inheritance and the title, while denying the claims of their brothers, and each one produced his ring as proof that he was right. But when they found the rings were so similar to one another that they could not tell which the true one was, the question of which son was their father's real heir was left pending. And so it still is to this day.'[17]

> Melchisedech willingly gave Saladin every last bit of the money he asked for, which Saladin later paid back in full. What is more, Saladin bestowed the most lavish gifts on Melchisedech, became his lifelong friend, and kept him at his side in a lofty position of honor.[18]

It is important to notice that Salahuddin speaks in his own terms, so that he says "laws" rather than "religion" or "faith." The stress on "the inheritance and the title" refers back to the feudal world and to the biblical struggles between Jacob and Esau. The exclusivist nature of the logic is here manifested by the fact that the father "himself, who had ordered them [the rings] made, was scarcely able to identify the true one."[19] This means that the father wanted to hide his preference, but also that such a preference is of a minimal degree.

---

[15] Shagir, *The Parable of the Three Rings*, 108.
[16] Shagir, *The Parable of the Three Rings*, 95. The translation is by Wayne. A. Rebhorn.
[17] Shagir, *The Parable of the Three Rings*, 96. It is Melchisedech speaking.
[18] Shagir, *The Parable of the Three Rings*, 96.
[19] Shagir, *The Parable of the Three Rings*, 96.

Similarly, God is taken to have given three laws such that one is true, and the other are truthlike. The other two are not merely false, yet they are not true. The reason why is simple, i.e. the heir is just one—" they all claimed the inheritance and the title, while denying the claims of their brothers." This juridical aspect of the metaphor has an ontological counterpart. In fact, only one religion is true, yet epistemologically no one can claim to possess the true ring: "they found the rings were so similar to one another that they could not tell which the true one was." Salahuddin is impressed by such a clever distinction between ontology and epistemology that was able to avoid his trap—the Sultan was not curious, rather he was in need of money. The final friendship starts with the Sultan openly admitting his plot and need, i.e. by telling the truth. The paradox of the story is that truth is both what is out of human reach and what unites the two friends. The moral is that human weakness cannot deal with an evident truth: no one of the sons could replicate the father's love. Mankind is responsible for the divine occultation of the true heir. Yet it is for heir's sake that truth is hidden so that he will not be haughty, and the others will not persecute him. Evidence for this could be the destiny of Abel implicitly evocated by the tale, that overt divine preference shall lead to murder: the Sultan was ready to turn into Cain. Ignorance is necessary for peace and friendship and this is precisely because there is just one indivisible and invisible truth. The inheritance is chosen as a metaphor of truth because it is exclusive; here is the reason why it co-occurs with "the title." The inheritance of a title is by definition exclusive and thus it works perfectly for representing truth, yet inheritance could be—as it is nowadays—shared. This possibility is opened by the logic of the best: turning from truth to goodness implies overcoming the inheritance of a title towards an inheritance shared by humanity.

Lessing

While Boccaccio's version displays the clear exclusivist implicature of the logic of the three rings, Lessing's variant is characterized by two main features. First, it reformulates exclusivism in terms of a natural religion of sorts which is immanent to each positive religion—Judaism is reduced to a humanitarian version of the natural religion and is functional to depict and fuel an identity crisis of Christianity.[20] Second, it denies revelation so much that there is no difference

---

[20] Cf. Price, "The Philosophical Jew and the Identity Crisis of Christianity in Lessing's "Nathan the Wise"," 203–23. Price shows how Lessing was inspired by the Illuminist figure of the rationalist Jew.

between Livy's history of Rome and the Bible.[21] This last point has been used to argue that Lessing is integral to the development of philosophical hermeneutics.[22] Thus, the Parable told in the drama *Nathan the Wise* seems to be modern as far as it uses the limits of human knowledge to solve the question about religious truth, and to be post-modern as far as it shows the irrelevance of truth as correctness while keeping truth as cultural transmission. Natural religion might be regarded as démodé nowadays, but truth as an interpretative experience is yet among us as much as philosophical hermeneutics is. Truth as ἀλήθεια in a Heideggerian and Gadamerian sense always implies concealment and situatedness, so that there cannot be a best religion (just good or authentic ones). Lessing stresses an ethical proof of truth in his own version of the parable, yet the primacy of the alethic over the ethical remains unshaken. It is not by chance that Celada Ballanti relies on Lessing's *Nathan* as one of the sources of inspiration for his own hermeneutically oriented philosophy of interreligious dialogue.[23]

The tale has two new endings. In fact, Lessing invents a whole background story as a frame for the parable and transforms the parable itself into a dialogue between Nathan the Jewish merchant and Salahuddin the Sultan where narrative sections are intertwined with argumentative ones. In the new part of the parable, good behaviour is a sign of the possible truth of a religion and so the truth-claim should turn into a moral and humanitarian engagement all faiths can contribute to before a day of final judgement that is always yet to come. This happens because the sons ask for the intervention of a judge who tells them:

> As each of you received his own ring from his father's hand, let each believe for certain that his ring is the original. Perhaps the father did not want to suffer any more the tyranny of one ring in his house. Certainly he loved all three of you, and loved you equally. He could not injure two of you and favor only one. Well then! Let each one strive to emulate his love, unbiased and unprejudiced. Let each one of you vie with the other two to bring to light the power of the stone in his own ring. And may this power be helped by gentleness, sincere good nature, charity and deepest of devotion to God. And when in time, the power of the stone shall find expression in your children's children's children, I invite you in a thousand, thousand years to come again before this court. A wiser man than I will then sit in this chair and speak. Now go![24]

---

[21] Cf. Leventhal, "The Parable as Performance: Interpretation, Cultural Transmission and Political Strategy in Lessing's Nathan Der Weise," 502–27.

[22] Cf. Leventhal, "The Parable as Performance," 503.

[23] Celada Ballanti, *Filosofia del Dialogo Interreligioso*.

[24] Lessing, *Nathan the Wise*, 83–84.

This novelty is remarkable, but is less relevant than the one concerning the father of the tale, i.e. he is not able at all to recognize which one is the true ring so that any trace of the original truth is lost. The importance of such an inability is grasped by Celada Ballanti in the following terms: "In Lessing... the indistinguishability of the rings becomes definitive from the father's perspective too: this deepens the abyss between heaven and earth that can be crossed solely by the merit of being able to activate the power of the ring."[25] The whole play ends with a vision of embrace: the three faiths are metaphorically pictured as a harmonic family, a human family. In this version, the Jew does not just become Salahuddin's friend but finds out that he adopted Salahuddin's dead brother's daughter and that the Templar knight graced by the Sultan was her brother and brings them back to him, who thought they were lost. Indeed, Nathan and his adoptive daughter still feel each other like relatives.[26] Moreover, Nathan takes the Templar knight to be his own son too and the children embrace their adoptive father.[27] To sum up, all are relatives either by blood or by adoptive parenthood. The historical kinship of the faiths has a spiritual counterpart pictured by this final embrace. The limits of human knowledge (it seems that there was a true ring—even this is not absolutely certain— but no one knows which one is the true one) are functional to advocating for a rational religion beyond positive religions based on the common origins and traits. To Salahuddin who argues that religions can be distinguished "**even down to food and drink,**" Nathan replies, "**But not the grounds on which they rest. For are they not all based on history, handed down or written? History we take on trust, on faith. Is that not true?**"[28] The quest for a true religion is eventually a quest for the essential elements among religions beyond the contingent and accidental ones. Such inessential elements are just cultural ones, yet they cannot be given up since they constitute the identity of each faith:

In whose good faith can we most put our trust? Our people's, those whose blood we share, and who, from childhood on have proved their love for us, who never have deceived us, save, perhaps, when it was good for us to be deceived? Can I believe less in my ancestors than you believe in yours? Or vice versa, can I demand of you that you accuse your own forebear of lies, just so that I don't contradict my own? —or vice versa. The same is true of Christians, isn't it?[29]

---

[25] Celada Ballanti, *Filosofia*, 86. Translation is mine.
[26] Cf. Lessing, *Nathan*, 136–37.
[27] Cf. Lessing, *Nathan*, 141.
[28] Lessing, *Nathan*, 82.
[29] Lessing, *Nathan*, 82.

Despite this, the message of the *Nathan* is that Christianity is good only in what it shares with the other religions, i.e. its intolerance is inauthenticity more than cultural identity. Thus, *Nathan* has been read in terms of a Christian identity crisis: "Lessing's overall perspective on Christian violence is similar to Voltaire's contention that the history of Christianity, in particular Christianity as an exclusivist creed, undermines its validity."[30] In this perspective, the best religion is what is best in all religions and this amounts to few principles selected by human reason and its limits. God speaks no more. Such is the price to overcome intolerance and persecution, i.e. an exclusivism that cuts across all religions. It is true that religion is meant to make human life a better life so that religious violations of human dignity come out of inauthenticity, yet Lessing seems to infer from this that human reason is the measure of religion. Such a substitution of the Christian exclusivism with a rationalist one is the result of the underlying logic of truth. On the other hand, truth as cultural transmission and interpretation is what turns revelation into silence. Indeed, revelation is nothing more than the education of mankind:

Education gives the individual nothing which he could not also acquire by himself; it merely gives him what he could acquire by himself, but more quickly and more easily. Thus revelation likewise gives the human race nothing which human reason, left to itself, could not also arrive at; it merely gave it, and gives it, the most important of these things sooner.[31]

Even if the truths were spoken by God, they are meant to be claimed by reason itself:

The word "mystery," in early Christian times, meant something quite different from what we understand by it now; and the development of revealed truths into truths of reason is absolutely necessary if they are to be of any help to the human race. When they were revealed, of course, they were not yet truths of reason; but they were revealed in order to become such truths.[32]

A Different Version of the Story

The version included in *Novellino*—a Medieval Florentine collection of tales—has been often compared with Boccaccio's Parable.[33] Such a

---

[30] Price, "The Philosophical Jew," 215.

[31] Lessing, *Philosophical and Theological Writings*, 218.

[32] Lessing, *Philosophical*, 236.

[33] See Poorthuis, "The Three Rings;" Celada Ballanti, *La Parabola dei Tre Anelli*; and Shagir, *The Parable of the Three Rings*. Shagir considers it the first modern version (cf. Shagir, *The Parable of the Three Rings*, 91).

comparison has somehow blinded scholars and prevented them from realizing that it manifests a different logic. It is true that the *Novellino* variant seems to interchangeably use the adjectives "true" and "best," but the symbol of the father is not a mere metaphor in this case and implies a participation between the godlikeness of the father in the tale and the transcendence of God.[34] The Eternal is labeled "Father on High" and truth is a divine possession, rather than a human one. In the text truth is always an opinion when it co-occurs with humanity, and the true religion as a human unwitting possession is referred to as the "best" one—consistently, the question is "What is the best faith?" Here is the full text:

The Sultan was in need of money, and so he was advised to proceed against a rich Jew who lived in his country, and to take away his property, which was abundant beyond measure. The Sultan sent for this Jew and asked him what was the best faith, thinking: "If he says 'The Jewish [faith]', I will say that he sins against mine. And if he says 'The Saracen [faith],' I shall say: 'Why then do you adhere to the Jewish [faith]?'". The Jew, upon hearing the Sultan's question, replied as follows: "My Lord, there once was a father who had three sons, and he owned a ring with a precious stone, the finest in the world. Each of the sons begged the father that upon dying he would give him the ring. Seeing that everyone desired it, the father went to a skillful jeweler, and said to him: 'Make me two identical rings to this one, and set each one with a similar stone.' The jeweler prepared rings that were so identical that no one, except the father, could recognize the genuine one. The father summoned his sons, one by one, and gave each a ring in secret, each one thinking he held the genuine ring, and no one but their father knew the truth. And so I say it is with the faiths, which are three. The Father on High knows which is best, and the sons—that is, we—each believes that he holds the true one." Well, upon hearing this, the Sultan did not know what he could accuse the Jew of, and let him go.[35]

---

[34] I use the notion of participation in Lucien Lévy-Bruhl's sense, i.e. the symbol is part of the symbolized reality (e.g., in pre-logical thinking smearing someone's name is like directly harming someone since the name is an integral part of the person—see also the importance of God's name in the Bible). On symbols and participative thinking, see Lévy-Bruhl, *L'Expérience Mystique et les Symboles chez les Primitifs.*

[35] Shagir, *The Parable of the Three Rings*, 90–91. Saghir translates from *Il Novellino*, ed. Alberto Conte, 123–24.

It is worth noticing that the text does not feature the word "God" at all: the father of the tale is in a way "the father on Earth," yet the word for God is the same with the only difference made by the capital letter. The neglect of the word "God" in the text is functional to strengthen the link between the symbolizing element and the symbolized one. Moreover, the godlikeness of the father of the three sons is not just internal to the text, but it can be highlighted by the comparison with Boccaccio's and Lessing's presentation of the father. Mind that this comparison is not blinding anymore, since it gives priority to *Novellino*: its variant is not inquired to reconstruct the tradition in which Boccaccio and Lessing find their place. Indeed, the aim of the present operation on the text is to deconstruct the modern tradition of thinking about religious diversity. The godlike aspect of the father on Earth is his exclusive knowledge of the truth. The divinity of truth makes the key question differ from Boccaccio's and Lessing's "Which is the true religion?" If the shift from "best" to "true" is taken seriously, it becomes evident that the modern versions preferred the truth. The original question is about goodness and invites the reader to follow a different path.[36] To turn back to the original meaning of religious diversity, the reader should invert the flow and move backwards from truth to goodness. As anticipated, this is already happening to some extent.

Boccaccio's father is almost unable to discern the true ring from the copies; Lessing's one is definitely unable to do so. This is a relevant sign of the fact that the story told by the anonymous author of the *Novellino* does not follow the logic of the three rings. The logic of the best implicitly acknowledges that other faiths can be good. It is highly relevant that the "Father on High knows which is best," so that, even if there is only one "genuine ring", there is no true religion outside of human mind—"the sons—that is, we—each believes that he holds the true one." It is essential that, while "each one [was] thinking he held the genuine ring," only the godlike father "knew the truth." The implied meaning is that "truth" is not a relevant concept in answering the question about religious diversity. The story told by the Jew in the text does not employ the concept of "best," but it uses the pair "true"/"genuine" to stress the difference of situation between the exceptional—"no one, except the"—father and the sons who do not know the truth. On the other hand, the story told by the *Novellino* does not employ the concept of truth by reducing it to what it actually is, namely a mere matter of belief. In fact, it is the Jew who performs this reduction while telling the moral of his own tale: "And so I say it is with the faiths, which are

---

[36] In Cicero we find a story concerning the best religion—rather than the true one—that was referred by Jean Bodin in his own work on religious diversity (cf. Celada Ballanti, *La Parabola dei Tre Anelli*, xv-vii).

three. The Father on High knows which is best, and the sons—that is, we—each believes that he holds the true one." It is the character who employs the truth in the tale about the father and his sons in order to dismiss it in the morale, so that the rest of the text works totally without even mentioning it:

The Sultan was in need of money, and so he was advised to proceed against a rich Jew who lived in his country, and to take away his property, which was abundant beyond measure. The Sultan sent for this Jew and asked him what was the best faith, thinking: "If he says 'The Jewish [faith]', I will say that he sins against mine. And if he says 'The Saracen [faith],' I shall say: 'Why then do you adhere to the Jewish [faith]?'". The Jew, upon hearing the Sultan's question, replied as follows:....Well, upon hearing this, the Sultan did not know what he could accuse the Jew of, and let him go.[37]

The text exhibits its own freedom from the logic of the three rings by including a storytelling in which the concept of truth is shown irrelevant for the encounter between the Sultan and the Jew. In fact, the Sultan uses the religious notions of sin and adherence, and then the text employs the juridical notion of accuse. The Jew takes advantage of the semantic possibility opened by the word "best": neither Islam nor Judaism is bad, but God alone knows what is best. Faced with the goodness of religions and the mystery about the best one, the Sultan learns that "the finest [ring] in the world" leaves room for good rings rather than for mere copies of the exclusivist ring. The wisdom of the moderns is doomed to think that most, if not all, of the religions must be wrong without knowing it. The implicit wisdom of the *Novellino* teaches that there is nothing we could accuse religious diversity of, and that each revelation happens "in secret" according to the will of the Father on High, who alone knows what is best. This does not prevent people from joining the quest for the best faith, but at the same time acknowledges that all are given by God.[38] Indeed, there is probably a perspective game played by the pair of words "true"/"genuine." The father knows which ring is the genuine one, but, when the reader thinks that this means the same as "their father knew the truth," the result is believing that someone has the true one, i.e. the reader endorses the attitude of the sons. The truth is that all the rings are good since they are identical, and that one is the best one for a very simple reason: "Make me two identical rings to this one, and

---

[37] Shagir, *The Parable of the Three Rings*, 90–91. Saghir translates from *Il Novellino*, ed. Alberto Conte, 123–24.
[38] In Italy, Salahuddin was commonly portrayed as looking for the best religion (cf. Shagir, *The Parable of the Three Rings*, 103–6).

set each one with a similar stone." It is the stone that makes one ring the best one, and the divine truth is that all rings are genuine—"The jeweler prepared rings that were so identical that no one, except the father, could recognize the genuine one." Lessing has removed this point, but Boccaccio was somehow keeping it: a father who gives his sons only genuine rings and hides from them who is his favorite son is a loving father. Eventually, the text suggests a sort of predestination or election: "Each of the sons begged the father that upon dying he would give him the ring." The actions of the sons are identical as much as the rings, yet the father choses only one of them as the hidden receiver of the finest ring. This is a further feature of godlikeness because the reason why that one is chosen is beyond human scope.

From the Truth to the Goodness

The transition from the logic of truth to the logic of the best should not underestimate ignorance and truthfulness as a basis for friendship (see Boccaccio) and the kinship beyond and above religious diversity (see Lessing). Furthermore, Lessing moved from a premise that is pivotal to an ethical rather than alethic approach to religious diversity, namely that religion is meant to make human life a better life so that religious violations of human dignity come from inauthenticity.

An ethical view of interreligious encounter is inherently paradoxical, when inspired by Lévinas. It implies that both sides are asymmetrically responsible and respectful towards the other, so it is by definition an approximation to an ideal situation.[39] The ideal dialogue is a meeting between infinite responsibilities, yet it is only a bilateral infinite responsibility that is able to build a relationship between two absolutely separated partners. According to Lévinas, language as conversation is "a relation in which the terms absolve themselves from the relation, remain absolute within the relation."[40] The interlocutors are proximate, but each one does not try to subsume the other under a concept. The other can only be spoken to. Trying to conceptualize the other is already an act of violence that turns conversation into domination. Thinking about Lévinas, Ryan Urbano states that nowadays philosophy has "to

---

[39] Cf. Burggraeve, "Dialogue of Transcendence: A Levinasian Perspective on the Anthropological-Ethical Conditions for Interreligious Dialogue," 2–28. The author makes extensive references to a large number of Lévinasian works, but the main source is Lévinas, "Dialogue," in *Of God Who Comes to Mind*, 137–51.

[40] Lévinas, *Totality and Infinity. An Essay on Exteriority*, 64.

clarify the true nature of dialogue."[41] The first step is to realize that dialogue is not mere communication or mutual understanding, i.e. it is much more than pragmatical analysis of conversation and ethnological interview. This implies the following awareness about the pivotal condition of possibility for an encounter where religious diversity is truly respected: "Interfaith dialogue will fail if it is construed mainly as a cognitive encounter where one makes an effort only to know and understand the other's religion. Knowledge, as Lévinas says, tends to assimilate and dominate the Other."[42] The reason why is stated thus: "One cannot help but understand the other person's religion through one's cultural and religious categories."[43] Therefore, conceptual violence is always behind the corner and is somehow a necessary outcome of a cognitive approach to interreligious happenings. Here comes the chief contribution from Lévinas to a philosophy of interreligious dialogue, at least according to Urbano:

Dialogue for Levinas is an asymmetrical interpersonal relation. It means that the relation is one of inequality because the self is a servant to the other person who is considered a master. Being a servant means that the self is indebted to his master in terms of responsibility. Moreover this responsibility is infinite, and so the debt cannot be fully repaid. To set a limitation to this responsibility is to put the self over the Other, and this breaks the asymmetry of the ethical relation.[44]

Even if one maintains to possess the whole truth, one must serve and protect the other—otherwise the risk is to transform dialogue into "violence due to persuasion and propaganda."[45] The unveiling of the asymmetrical structure of dialogue states the conditions for its effectiveness, i.e. entering interreligious encounter is serving the other as a master. This metaphor is enlightening since a servant is forced by social status to contradict the master only in a respectful way. Even though the master seems wrong, the servant should find a way to intervene without threatening the roles they both play and at the same time the master would take the servant to be a bad one in case of an omission of intervention. Truth claim works as a limitation of responsibility since one can think to be doing what is best for the other and being thus justified to act in a certain manner. On the other hand, the infinite responsibility of the I for the

[41] Urbano, "Levinas and Interfaith Dialogue," 148–61, 149.
[42] Urbano, "Levinas," 153.
[43] Urbano, "Levinas," 154.
[44] Urbano, "Levinas," 154.
[45] Urbano, "Levinas," 158.

Other prevents from giving up too easily during the effort of acting ethically. Dialogue is supposed to be a pleasant and ideal alternative to violence, yet only when it conforms to Lévinas' requirements can it really avoid violence. Sadly, such requirements show that dialogue is neither pleasant nor ideal. Dialogue is harsh as slavery. This service is also what makes dialogue a religious practice, since Lévinas conceives of religion in ethical terms.[46]

A less thorny model is the one Marion Larson and Sara Shady could find in Buber's life and thought. They are aware that Buber is not interested in the question of truth:

> When applying Buber's model of inclusive dialogue to the topic of interreligious conversation, it is important to recognize that Buber does not present a theory for how to evaluate the truth of competing views, nor does he argue that the truth of one's view is irrelevant. Rather, his priority is placed on how to live with others in the midst of diversity in a manner that maintains genuine commitment to personal belief and genuine respect for the position of the other.[47]

Once again, a philosophical analysis of dialogue tells us how it is possible that interreligious encounters and communities can take place. A possible image is indeed the family: more than before, families are constituted by members who take life in different ways even in terms of religious beliefs, but they are still communities in which people love and respect each other. In fact, Larson and Shady sum up Buber's point thus: "In genuine dialogue, the encounter between self and other forms a living foundation for community and meaningful relationship, even if they hold very different beliefs."[48] Rather than family, the two scholars adopt a class stimulated by a teacher to engage in inclusive talk as an example.[49] The two examples are complementary in showing how families, schools, and universities are the main venues of interreligious encounter, where missing the opportunity for dialogue is a real pithy and inclusive relations are a pressing necessity.[50] Furthermore, this model

---

[46] Cf. Urbano, "Levinas," 152–53.

[47] Larson and Shady, "Interfaith Dialogue in a Pluralistic World: Insights from Martin Buber and Miroslav Volf," 5.

[48] Larson and Shady, "Interfaith Dialogue," 3.

[49] Cf. Larson and Shady, "Interfaith Dialogue," 4.

[50] Cf. Scuderi, "Interfaith Dialogue in Italy: A School Project Suggestion," *Ricerche di Pedagogia e Didattica,* 169–86.

is exactly what is needed to keep the best of Boccaccio's and Lessing's going far beyond mere tolerance:

> Buber's concept of inclusion provides a viable alternative to both tolerance and empathy. Unlike tolerance, inclusion seeks to break down boundaries and develop deep relationships with other people....For openness to occur, one must be willing to let the other change one's perspective rather than seeking to impose one's own views. Such an attitude of absolute receptiveness may sound like the boundary-erasing stance of the type of empathy that Buber rejects. It does not have to be, though. While one seeks to cultivate openness and receptiveness, at the same time, there is a recognition of the distance....He is careful to note that this does not mean that we form a "union of the like-minded." Rather, inclusive community arises when we live meaningfully together in the midst of different opinions and perspectives.[51]

On the other hand, it is evident that Buber's view is far away from Lessing's rational religion and, unlike Boccaccio's suspended dispute about the "father's real heir," makes a shared inheritance possible.

If Lévinas provides the condition of possibility of interfaith dialogue, Buber finds out what should be its goal: "The goal of such dialogue is the relationship itself, the opportunity it provides to be confirmed by the other as well as experience the other's side. Genuine dialogue seeks to confirm rather than convert or coerce."[52] The two accounts of interreligious dialogue then show some similarity, but their premises are still conflicting.[53] Buber, while taking the relation with the other as nonconceptual, keeps thinking of it in ontological terms:

> Relation is mutual. My *Thou* affects me, as I affect it. We are moulded by our pupils and built up by our works. The 'bad' man, lightly touched by the holy primary word, becomes one who reveals. How we are educated by children and by animals! We live our lives inscrutably included within the streaming mutual life of the universe.[54]

---

[51] Larson and Shady, "Interfaith Dialogue," 4.

[52] Larson and Shady, "Interfaith Dialogue," 4.

[53] Urbano, "Levinas" is well aware of this, while Burggraeve, "Dialogue" does not give any particular relevance to the tensions between Buber and Lévinas.

[54] Buber, *I and Thou*, 15–16.

On the other hand, Lévinas openly criticizes Buber for his stress on such a vitalist mutuality:

> The worth of the You, the deaconship [service] of the I—such are the semantic depths of the "primary word", the ethical depths. There would be an inequality, a dissymmetry, in the Relation, contrary to the "reciprocity" upon which Buber insists, no doubt in error. Without a possible evasion, as though it were elected for this, as though it were thus irreplaceable and unique, the I as I is the servant of the You in Dialogue. An inequality that may appear arbitrary, unless it be—in the word addressed to the other man, in the ethics of the welcome—the first religious service, the first prayer, the first liturgy, the religion out of which God could first have come to mind and the word "God" have made its entry into language and into good philosophy. It is not, of course, that the other man must be taken for God or that God, the Eternal Thou, be found simply in some extension of the You.[55]

The "Eternal Thou" is a Buberian phrase, so Lévinas is clearly engaging in a polemical correction of the dialogical principle as formulated by Buber. In a sense, Lévinas' You is akin to *Novellino*'s father, since it is granted a godlike aura while being a trace of the Eternal Thou—as much as the father symbolizes the Father on High. It is tempting to notice that in the passage the notion of election is referred to. In terms of the logic of the best, the I as I is predestinated by the Eternal to be a servant of the You, i.e. the possession of the finest ring does not imply elevation above the other—it rather means an infinite responsibility. On the other hand, the logic of the best calls for mutuality: the other religions are good and only with their help can the chosen one bare its infinite burden. Such a logic requires a synthesis of reciprocity and dissymmetry. What should occur is a co-agency involving the Father on High, the sons and this world. Such is the human condition in Buber's opinion: "Neither the world of things, nor his fellow-man and community, nor the mystery which points beyond these, and also beyond himself, can be dismissed from a man's situation."[56] This recalls the vision underlying Panikkar's conception of inter-in-dependence:

> The inter-in-dependence of the three dimensions of reality is essential to the cosmotheandric experience. Otherwise we have only a mental construct.

---

[55] Lévinas, "Dialogue," 150–1.
[56] Buber, *Between Man and Man*, 214.

Matter, Man, and God are interrelated and connected, but the nexus is not determined by any of the three "factors" independently of the others. The connection is a free connection, the fruit of the spontaneous response to the free actions of the others....The repercussions are mutual.[57]

This looks like "a relation in which the terms absolve themselves from the relation, remain absolute within the relation,"[58] yet this does not prevent the "cosmotheandric" conversation from resulting into mutuality.[59] Moreover, Josef Boehle uncovers Buber's affinity with Panikkar by adapting the I-You dialogue model in terms of trialogue for interreligious ends:

The dialogical encounter between persons should be viewed as a *Trialogue*: a dialogue and relation between concrete persons in the presence of Ultimate Reality and Ultimate Self of each dialoguing partner. A major difference between Buber's dialogue and the Trialogue model is that, in his understanding, the "I" is only existent as *I-It* or *I-Thou*, not in itself, whereas the Ultimate Self in the Trialogue model is Self-existent as well as interrelated with everything, and this, not through mental unity but through spiritual unity, transcending thus the dualisms of mental concepts of the Self.[60]

Clearly, such a development is implicit in the passage quoted from Buber on human condition. The only limit posed by Buber to Boehle's reformulations is the very fact that such an Ultimate human Self is intertwined with "fellow-man and community." Nevertheless, the trialogue model is here functional to understand that the experience of inter-in-dependence in dialogue partakes to living accordingly with the material, human, and divine nature of Reality. Panikkar's dialogue is a microcosm in which the macrocosmic triunity or inter-in-dependence is reflected:

The relational energy at the heart of Panikkar's ontology is given expression in his theory and practice of dialogue for which he is best

---

[57] Panikkar, *The Rhythm of Being: The Gifford Lectures*, 1789–97.

[58] Lévinas, *Totality and Infinity. An Essay on Exteriority*, 64.

[59] Cf. Prabhu, "The Encounter of Religions in a Globalized World: Provocations from Panikkar," 142–58, esp. 154–55; and Chiricosta, *Filosofia Interculturale e Valori Asiatici*, esp. 163–73.

[60] Boehle, "Trialogue in an Interreligious Context: Reinterpreting the Dialogue Model of Martin Buber," 126–50, 150.

known, at least in large parts of the West. Dialogue can be seen as a personalizing of this relational energy. At its deepest level, it can be regarded as a mutual recognition of the cosmotheandric Mystery expressing itself in oneself and the other.[61]

Inter-in-dependence is thus strictly connected to the mythical and symbolic harmony between microcosm and macrocosm, while Lévinas seems to avoid such a background. The context in which the word "God" entered language is the "ethics of welcome," yet the sacrality of hospitality is a well rooted element of Mediterranean myths.[62] Despite this, Lévinas can be read as arguing for a genealogy of the usage of the word "God," without implying any precise worldview. However, Panikkar attempted to speak about interreligious encounter in terms of inter-in-dependence also by using metaphors and examples, even if the reflection of macrocosm in it "provides the ontological ground for Panikkar's philosophy of interpersonal dialogue."[63] Here is what he writes in *Human Dialogue and Religious Interindependence*:

> We believe that we are interdependent, and indeed it is true that we are not alone and that everything is interrelated, but is equally true that it is the weaker or poorer or less intelligent people who depend on the stronger, richer, and more intelligent ones. In southern India we say that when an ant is tied by a rope to an elephant, it is hardly the elephant that moves in the direction of the ant, but exactly the contrary….if one person possesses atom bombs, a thousand allies, or a thousand dollars, and the other person has only a sword and is alone and poor, interdependence is merely a euphemism.[64]

These are simple observations, but they imply that, since inter-in-dependence is based on human uniqueness, human beings are endowed with dignity and responsibility. None of them is like the others, but this does not result in absolute difference or indifference. Responsibility depends on the degree of freedom that each one has. Humans have the same dignity, but not the same responsibilities. There are consequences for both religion and cultures: "If religion means an openness to the Mystery, it follows that no one has a

---

[61] Prabhu, "The Encounter of Religions," 147.

[62] On this topic, see Falcioni, "Cosa Significa Ospitare? Forme di Ospitalità Mediterranea," 117–27.

[63] Prabhu, "The encounter of religions," 147.

[64] Panikkar, "Human Dialogue and Religious Interindependence," 141–45, 142.

monopoly on it, because the Mystery is infinite…To cultivate religious dialogue, the interindependence of all cultures and all men must be recognized."[65] The conclusion is simple: "We know how to use things, but we do not know the mystery of reality: we must be humble….True religiosity leads us to listen to others, because no one is self-sufficient."[66] In short, we need even the ones who depend on us. Much more than in the passage on the "three dimensions of reality," Panikkar gets close to Buber's terminology when speaking about human condition in *Human Dialogue and Religious Interindependence*. Yet he never gives up the reference to uniqueness and inequality that is typical of Lévinas' account of human condition. To sum up, Panikkar helps us to reactivate the best elements of ancient Indian emperor Asoka's wisdom:

King Beloved by Gods Priyadarsin is honoring all sects: (both) ascetics and householders, with gifts and with honors of various kinds. But the Beloved by Gods does not value either gifts or honors so (highly) as (this), (viz.) that a promotion of the essentials of all sects should take place….its root is this, viz. guarding (one's) speech, (i.e.) that neither praising one's own sect nor blaming other sects should take place on improper occasion, or (that) it should be moderate in every case. But other sects ought to be duly honored in every way. If one is acting this, he is promoting his own sect and is benefiting other sects as well. If one is acting otherwise than thus, he is hurting his own sect and wronging other sects. For whosoever praises his own sect (or) blames other sects—all (this) out of pure devotion to his own sect, (i.e.) with the view of glorifying his own sect,—if he is acting thus, he rather injures his own sect very severely.[67]

Conclusion

Cosmotheandric vision is not just connected to Panikkar's inter-in-dependence view of dialogue. It implies ecosophy too, i.e. a nondualist ecology. The relationship between mankind and environment misses the cosmical dimension of nature lived by many religions and reduces it to a pure matter of science and climate policy, while the consideration of the dimension of mystery

---

[65] Panikkar, "Human Dialogue," 143.

[66] Panikkar, "Human Dialogue," 144.

[67] Hultzsch, ed., *Inscriptions of Asoka*, 65. The translation is slightly modified. On the relevance of this approach for interreligious matters, see Colagrossi, "Un'Altra India. Il Dialogo Interreligioso nella Tradizione Indiana: Da Aśoka a Gandhi," 28–40.

could reactivate the awareness of the inter-in-dependence among environment, mankind and the divine.[68] Thus, a Panikkarian account of interreligious encounter can enrich the goal suggested by Buber for it, namely the construction of a community that goes beyond religious diversity while preserving it: such a communion should and could include environment itself. Therefore, interreligious dialogue might become the key for a new ecology and play an incisive role in taking care of our planet—a more realistic objective than interfaith encounter as a prevention of wars.[69] Despite this, it remains true that cosmotheandric experience cannot be preliminary to the practice of interreligious dialogue. It could be the outcome, but it cannot be the input. A first step in introducing inter-in-dependence as a premise to dialogue and as a way to conduct it can be made in terms of *philosophy as comparison*: Giangiorgio Pasqualotto describes this practice, exemplified by Nishida Kitarō's work, as happening "in the awareness that none of the 'terms' of the relation (himself as a questioning subject, and the two different domains assumed as speculative touchstones) exists and functions alone, independently from the other two."[70] The second step is provided by François Jullien's notion of 'gap' (*écart*).[71] The thinking of alterity in terms of gap is an alternative both to the concept of difference and to the godlike aura of the other:

> I thus stress on the virtue of the *gap* that generates the *between*, and of the *between* that generates the *other* because I believe that the notion of alterity is nowadays menaced from two sides. Either it is left to a sacralization that makes it absolute and always emerges from forms of divinization or it is

---

[68] Cf. Pizarro, "'Ecosofía': hacia una Comprensión de la Sabiduría de la Tierra desde la Noción de 'Ritmo del Ser' de Raimon Pannikar," 263–78.

[69] This does not imply that interfaith dialogue does not work as a deradicalization and peacebuilding tool (see Byron, "Interfaith Dialogue to De-Radicalize Radicalization: Storytelling as Peacebuilding in Indonesia," 92–102).

[70] Pasqualotto, ed., *Per una Filosofia Interculturale*, 50. The translation is mine. Nishida's philosophy was actually a dialogue between the western philosophical tradition and the Zen culture and practices of Japan, yet Nishida was not just a questioning subject since he was moved by his bodily experience of zazen and calligraphy and by the need for a way to express philosophically the insights of Zen—see Vendruscolo, "L'Esperienza del Corpo in Nishida Kitarō." The dialogue somehow transformed at the same time Nishida, philosophy, and Zen culture. Furthermore, it is noteworthy that Nishida wrote a book titled *I and You*, even if his account of the role of the You in the self-contradictory definition of the I differs sensibly from Buber's dialogical approach—cf. Heisig, *Philosophers of Nothingness: An Essay on the Kyoto School*, esp. 79–86.

[71] Pasqualotto himself refers to Jullien as a second example of comparison based on intercultural philosophy (cf. Pasqualotto, *Per una Filosofia*, 50–51).

abandoned to standardizing and sterilizing assimilation that leaves the world identical and inert.[72]

Indeed, Jullien—as much as Panikkar—takes linguistic and cultural diversity as the very life of cultures: "Babel is not a malediction, it is the fortune of thought."[73] Semantic gaps are what is always there as a tool to avoid conceptual violence and warrants the separation thought by Lévinas in terms of "a relation in which the terms absolve themselves from the relation, remain absolute within the relation."[74] Here comes the third step, i.e. going back to ecosophy. As much as biodiversity, cultural and religious diversities are the ecosophical traces of the triunity of Reality. Eventually, an open question is to what extent this approach to dialogue can take place in our conflictual world. It is clear from this paper that the most powerful institutions have the lion's share of responsibility. We might not be able to do much to remind them about their responsibility, but this means that one has at least to write it down. On the other hand, Pasqualotto tells us what we can do for those who have less responsibility: "an intercultural project endowed with realistic awareness… can positively present itself only as a *preventive therapy* for the individual and social catastrophes brought about by economic globalization and as a *rehabilitative therapy* for the victims already suffering from the effects of such catastrophes."[75]

BIBLIOGRAPHY

Boehle, Josef. "Trialogue in an Interreligious Context: Reinterpreting the Dialogue Model of Martin Buber." *Culture and Dialogue* 6, no. 2 (2018): 126–50.

Buber, Martin. *I and Thou*, translated by Ronald G. Smith. Edinburgh: T. & T. Clark, 1937.

———. *Between Man and Man*, translated by Ronald G. Smith. London New York: Routledge, 2002.

---

[72] Jullien, *Contro la Comparazione: lo "Scarto" e il "Tra"*, 723. The translation is mine.

[73] Jullien, *Contro la Comparazione*, 49.

[74] Lévinas, *Totality and Infinity. An Essay on Exteriority*, 64.

[75] Pasqualotto, *Per una Filosofia*, 29.

Buck, Christopher. "Bahá'í Contributions to Interfaith Relations." *Journal of Ecumenical Studies* 54, no. 2 (Spring 2019): 260–77.

Burggraeve, Roger. "Dialogue of Transcendence: A Levinasian Perspective on the Anthropological-Ethical Conditions for Interreligious Dialogue." *Journal of Communication and Religion* 37, no. 1 (Spring 2014): 2–28.

Celada Ballanti, Roberto. *La Parabola dei Tre Anelli: Migrazioni e Metamorfosi di Un Racconto Tra Oriente e Occidente*. Rome: Edizioni di storia e letteratura, 2017.

———. *Filosofia del Dialogo Interreligioso*. Brescia: Morcelliana, 2020.

Chiricosta, Alessandra. *Filosofia Interculturale e Valori Asiatici*. Milano: O barra o, 2013.

Colagrossi, Elisabetta. "Un'Altra India. Il Dialogo Interreligioso nella Tradizione Indiana: Da Aśoka a Gandhi." *Nuovo Giornale di Filosofia della Religione* 13/14 (May-December 2020): 28–40.

Falcioni, Daniela. "Cosa Significa Ospitare? Forme di Ospitalità Mediterranea." *postfilosofie* 9, no. 9 (2016): 117–27.

Heisig, James W. *Philosophers of Nothingness: An Essay on the Kyoto School*. Honolulu: University of Hawai'i Press, 2001.

Hultzsch, Eugen, ed. *Inscriptions of Asoka*. Oxford: Clarendon Press, 1925.

Jullien, François. *Contro la Comparazione: lo "Scarto" e il "Tra"*, edited and translated by Marcello Ghilardi. Milano-Udine: Mimesis, 2014.

Kelly, Andrew. "Reciprocity and the Height of God: A Defence of Buber against Levinas." *Sophia* 34, no. 1 (April 1995): 65–73.

Larson, Marion, and Sara Shady. "Interfaith Dialogue in a Pluralistic World: Insights from Martin Buber and Miroslav Volf." *Journal of College and Character* 10, no. 3 (February 2009).

Leirvik, Oddbjørn. "Philosophies of Interreligious Dialogue: Practice in Search of Theory." *Approaching Religion* 1, no. 1 (May 2011): 16–24.

Lessing, Gotthold Ephraim. *Nathan The Wise*, translated by Stephanie Clennell and Robert Philip, Milton Keynes: Open University, 1992.

―――. *Philosophical and Theological Writings*, edited and translated by H. B. Nisbet. Cambridge, U.K.: Cambridge University Press, 2005.

Leventhal, Robert S. "The Parable as Performance: Interpretation, Cultural Transmission and Political Strategy in Lessing's Nathan Der Weise." *The German Quarterly* 61, no. 4 (Autumn 1988): 502–27.

Lévinas, Emmanuel. *Totality and Infinity. An Essay on Exteriority*. 3rd ed. Translated by Alphonso Lingis. Dordrecht: Kluwer, 1991.

―――. "Dialogue." In *Of God Who Comes to Mind*. 2nd ed., 137–51. Translated by Bettina Bergo. Stanford, Calif.: Stanford University Press, 1998.

Lévy-Bruhl, Lucien. *L'Expérience Mystique et les Symboles chez les Primitifs*. Paris: Librairie Félix Alcan, 1938.

Il Novellino, edited by Alberto Conte. Rome: Salerno Editrice, 2001.

Panikkar, Raimon. *The Rhythm of Being: The Gifford Lectures*. ebook. Maryknoll: Orbis Books, 2010.

―――. "Human Dialogue and Religious Interindependence." In *Opera Omnia*. English ed. Volume VI, Part Two, *Cultures and Religions in Dialogue*, 141–45. Maryknoll: Orbis Books, 2018.

Pasqualotto, Giangiorgio, ed. *Per una Filosofia Interculturale*. Milano-Udine: Mimesis, 2008.

Poorthuis, Marcel. "The Three Rings. Between Exclusiveness and Tolerance." In *The Three Rings: Textual Studies in the Historical Trialogue of Judaism, Christianity, and Islam*, edited by Marcel Poorthuis, Barbara Roggema, and Pim Valkenberg, 257–85. Leuven: Peeters Publishing, 2005.

Prabhu, Joseph. "The Encounter of Religions in a Globalized World: Provocations from Panikkar." In *Raimon Panikkar. Intercultural and Interreligious Dialogue*, edited by Joan Vergés Gifra, 142–58. Girona: Documenta Universitaria, 2017.

Sclafani, Robin. "A Jewish Educational Approach to Religious Pluralism." In *Religious Literacy, Law and History: Perspectives on European Pluralist Societies*, edited by Alberto Melloni and Francesca Cadeddu, 189–98. London and New York: Routledge, 2018.

Scuderi, Marzia. "Interfaith Dialogue in Italy: A School Project Suggestion." *Ricerche di Pedagogia e Didattica. Journal of Theories and Research in Education* 10, no. 1 (February 2015): 169–86.

Sepúlveda Pizarro, Jéssica. "'Ecosofía': hacia una Comprensión de la Sabiduría de la Tierra desde la Noción de 'Ritmo del Ser' de Raimon Pannikar." *'Ilu. Revista de Ciencias de las Religiones* 23 (November 2018): 263–78.

Shagrir, Iris. *The Parable of the Three Rings and the Idea of Religious Toleration in European Culture.* Cham: Springer International Publishing, 2019.

Smith Byron, Amanda. "Interfaith Dialogue to De-Radicalize Radicalization: Storytelling as Peacebuilding in Indonesia." *Journal of Living Together*, 2–3, no. 1 (2016): 92–102.

Urbano, Ryan C. "Levinas and Interfaith Dialogue." *The Heythrop Journal* 53, no. 1 (November 2010): 148–61.

Vendruscolo, Pietro. "L'Esperienza del Corpo in Nishida Kitarō." Master's thesis, University of Padua, 2017–2018.

Volf, Miroslav. *Exclusion and Embrace: A Theological Exploration of Identity, Otherness, and Reconciliation.* Nashville: Abingdon Press, 1996.

ABOUT THE AUTHOR

Valerio Marconi has a PhD in Humanities and is Adjunct Professor of Philosophy of Language at the University of Urbino (Italy). His main topic of research is the dialogical and relational nature of sign and meaning. He spent periods of study and research in St Andrews (Scotland, UK) and Munich (Germany). Dr. Marconi published on mysticism and semiotics too. He worked often on Aristotle, Hjelmslev and Peirce, and wrote on della Volpe, Cassirer and Todorov focusing on their contributions to Structuralism.

ACKNOWLEDGMENT

I am grateful to Aleksandar Georgiev for his help in revising the text of this paper and for our conversations about Lévinas.

MORE FROM THE AUTHORS

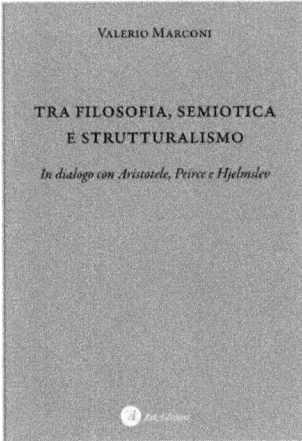

VALERIO MARCONI

TRA FILOSOFIA, SEMIOTICA
E STRUTTURALISMO

In dialogo con Aristotele, Peirce e Hjelmslev

Tra filosofia, semiotica e
strutturalismo
ZeL, 2020

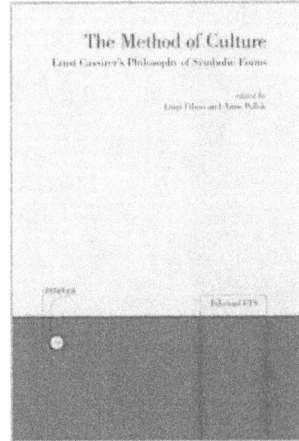

The Method of Culture
Ernst Cassirer's Philosophy of Symbolic Forms

edited by
Luigi Filieri and Anne Pollok

"Cassirer and Cognitive
Structuralism"
ETS, 2021

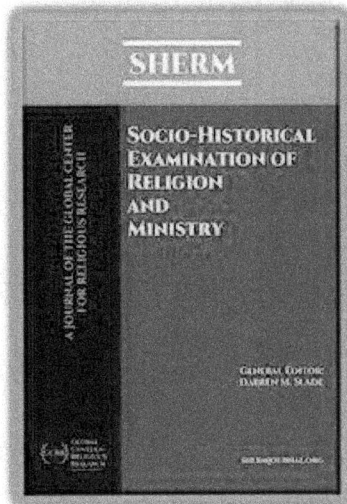

SHERM

SOCIO-HISTORICAL
EXAMINATION OF
RELIGION
AND
MINISTRY

A JOURNAL OF THE GLOBAL CENTER
FOR RELIGIOUS RESEARCH

GENERAL EDITOR:
DARREN M. SLADE

DESTROYING
EVERYTHING
BAD IN THE LAND

IMPLEMENTING CHARLES
SPURGEON'S GOSPEL-CENTERED
ETHIC TOWARD THE VULNERABLE

MATTHEW R. PERRY

from

GCRR PRESS

WWW.GCRR.ORG/GCRR-PRESS

SHERM 5/1 (2023): 96–108

Understanding Understanding, the Foundation of Interreligious Dialogue

A Paper Presented at the
International eConference on Interreligious Dialogue

Dominic McGann,
Exeter College, University of Oxford

Abstract: *This paper seeks to explore the academic approach to interreligious dialogue by outlining some key features of what the author sees as its philosophical foundation: understanding. It argues that understanding what it is to understand is crucial to developing interreligious dialogue because, at its core, the goal of such dialogue is the exchange of differing religious understandings for mutual benefit. Thus, the author contends that a thorough academic perspective on interreligious dialogue can only be established if a robust account of understanding is first constructed. Having addressed this, the author outlines three key features of understanding: subjectivity, internality, and appreciation of the whole. Following this, a curious aspect of the generation of new understanding is explored, namely the seeming link between leisure, the absence of so-called "servile" work, and the generation of new insights. Whilst this collection of key features is by no means exhaustive, this paper seeks only to open a conversation on the nature of understanding that has been noticeably absent from philosophical and theological discussion in recent years. Given this, the author hopes to open avenues through which others might critique, explore, or add to the features identified in this article in order to expand the neglected field of the Philosophy of Understanding.*

Keywords: Understanding, Interreligious Dialogue, Insight, Internality, Leisure

Interreligious Dialogue and the Necessity of Understanding

The necessity of the academic study of interreligious dialogue is only increasing in the modern day. In our so-called "Information Age," it has never been easier to converse with people from a diverse range of religious cultures and worldviews, which naturally increases the importance of understanding how such conversations can best be used to benefit cross-cultural intellectual development. In order to make the most of this discourse, however, we must first come to know exactly what it involves.

Socio-Historical Examination of Religion and Ministry
Volume 5, Issue 1, Summer 2023 shermjournal.org
© Dominic McGann
Permissions: editor@shermjournal.org
ISSN 2637-7519 (print), ISSN 2637-7500 (online)
https://doi.org/10.33929/sherm.2023.vol5.no1.05 (article)

It seems that the main purpose of interreligious dialogue is the exchange and cross-pollination of religious worldviews. A priest should make it their business to seek the wisdom and perspective of a rabbi in order that their conversations might provide new insights into their own impression of the world. Rather than such conversations leading to conflict or religious doubt in any of the participants, such interreligious dialogue, *when conducted properly*, can instead act as an opportunity for the expansion of each religious worldview in reflection of the wisdom of others.

How then, are we to know how to conduct interreligious dialogue properly? Well, as with most subjects, the best place to start with such an inquiry is at the intellectual foundations. It has already been stated that the main reason we should seek out interreligious dialogue is to better our own religious worldviews through learning from the worldviews of others; so, the intellectually foundational question becomes "What is a religious worldview?", which in turn yields the question "What is a worldview?"

The term "worldview" saw its philosophical definition crystallized in the work of Thomas Kuhn,[1] whose use of this word applies most explicitly to the philosophy of science. Despite the scientific basis of Kuhn's work, however, it takes little effort to make his theories more generally applicable, as the general foundation of Kuhn's theory is that worldviews consist of a network of understandings of the world. At any given stage of a person's intellectual development, they will have a worldview made of a patchwork of different understandings, be they scientific, theological, political, *et cetera*.

If worldviews are composed of a patchwork of varying understandings of the world, then the job of clarifying the notion of a worldview must start with an understanding of what it is to understand. Furthermore, since clarifying the nature of a worldview is necessary in order to understand how interreligious dialogue can be most effectively carried out, a clear picture of what is necessary for such dialogue to operate effectively is only possible after a satisfactory account of understanding is established.

With this goal in mind, the following two sections of this paper seek to lay out some of the philosophical foundations of understanding in a theological context. First, I will lay out and explain three key features of understanding, before developing a section devoted to the ways in which new understanding can be catalyzed. By establishing these features of understanding and coming to understand, it is my hope to clarify some of the foundations of interreligious dialogue in order to establish an academic picture of this all-important practice.

---

[1] Kuhn, *The Structure of Scientific Revolutions*.

Three Features of Understanding

The elusive nature of understanding is reflected in the dictionary definitions of the term. The *Oxford English Dictionary* (*OED*) defines understanding in a number of ways, including:

> 1a. To comprehend; to apprehend the meaning or import of; to grasp the idea of.
>
> 4a. To grasp as a fixed or established fact or principle; to regard as settled or implied without specific mention.
>
> 5a. To take, interpret, or view in a certain way.[2]

These definitions are noticeably vague and achieve their definition by outsourcing the burden of inquiry to other terms. By defining understanding in terms of apprehending, comprehending, or grasping, these definitions have not helped much, as those who wish to get to the root of understanding must now ask what it means to apprehend, comprehend, or grasp. In what follows, I will attempt to outline three key features of understanding: that understanding involves an appreciation of the whole rather than an appreciation of its parts, that understanding is an internal state of the understander, and that each person's understanding is subjectively unique.

Studying the etymology of the word "understanding" reveals its ancestral link with the Old English word *understanden*.[3] This word, unsurprisingly similar to its modern English counterpart, can be broken down into two atoms: *under-*, which means more or less the same as it does today, and *-standan*, meaning 'to stand' in the context of standing "between or amongst" something.[4] This etymology hints at the nature of understanding in two subtly different ways. First, it implies that understanding involves the "gathering together" of several ideas under one heading, as one might gather children under one umbrella in the rain. For example, to "understand someone" in terms of understanding them as a person, is to bring several complex elements of who they are (their emotions, motivations, aspirations, etc.) under the same heading that might be referred to as their personality.

The second, and more important aspect of understanding indicated by this etymology, however, is that to understand something, to "stand under" it, is to be situated in the midst of whatever it is we are apprehending—to be at its

---

[2] *OED Online*, s.v. "Understand."

[3] *Online Etymology Dictionary*, s.v. "Understand."

[4] *Online Etymology Dictionary*, s.v. "Understand."

centre and appreciate it as a greater whole. Understanding something as a whole in this way is the first key feature of understanding that this paper will focus upon.

Understanding the Whole

In an attempt to clarify the relationship between understanding and unified wholes, I ask you to consider the following situation. Imagine that you are in an art gallery viewing a painting with a magnifying glass such that the painting appears as a macroscopic blend of formless pigments and lines. When you look at the painting in this way, you know it is a painting, and you know what you are seeing are brushstrokes and pigments, but this is all you see it as: a collection of formal elements. Given how closely you are examining these individual parts of the painting, you cannot see the greater image to which they contribute.

Were you to view the painting from a distance, however, you would get a chance to appreciate the work as a whole. This change of perspective will, in turn, allow you to begin *understanding* those formless swirls of pigment as a part of a cohesive object because you can now see it in its entirety, as it was meant to be seen. What, when viewed up-close, seems to be nothing more than a mass of formal strokes and colors becomes an image with meaning when considered as a unified whole.

In this way, one can only understand a painting if one appreciates it as a unified whole, rather than a collection of smaller features. Certainly, you can *know* a painting in the sense of intellectual acquaintance simply through an awareness of the emblematic brushstrokes in, say, Van Gogh's *Starry Night*, but without viewing the whole painting, it becomes impossible to understand the work in any meaningful way.

As a further example of this relationship between understanding and an awareness of unified wholes, consider the distinction between knowing and understanding Shakespeare's *Hamlet*. Many people, including actors, well-read adults, or high school English students, can claim to know Shakespeare's *Hamlet* insofar as they recognize its characters, famous passages and themes. Far fewer people, however, truly understand *Hamlet* insofar as they can combine their knowledge of these individual parts of the play and formulate a complete picture of the themes, meanings, and the possible intentions of the author.

Understanding as 'Internal'

In an epistemological context, the comparison of understanding and knowledge has been utilized as a way of highlighting other unique aspects of understanding.[5] Such a strategy is adopted by both Linda Zagzebski and Jonathan Kvanvig, who stress what they call the "internal" nature of understanding that is lacking from knowledge.[6]

The internal nature of understanding is the second key feature of understanding on which this section will focus. Unlike knowledge, which necessarily requires the correspondence of a belief to the external world, Zagzebski and Kvanvig rightly highlight that understanding a subject or group of facts is an internal mental attitude that does not necessarily require additional external input from the outside world. Whilst one's understanding can be hastened in some cases by the input of those with expertise in a relevant subject area, a link to the external world is not a necessary part of understanding, as it is for factual knowledge. This second key element of understanding can be developed further through reference to a thought experiment drawn from the Philosophy of Mind, Searle's Chinese Room.[7]

In this thought experiment, Searle asks us to imagine a room that can perform the function of responding to Mandarin documents such that if one were to put a passage of Mandarin into its input slot, a corresponding passage of Mandarin would come out of the output slot after some time. This room functions with the help of an operator who sits at a table in its centre. On the operator's table is a comprehensive book of rules for writing outgoing messages according to the shape and order of characters on the page received in the input slot. When one posts the Mandarin document through the input slot, the operator cross-references the syntactic properties of the characters with the rulebook and transcribes the correct Mandarin response.

From the outside, whatever is in the room appears to understand Mandarin insofar as it can generate correct responses to the inputted documents. What is crucial to Searle's point, however, is that the operator, whilst adept at identifying characters based on their shape and cross-referencing them with the rulebook, *does not understand Mandarin*. This thought experiment illustrates the internality of understanding. The operator has all the external tools

---

[5] For a detailed discussion of the major positions in this debate, see Grimm, "Is Understanding A Species Of Knowledge?" 515–35.

[6] See Zagzebski, "Recovering Understanding," 235–49. and Fine, "Knowledge and Belief in Republic V," 198–99.

[7] See Searle, "Minds, Brains, and Programs," *Behavioral and Brain Sciences*, 417–57.

necessary to *act as if* they understand Mandarin, but they do not actually understand it; they have not internalized those external tools within their own mind. Whilst the operator, with their external rulebook-bound knowledge, can perform the same function as someone who understands Mandarin, if you took the rulebook away, they would not be able to do their job. This demonstrates the fact that the operator does not possess the internal mental state of understanding Mandarin, which in turn illustrates the necessity of internalization for true understanding.

This idea is furthered by Frank Jackson's case of Mary in the Black and White Room.[8] In this thought experiment, Mary is a scientist who specializes in the study of color. Her expertise is such that she knows everything there is to know about light, color, and the mechanisms by which it is perceived and interpreted by the brain. Despite this knowledge, however, Mary has never seen color herself. She lives in a completely black and white room and can only view the outside world through a black and white monitor. The key question is can Mary, with her expert knowledge, be considered equivalent to someone who has experienced red? In other words, does she understand what red is?

Jackson's arguments allude to the fact that Mary does not understand color, based on the assumption that Mary would learn something new if she was allowed to leave the room and witness colors for herself. Given that Mary has never experienced color before, it seems intuitive that, once she exits the room, she will gain a new intellectual grasp of red. In spite of her prior extensive knowledge, she will finally have experienced color herself, and will therefore have gained a new understanding of the experience of red.

This thought experiment further highlights the internal nature of understanding. Despite Mary's extensive knowledge of the external facts about color (wavelengths of light, refraction, etc.), she lacks the internal, subjective understanding of what it is to experience color before she leaves the room. To understand something, in this case color, requires something more subjective and internal than the acquisition of knowledge through the apprehension of external facts.

Notably, the clearest moments of our appreciation of the internal nature of understanding come in moments in which understanding changes. Consider, for example, this famous image:

---

[8] Jackson, "Epiphenomenal Qualia," 127–36.

Wittgenstein's Duck-Rabbit [9]

This duck-rabbit is famous for illustrating how one's understanding of something can change without the object of understanding being altered. When I look at this image, I can shift how I view this drawing from understanding it as a drawing of a duck to understanding it as a drawing of a rabbit *without the marks on the page changing*. What is changing when I view the drawing as a duck or a rabbit is not an aspect of the external world, but an aspect of my internal mental attitudes and appreciations of elements of that external world—namely, the drawing.

This internal character of understanding yields clues as to what it is to understand a subject. As in the case of the duck-rabbit, understanding does not necessarily involve the acquisition of new knowledge. Therefore, in the context of Wittgenstein's diagram, understanding seems to be a contextualization or interpretation of the knowledge that has already been gained—a framework in which known facts are placed.

The Subjectivity of Understanding

The third and final feature of understanding that will be mentioned briefly here is the uniquely subjective character of understanding. Unlike knowledge, which can be described objectively and can belong to many people at once in much the same way, understanding is subjective and belongs, in its specific instantiation, to the one who gained that understanding. Whilst two students could both understand long division such that they can produce correct equations, their subjective understandings—the ways in which each of them personally came to that understanding and the manner in which they personally think about it—will be distinct. Such a subjective understanding can arise only

---

[9] See Wittgenstein, *Philosophical Investigations*, 194.

from a synthesis of the person with what they are coming to understand through experience.[10]

This subjective aspect of understanding links back to Mary in the Black and White Room. Mary's understanding is not associated with her knowledge of the objective scientific facts of color, but rather with her subjective experience of color when she leaves the room. Jackson's thought experiment therefore illustrates the importance of subjectivity, as well as internality, for understanding; Mary must comprehend the external world through her own subjective experience in order to gain an understanding of it.

This principle can be seen in the real world through the study of the roots of dictionary definitions. Some definitions can be understood in terms of the definitions of other words; consider, for example, the definition of "Man" as "a rational animal," which is derived from the separate definitions of "rational" and "animal." Such definitions, however, cannot refer to other definitions *ad infinitum* as there must, eventually, be some word that does not defer its meaning to a combination of other words.

So, in what is the meaning of language rooted? According to recent work by Iain McGilchrist that focuses on the operation of the right brain hemisphere and its relationships to how we understand,[11] eventually, all definitions, and indeed all words, must lead back to some kind of subjective, embodied experience.[12] As an example of this, consider the notion of "grasping a concept," the use of which has been scattered throughout this paper. This concept is understandable, at least in part, because we are all familiar with the notion of grasping an object. Although a concept is something abstract and ungraspable, the metaphor of an embodied experience makes this notion of "grasping a concept" understandable without reference to further layers of verbal explanation. Our subjective experiences of grasping an apple from a bowl of fruit enable us to understand the objective, abstract concept of grasping an idea.

According to McGilchrist, metaphors such as the metaphor of "grasping" provide a connection between the external world and our internal understanding of it by bridging the gap between objective reality and subjective experience.[13] Metaphors and narratives pertaining to certain concepts allow

---

[10] McGilchrist, *The Master and His Emissary*, 133–34.

[11] McGilchrist, *The Master and His Emissary*.

[12] For a further explanation of this, see McGilchrist, *The Master and His Emissary*, 118. See also, Lonergan, *Insight*, 36. Specifically, the beginning of section 2.7.

[13] A term the etymological roots of which stem from the Ancient Greek word for "to carry over." See *OED Online*, s.v. "Metaphor."

those that hear them to comprehend abstract ideas in terms of their own bodies, a frame of reference with which they are innately familiar, and thereby promote the gaining of understanding.

Such mechanisms are the very backbone of teaching. A good educator does not simply explain a concept externally by listing facts about it, they contextualize the concept within situations with which their audience would be familiar. By allowing the audience to understand concepts in these terms, the educator enables them to embed these objective facts within their subjective experience of the world, thereby catalyzing the transition of their knowledge of something into an understanding of it.

The Operation of Leisure
in Coming to Understand

In addition to exploring these three key features, a discussion of understanding would be incomplete without a brief mention of the unique aspects of the process of *coming to understand*. Whilst my arguments so far have aimed to outline an understanding of understanding as a static mental attitude, the active process of coming to understand, sometimes referred to as "gaining insight," is equally as important for the purpose of developing an academic understanding of interreligious dialogue. Given that the purpose of interreligious dialogue, as laid out in the first section of this paper, is the cross-pollination and exchange of differing religious worldviews in order for the dialogue's participants to gain new understanding, laying out how new understanding can be gained will serve this essay's purpose well.

As was mentioned in the end of the previous section, the process of coming to understand something can be catalyzed by education. The deep understanding and experience of a good teacher can speed up the process of gaining insights by providing a "shortcut" to the internalization of the knowledge that they communicate. Such catalysis can be provided by well-crafted metaphors, diagrams, or even asking crafted questions that guide a pupil's brain to understanding at a quicker pace, and the skill of teaching lies in constructing and presenting these tools to their classes.

Beyond this active method through which the process of coming to understanding can be hastened, however, one of understanding's most unique features is that it is often best gained passively, without direct effort or the immediate input of an expert. Consider, for example, the case of August Kekulé, the discoverer of the molecular structure of benzene. Benzene, a ring-shaped hydrocarbon commonly employed in organic chemistry, perplexed the chemists of the early 19ᵗʰ century due to its bizarre chemical properties. These properties, unlike those of any other known hydrocarbon at the time, led chemists of the time to wonder about the physical structure of the benzene molecule and how its then-unknown shape might contribute to its equally strange chemical properties.

It was this quest to discover the shape of benzene that consumed the waking hours of Kekulé. He went through many hours of research, actively trying to find the shape of the molecule through diagrams and experimentation without any part of the puzzle becoming clearer. This was, at least, until Kekulé reportedly fell asleep in front of the fire after a long session of working at the problem. During this sleep, Kekulé claimed that he dreamt of several floating serpents biting their own tails to make a ring-shaped ouroboros. Waking suddenly from this dream, he had an insight into what he had been missing throughout his hours of active research. Following the imagery in his dream, Kekulé postulated that a ring of carbon atoms would explain benzene's bizarre chemical properties, a postulation that would be proven true some years later.[14]

This anecdote about Kekulé's discovery of the shape of benzene highlights a key feature about understanding—insights can be gained *without* actively working for them. Furthermore, sometimes these passive insights can be better or more profound than those that might have been gained with hours of endless study at one's desk. As was seen in the case of Kekulé, hours of active searching can yield fewer insights than a single nap in front of a fire; the tension of wrestling with intellectual problems can often be broken by resting and removing oneself from the active search for it.

In addition to being visible in the natural sciences, the importance of passive insight can be seen in religious history. Over the course of the European Middle Ages, many Christian mystics chose to sequester themselves from society in order to increase their understanding of God and their faith. A particularly extreme example of this can be found in St. Julian of Norwich, who lived in almost permanent seclusion during her life as an anchoress and wrote on the profound divine revelations she experienced during this period.[15] I contend that this type of seclusion is an extreme way of promoting the same kind of passive insight that might otherwise occur accidentally by resting or, as Darwin often did, taking a walk through a forest.

---

[14] The exact details of Kekulé's anecdote are ambiguous, but details can be found in "Molecular Dreams," the second chapter of Rocke, *Image and Reality*.

[15] See Norwich, *Revelations of Divine Love by Julian of Norwich*.

Whilst the exact neurological mechanism by which seclusion can catalyze the generation of new insights is scientifically unclear, it seems intuitive that the absence of distraction caused by removing oneself from society allows greater mental energy to be spent passively internalizing what one knows, thereby increasing the rate of acquisition of understanding.

This postulation would quite happily explain the link between heightened theological understanding and the seclusion of monastic life. Through their vows of poverty, removal from the wage-earning busy-work of ordinary society, and their occasional observations of the Great Silence, those who are called to the religious life are in a privileged position to gain understanding through passive insight. Whereas the average person has to contend with the servile hardships of paying bills and furthering their career, those who follow the monastic way of living have the freedom, in many cases, to dedicate their time to the passive contemplation of the divine in every aspect of their life.

This link between passive insight and monastic traditions was noticed by Josef Pieper, who framed secluded and contemplative life of monks/nuns in terms of a life of "intellectual leisure."[16] Pieper argues that, rather than leisure being seen through the capitalist lens and defined as "the time when you are not working," it should instead be seen as a form of "...silence which is the prerequisite of the apprehension of reality."[17] Through leisure, here defined as the absence of servile work or a utilitarian purpose, a person can better understand their reality due to the lack of the burdensome tasks that might otherwise distract their contemplative processes.

The apparent fact that understanding can be gained through passive contemplation/leisure as well as active study is crucial for clarifying the methods of interreligious dialogue. If understanding is sometimes best gained through intellectual leisure rather than the academic work of, say, an involved debate, then perhaps the best interreligious dialogues will involve periods of discourse followed by periods of quiet, leisurely reflection. In these times of reflection, it is possible, or even likely, that the contents of a dialogue performed throughout a period of time will trigger insights in the participants' minds, just as Kekulé's ideas crystallized, which will ultimately lead to a more fruitful exchange of religious understanding.

---

[16] Pieper and Schall, *Leisure*, §3–4.
[17] Pieper and Schall, *Leisure*, 46.

Conclusion

Throughout the course of this paper, I have endeavoured to lay out the importance of gaining an understanding of understanding for the academic discussion of interreligious dialogue. Furthermore, I have sought to lay out both three key features of the mental attitude of understanding—internality, subjectivity and appreciation of the whole—and a notable contributing factor to the process of coming to understand, namely passive or leisurely insight. It is my hope that the content of this paper might spark further discussions in this field and that, through these continued conversations, our academic picture of interreligious dialogue, and our understanding of understanding, will become clearer in years to come.

BIBLIOGRAPHY

Fine, Gail. "Knowledge and Belief in Republic V." *Archiv Für Geschichte Der Philosophie* 60, no. 2 (1978): 121–39.

Grimm, Stephen R. "Is Understanding a Species Of Knowledge?" *The British Journal for the Philosophy of Science* 57, no. 3 (2006): 515–35.

Jackson, Frank. "Epiphenomenal Qualia." *The Philosophical Quarterly* 32, no. 127 (1982): 127–36.

Kuhn, Thomas S. *The Structure of Scientific Revolutions*. 4th ed. Chicago; London: University of Chicago Press, 2012.

Lonergan, Bernard J. F. *Insight: A Study of Human Understanding*. London: Darton Longman and Todd, 1983.

McGilchrist, Iain. *The Master and His Emissary: The Divided Brain and the Making of the Western World*. New Haven: Yale University Press, 2009.

Norwich, Julian of. *Revelations of Divine Love* by Julian of Norwich, 2020.

OED Online. Oxford University Press.

Online Etymology Dictionary.

Pieper, Josef, and James Schall. *Leisure: The Basis of Culture*, 2009.

Rocke, Alan J. *Image and Reality: Kekulé, Kopp, and the Scientific Imagination.* Chicago: University of Chicago Press, 2010.

Searle, John R. "Minds, Brains, and Programs." *Behavioral and Brain Sciences* 3, no. 3 (1980): 417–57. https://doi.org/10.1017/s0140525x00005756.

Wittgenstein, Ludwig. *Philosophical Investigations.* 3d ed. Oxford: Blackwell, 1968.

Zagzebski, Linda. *Recovering Understanding.* Oxford University Press, 2001.

ABOUT THE AUTHOR

Dominic McGann *BA (Hons), MPhil (Oxon)* is a DPhil Candidate in Theology and Religion at the University of Oxford. He is currently in the third year of his doctoral research into the relationship between religious understanding and sacred music, a project he is conducting under the supervision of Dr. Andrew Pinsent in the Ian Ramsey Centre for Science and Religion. At the time of publication, he is the Arthur Peacocke Scholar in Theology at Exeter College, Oxford.

ACKNOWLEDGMENT

I would like to thank Dr. Andrew Pinsent for his expert supervision and guidance in my studies of religious understanding. Furthermore, time should be taken to thank Rosemary Peacocke, whose kind donation of the legacy of her late husband, Prof. Arthur Peacocke, funds my doctoral research.

HEBREW MATTERS

BY JOSEPH LOWIN

"NOBODY KNOWS THE HEBREW LANGUAGE THE WAY JOSEPH LOWIN DOES." —FRANCINE KLAGSBURN.

110 HEBREW ROOTS
THE ROADS THEY TAKE
THE STORIES THEY TELL

SHERM 5/1 (2023): 110–119

Jesus, Socialism, and "Judeo-topia"

A Paper Presented at the
International eConference on the Historical Jesus

Kenneth L. Hanson,
University of Central Florida

Abstract: *This article addresses the contention commonly expressed among liberal theologians and commentators that the Jesus of history, to the extent that he may be identified, was essentially a social revolutionary, broadly sympathetic to what might be identified in contemporary terms as ideological "socialism." It is often conceived that Jesus' concern for the poor, the disenfranchised, and the underclass of Second Temple Judea endows him with a broad egalitarian ethic, making him akin to an ancient "redistributionist." I will argue, however, that "socialism" did indeed exist in those days, in the form of the Dead Sea sect, and that the historical Jesus was profoundly opposed to the community of property it represented. For him, "social justice" was part of the embedded ethics of Judaism itself, divorced from the "redistributionist" theories of Marxist and neo-Marxist adherents. Whereas the Essene sectarians withdrew from what they called "the material wealth of wickedness," Jesus admonished his disciples to pursue dealings out of economic contact with the world at large.*

Keywords: Historical Jesus, Socialism, Dead Sea Scrolls, Social Justice, Tzedakah

Jesus, Proto-Rabbi

It is a truism that almost every brand of religionist, philosopher, and moral commentator, not to mention political theorist, has attempted to lay claim to the person of Jesus of Nazareth, as if doing so lends unimpeachable stature to one's cause or perspective. As Thomas Jefferson wrote, "Rogueries, absurdities and untruths were perpetrated upon the teachings of Jesus by a large band of dupes…"[1] As a result, it is arguably the case that much if not most of what is common knowledge with respect to the great Nazarene amounts to anachronistic stereotype. That, commingled with religious doctrine and dogma, leaves the serious scholar and researcher endeavoring to uncover even the slightest trace of the real man and his message, unvarnished by two millennia

---

[1] Jefferson, "Letter to the Danbury Baptist Association," January 1, 1802.

Socio-Historical Examination of Religion and Ministry
Volume 5, Issue 1, Summer 2023 shermjournal.org
© Kenneth L. Hanson
Permissions: editor@shermjournal.org
ISSN 2637-7519 (print), ISSN 2637-7500 (online)
https://doi.org/10.33929/sherm.2023.vol5.no1.06 (article)

of force-fitting him into one mold or another. Moreover, when occasional voices from the religious left chime in, justifying everything from social welfare, to woke egalitarianism, to outright Marxism under the guise of "liberation theology," one wonders whether looking at Jesus through the simple lens of the Judaism of his day, albeit filtered through the teachings of the rabbinic sages, might shine a more reliable light on an ancient proto-rabbi, who was, at his core, a Galilean, an Israelite, and a piously observant Jew. Is it fair to assert, given what we know or think we know about the historical Jesus, that he might have been at least somewhat sympathetic to what today might be thought of as socialism? I will argue, however, that faithful Torah observance, the kind to which the historical Jesus certainly adhered, does not a woke socialist make.

The one thing we know with certainty about Jesus is that we know very little with certainty. That being the case, it is fair to ask why anyone would be inclined to turn history's most celebrated Galilean into a dedicated socialist, or even a fellow "traveler" on Karl Marx's utopian journey. Most likely such a perspective is gleaned from Jesus' sensitivity, as recorded in the Christian Gospels, to the poor and downtrodden in tandem with his unrelenting attacks on the rich. Jesus is said to have declared to a certain "rich young ruler," "Sell all that you have and distribute to the poor, and you will have treasure in heaven" (Luke 18:22, NKJV). He is also credited with declaring: "It is easier for a camel to go through the eye of a needle than for a rich man to enter the kingdom of God" (Matthew 19:24, NKJV). Not a few contemporary exegetes gleefully rely on such passages to cast Jesus in the role of Robin Hood.

Ayn Rand, noted for her spite for socialist/Marxist theory, was also known to have despised Jesus, since in her words: "Jesus (or perhaps His interpreters) gave men a code of altruism, that is, a code which told them that in order to save one's soul, one must love or help or live for others."[2] In her mind, Jesus, as any good socialist, promoted the collective over the interests of the individual. Or did he? Perhaps it was his interpreters who gave us this image. Perhaps Ayn Rand, like the Marxist theorists she abhorred, was inclined to filter Jesus through John's Gospel, which declares that Jesus came, "that the world [not isolated individuals] through him might be saved" (John 3:17, KJV). That of course is John, which paints Jesus as a self-denying Greco-Hellenistic philosopher. The synoptic Gospels by contrast find room to depict a Jesus who was fully a product of the Jewish world of the pre-rabbinic Sages. Certainly Judaism, in antiquity as well as in the modern world, represents a collective, but

---

[2] Rand, *Letters of Ayn Rand*, 287.

it does not involve, as Ayn Rand described Jesus' message, "the subordination of one's soul (or ego) to the wishes, desires or needs of others."[3]

Judaism classically taught that one should love others "as oneself." However, neither the Jesus of the synoptics nor the religion to which he belonged taught subordinating one's soul to anyone. Hillel summed it up, expressing the "golden rule" later attributed to Jesus, in the negative: "That which is hateful to yourself do not do to others."[4] Obviously, the self should not and cannot be subordinated, for it is the measure by which others should or should not be treated. In a larger context, the Jewish collective historically celebrated individual contributions, and while Jews have never quibbled with the notion that it takes a village, the Jewish village has historically been composed of individuals, whose altruism leaves healthy self-interest undiminished. Indeed, a cursory overview of history finds legions of Jewish merchants, entrepreneurs, and capitalists of every variety, and even the rabbis and sages of late antiquity preferred to have a trade, earning their own living rather than subsisting from the contributions of others.[5]

Are we to conclude that Jesus the Jew, the son of a carpenter, was somehow different, even a "social revolutionary" of sorts? Renowned Jesus scholar John Dominic Crossan summed up the great Galilean in one of his tomes, titled *Jesus: A Revolutionary Biography*. He repeatedly refers to Jesus as a presumably impoverished "peasant."[6] Yet, contrary to popular perceptions, Jesus' family was well enough off to afford pilgrimage to Jerusalem, which is hardly what we would expect from those who hailed from an impoverished, pastoral society.[7] If the Gospel narratives are to be trusted at all, this Jesus was not, in Crossan's words, a "Mediterranean Jewish peasant," or an exploited "peasant with an attitude."[8] Josephus attests that Galilee was a land of rich fertility and very highly cultivated. He observes: "Moreover the cities lie here very thick; and the very many villages are everywhere so full of people by the richness of the soil that the very least of them contain above 15,000 inhabitants"

---

[3] Rand, *Letters*, 287.

[4] b, *Shabbat* 31a.

[5] See Muller, *Capitalism and the Jews*, 115-16; see also Rosenfeld and Perlmutter, "The Attitude to Poverty and the Poor in Early Rabbinic Sources (70-250 CE)," 411–38.

[6] Crossan, *The Birth of Christianity*, 235; *The Historical Jesus: The Life of a Mediterranean Jewish Peasant.*

[7] See Luke 2:41–52; see also Gibson, *The Final Days of Jesus: The Archaeological Evidence*, 4.

[8] Crossan, *Jesus: A Revolutionary Biography*, 198.

(Josephus, *B.J.* III, iii, 2).[9] Arguably, the whole notion of a poverty-stricken population, desperate for social revolution, needs to be reconsidered.

Jesus and Social Justice

When it comes to what is fondly referred to as "social justice," it is fair to point not only to the Torah, but to ancient Israel's prophetic class as the originators of the concept of equity and compassion for all people, and special concern for those in need. Noted religious historian Karen Armstrong has argued that the Jewish society of this period spawned an "egalitarian and socialist ethic."[10] Socialist? Perhaps the religious left, Karen Armstrong included, needs reminding that caring for the poor and needy was something that this ancient society practiced, not by governmental fiat, but as a religious obligation only. The amount of "charity" to be distributed was a matter of interpretation. Leviticus 19:9-10 instructs the Israelites not to reap the corners of their fields or pick their vines bare, thereby leaving them for the poor. However, the size of the corners which remain unharvested and the number of grapes which should be left on the vines is not specified.

Ancient Israel was not the Roman empire, where the centralized state was the guarantor of both bread and circuses. For Jews, charity became synonymous with upright conduct on an individual level, and was therefore called in Hebrew *tzedakah*, literally meaning "righteousness." It became a tradition carried forth by Israel's great Sages, throughout Talmudic times and beyond. It should also be recognized that Judaism, except on rare occasions when the state itself was Jewish (as in David's ancient kingdom and the later Hasmonean dynasty), operated independently of the secular government, which in Jesus' day was a mere proxy of Rome. Unlike Islam, where charity was instituted as a tax, an obligation known as *zakat*, paid to the religiously dominated state, in Judaism charity was strongly recommended but never coerced. The best situation for which Jews could hope was to be left alone by the state, not sublimated to a governmental collective. The only option, when the land was held captive to an occupying power, was to throw off the foreign yoke, which was certainly an aspect of the geopolitical climate in which the historical Jesus found himself.

---

[9] See Masterman, *Studies in Galilee*, 131.

[10] Armstrong, *A History of God: The 4,000 Year Quest of Judaism, Christianity and Islam* 26–7. See also Houston, *Contending for Justice: Ideologies and Theologies of Social Justice in the Old Testament*, 77ff.

Jesus certainly lauded almsgiving, but he was likely of the same mind as his Pharisaic counterparts, that charity (*tzedakah*) works best when it is distributed privately.[11] This was in sharp contrast to the communal lifestyle of the Dead Sea sect, who collectivized their wealth and redistributed (in Marxist lingo) "to each according to his need." It is in this cultural context that his remarks to the rich young ruler should be understood. Rabbinic literature does go into detail about *tzedakah*, citing various levels of giving, ranking them from lowest to highest. Though the source is medieval, it has much to say about Jewish attitudes going back to antiquity. The third highest level is when the donor is aware of the recipient's identity, but the recipient is unaware of the source. The second highest is when both donor and recipient are unknown to each other. The highest level of charity, however, is to help sustain someone before that individual becomes impoverished, by helping the person find employment or some form of business, so that dependence on others becomes unnecessary.[12] Nowhere is what we might conceive as the welfare state referenced in any of this.

In ancient Judea, King Herod the Great, himself a lackey of Rome, pretended to care for all elements of his ethnically diverse population, Israelites and non-Israelites as well, all the while crushing his subjects under burdensome taxation and forced labor/slavery. Those who were more well off, the so-called Herodians and their allies—including the Sadducees in their multiple priestly orders, government officials, and the landed gentry—thrived precisely because of their connections with the ruling authorities. In Ayn Rand's world, the "rich" were the bloat-bellied bureaucrats of centralized government; in ancient Israel under the Herodian dynasty, they were much the same. Given the socio-historical realities of his day, does Jesus still sound like a socialist/Marxist? Who were the oppressed souls he represented? The Galilean fisherman, selling his daily catch for as much hard coinage as he could earn? Or the industrious craftsman, the carpenter, the tool maker, or the tanner, involved in what amounted to cottage industries? These were the "small businesses" of the day, engaged in by generations of what we might think of as early "entrepreneurs"—bourgeois elements capable of warming the cockles of Adam Smith's capitalist

---

[11] Eight levels of charity were later codified by Maimonides: "The greatest level, above which there is no greater, is to support a fellow Jew by endowing him with a gift or loan, or entering into a partnership with him, or finding employment for him, in order to strengthen his hand so that he will not need to be dependent upon others..." Individuals, together with the religious community (not the state) were viewed as the dispensers of *tzedakah*. See *Mishneh, Yad, Matanot Ani'im* X, 7–14.

[12] Donin, *To Be a Jew: A Guide to Jewish Observance in Contemporary Life,* 50.

heart. Were those the ones Jesus chastised? Or was his castigation of the "rich" code language for a subversive broadside against ancient Israel's version of big-government autocracy, imposed by a foreign power?

The Essenes and "Proto-Communism"

Interestingly, there was indeed an ancient form of socialism/qua "proto-Communism" to be found in the society of Jesus' day. To encounter it, one need look no further than the Dead Sea sect (presumably the Essenes), whom Josephus describes as follows:

> These men are despisers of riches…. Nor is there any one to be found among them who hath more than another; for it is a law among them, that those who come to them must let what they have be common to the whole order, – insomuch, that among them all there is no appearance of poverty or excess of riches… and so there is, as it were, patrimony among all the brethren. (*Wars* II, viii, 3)

Elsewhere Josephus notes: "Nor do they allow of the change of garments, or of shoes, till they be first entirely torn to pieces, or worn out by time. Nor do they either buy or sell anything to one another; but every one of them gives what he has to him who wants it…" (*Wars*, II, viii, 4).

Indeed, their egalitarian ideal amounted to what could well be termed "Judeo-topia." The Dead Sea sectarians repeatedly referred to themselves as "the poor" (Heb. *evionim*), likely because as committed "proto-socialists," none of them owned anything privately. Jesus, when berated by his disciples for allowing himself to be anointed with costly fragrant oil, quibbles not with such apparent excess, but notes the simple economic reality that "you have the poor with you always" (Mark, 14:7; Matthew 26:11 NKJV). In this he is echoing Deuteronomy 15:11: "For the poor shall never cease out of the land…" Although it flatly contradicts Deuteronomy 15:4: "Howbeit there shall be no needy among you," Jesus cites the verse which acknowledges the presence of poverty, accepting it as a reality that no amount of utopian well-wishing can eradicate.

It is also more than plausible that he takes direct aim at the Dead Sea sect, in telling a parable of an unrighteous steward, who learned that his master was dismissing him. The steward then forgave the debts owed by others to his master, so that they would receive him into their homes when the day came. Jesus concludes the story, saying: "So the master commended the unjust steward because he had dealt shrewdly. For the sons of this world are more shrewd in their generation than the sons of light" (Luke 16:8, NKJV). In Christian circles this saying has long been interpreted to mean that "unbelievers," that is, "non-Christians," often act more wisely than people of faith, when Jesus' intent is most likely the exact opposite. Thanks to the Dead Sea Scrolls, we can see him, with a wry sense of humor, *mocking* the Essene sectarians, who, in multiple Qumranic passages, refer to all outsiders as "sons of darkness."[13] Jesus' disciples would presumably be among them. By contrast, Jesus quips, we so-called "sons of darkness," or "sons of this world," are wiser than you "sons of light," as the sectarians repeatedly call themselves in the Scrolls.[14]

Some interpret the parable with a broad socialist brush, since the unrighteous steward is forgiving the debt of those less well-off, at the expense of a wealthy master. He is Robin Hood. However, Jesus' next statement is perhaps even more telling: "And I say to you, make friends for yourselves by unrighteous mammon," i.e. "capital" (Luke 16:9, NKJV).[15] The Dead Sea Scrolls speak frequently of the "mammon of unrighteousness," as emblematic of the wealth, currency, and commerce of the outside world. By cutting themselves off from material wealth, the sectarians took one more step toward complete isolation, while bringing to fruition their own brand of socialist Judeo-topia. Jesus, with classic sarcasm and sharp wit, charges that, in refusing all commercial dealings involving "unrighteous" material wealth, the members of the sect, notwithstanding their obvious piety, are on the short end of wisdom. In Jesus' mind, *mammon* should be used shrewdly and certainly to advance self-interest. Indeed, *mammon* has value when it comes to living in the real world. As Benjamin Franklin observed, "If you would like to know the value of money, go and try to borrow some." As far as Jesus is concerned, those who appropriate and employ capital shrewdly are "wiser than the sons of light." On that level, as Ayn Rand pointed out in a 1946 letter to a fan, "Jesus was one of the first great teachers to proclaim the basic principle of individualism."[16]

---

[13] Note CD 1:9-10: "…love all the sons of light and hate all the sons of darkness."

[14] Note 1QM 1:1: "The first attack of the Sons of Light shall be undertaken against the forces of the Sons of Darkness, the army of Belial…"

[15] Note the Dead Sea Scrolls terminology: הון אנשי רמיה and הון הרשעה (CD 6:14; 1QS 9:8); also הון חמס 1QS 10:14). The Greek ἐκ ("by") is too literal. The text should be understood as saying" from" (מן): "Make friends *from* (not by) the mammon of unrighteousness." Hypothetical Hebrew reconstruction: עשו לכם ידידים מממון החמס. Jesus is not telling his disciples to give alms, but to pursue dealings "*out of* economic contact with the world at large."

[16] See Byrd, *A Cyritique of Ayn Rand's Philosophy of Religion: The Gospel According to John Galt*, 32.

In the final analysis, there will be no end of debates about Jesus' meaning, his message, and his sympathies. Some scholars see him as a "pacifistic" Pharisee, aware of the rumbles of anti-Roman sentiment, yet counseling a non-violent approach focused on what the modern left calls "social justice." Others see him, not as "Jesus the Jewish socialist," but as "Jesus the Zealot patriot," an insurrectionist in his own right, in league with the equivalent of an ancient Galilean "Tea Party." Interestingly, there is additional evidence in the Gospel itself for the latter interpretation. Specifically, when Jesus is tried before Pontius Pilate before his crucifixion, we are told that his opponents: "began to accuse Him, saying, 'We found this fellow perverting the nation, and forbidding to pay taxes to Caesar, saying that He Himself is Christ, a King'" (Luke 23:1, NKJV). The accusation is not that Jesus was a social revolutionary, but a tax revolutionary. Perhaps the most pertinent question to be asked is: WWJT—"What would Jesus tax?" Of course, Jesus is earlier quoted as uttering the famous expression, "Render unto Caesar that which is Caesar's, and unto God that which is God's" (Matthew 22:21). The passage may in fact represent a later interpolation, emphasizing the importance of maintaining good citizenship and proving that the evolving Christian faith represented no threat to Roman hegemony. However, it might also be taken as a subtle form of sedition, for the Israelite inherently knows that if everything belongs to God, nothing belongs to Caesar. One might reconstruct Jesus' saying: "As a Jew, you decide what belongs to Caesar."

Who, we may ask, were Jesus' genuine opponents? Doubtless, they were the Sadducean priesthood, ever at odds with Israel's Zealot "patriots" and ready to repeat to the authorities the incriminating rumors that had spread through the land. They knew, like the British dealing with their colonies seventeen centuries later, that tyrannical taxation, even to ostensibly advance the general welfare of the citizenry, is the seedbed of revolt. As far as the Jewish population was concerned, neither Rome nor the Herodian state was needed to dispense charity. What belongs to Caesar? Neither taxation nor *tzedakah*; indeed, nothing. As for Jesus, there is no question that he, like all observant Jews, is deeply concerned with the poor, with the underclass—the "people of the land" (*amme ha-aretz*). Ultimately, however, his concern derives not because he is a socialist, nor a proto-Marxist, nor a radical redistributionist, but because he is (borrowing a Yiddish-ism) a *mensch*.

BIBLIOGRAPHY

Armstrong, Karen. *A History of God: The 4,000-Year Quest of Judaism, Christianity and Islam*. New York: Ballantine Books, 1994.

Byrd, Dustin J. *A Cyritique of Ayn Rand's Philosophy of Religion: The Gospel According to John Galt*. London: Lexington Books, 2015.

Crossan, John Dominic. *The Birth of Christianity*. Edinburgh: T&T Clark, 1989.

———. *The Historical Jesus: The Life of a Mediterranean Jewish Peasant*. Edinburgh: T&T Clark, 1991.

———. *Jesus: A Revolutionary Biography*. New York: HarperOne, 2009.

Donin, Hayim. *To Be a Jew: A Guide to Jewish Observance in Contemporary Life*. New York: Basic Books, 2001.

Gibson, Shimon. The Final Days of Jesus: The Archaeological Evidence. New York: HarperCollins, 2009.

Houston, Walter J. *Contending for Justice: Ideologies and Theologies of Social Justice in the Old Testament*. Edinburgh: T & T Clark, 2006.

Josephus, Flavius, and William Whiston. *The Complete Works of Flavius Josephus*. Green Forest, AR: Master Books, 2008.

Masterman Ernest W. Gurney. *Studies in Galilee*. Chicago: University of Chicago Press, 1909.

Muller, Jerry Z. *Capitalism and the Jews*. Princeton, NJ: Princeton University Press, 2010.

Rand, Ayn. *Letters of Ayn Rand*. New York: Penguin Group, 1995.

Rosenfeld, B. Z. and H. Perlmutter, "The Attitude to Poverty and the Poor in Early Rabbinic Sources (70-250 CE)," *Journal for the Study of Judaism in the Persian, Hellenistic, and Roman Period* 47, no. 3 (2016): 411–38.

ABOUT THE AUTHOR

Kenneth L. Hanson is an associate professor and coordinator of the University of Central Florida Judaic Studies Program. He earned a Ph.D. in Hebrew Studies from the University of Texas at Austin, in 1991. His many scholarly articles focus on the Second Jewish Commonwealth, the Dead Sea Scrolls, the historical Jesus and Jewish Christianity. He has also published several books of popular scholarship, including: *Dead Sea Scrolls: The Untold Story, Kabbalah: Three Thousand Years of Mystic Tradition*, and *Secrets from the Lost Bible*. He has been interviewed multiple times on nationally syndicated radio, and his research was featured on the History Channel documentary, "Banned from the Bible." He teaches a wide range of Judaic Studies courses, including the Hebrew language, the Hebrew Bible, Jewish history and culture, and the history of the Holocaust.

MORE FROM THE AUTHORS

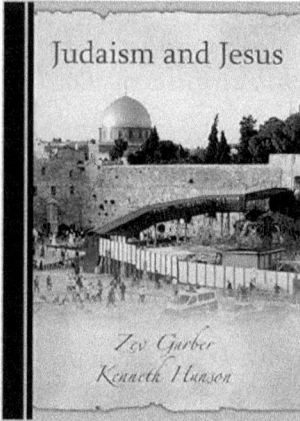

Judaism and Jesus
Cambridge Scholars
Publishing, 2020

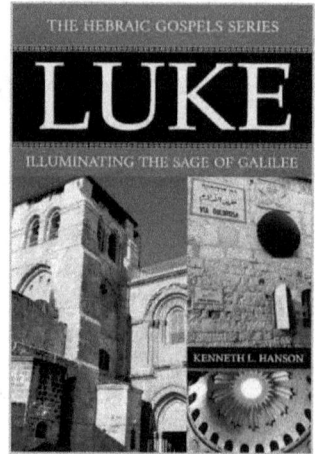

Luke: Illuminating the
Sage of Galilee
GCRR Press, 2021

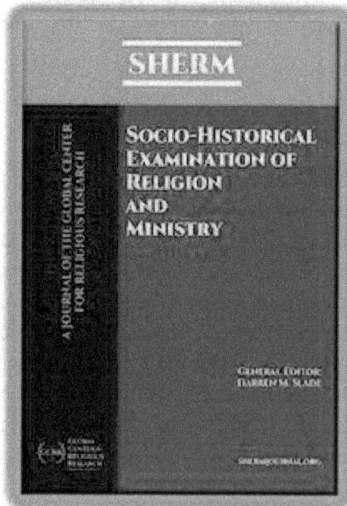

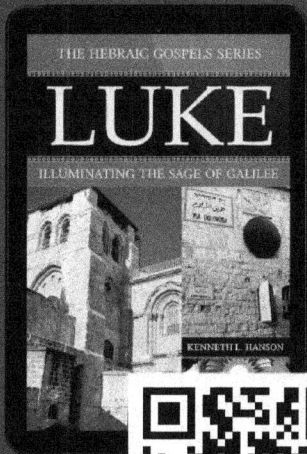

SHERM 5/1 (2023): 121–159

Religion as Brand:
ISIS and Al-Qaeda as Sub-brands of Islam

Razieh Mahdieh Najafabadi,
University of Tehran

Abstract: *Theorists emphasize the significance of the conceptualizing phenomena before any quantification in the scientific work process. The role of analogy among all human-beings' cognitive tools in the process of problem solving and concept creation is undeniable according to experts. Accordingly, this paper defines the analogy of "religion as brand" as an analogical model to shed light on political and religious marketing aspects of two terrorist organizations and religious brands in the Middle East. The concept of "ISIS and Al-Qaeda are sub-brands of Islam" was extracted from this metaphorical structure. The paper illuminates different branding attributes of these two terrorist groups through reviewing approximately fifty first-hand and second-hand materials on the issue. This review reveals how Islam functions as a master-brand and nourishes these two brands ideologically. The analogy entails a variety of attributes among which five aspects of branding including communication, brand mythology, competition, attracting social and symbolic capital, and brand promise are discussed and religious associations which endorse these two groups' political functions are examined.*

Keywords: Religion, Brand, Analogy, ISIS, Al-Qaeda

Introduction

The relationship between religion and market has been the main focus of many studies, from arguments on supply and demand for meaning as a commodity in the religious marketplace[1] to critical approaches on the emersion of religious brands such as churches and consumer goods based on capitalist culture.[2]

The first precondition in researching a phenomenon is the concept which is defined and appropriately operationalized[3] or, as Sartori warns,

---

[1] Finke and Stark, *Acts of Faith: Explaining the Human Side of Religion*
[2] Einstein, *Brands of Faith, Marketing Religion in a Commercial Age.*
[3] Sartori, *Social Science Concepts, a Systematic Analysis.*

Socio-Historical Examination of Religion and Ministry
Volume 5, Issue 1, Summer 2023 shermjournal.org
© Razieh Mahdieh Najafabadi
Permissions: editor@shermjournal.org
ISSN 2637-7519 (print), ISSN 2637-7500 (online)
https://doi.org/10.33929/sherm.2023.vol5.no1.07 (article)

"concept formation stands prior to quantification."[4] One of the cognitive tools in creating concepts is the analogy, the role of which human scientists have approved in creating knowledge[5], developing theories[6], and revealing generic properties of phenomena.[7] Isaiah Berlin even believes that thinking without metaphors is impossible[8], and Rosenthal asserts that metaphors and analogies are central features of the social scientific enterprise.[9]

Accordingly, by considering the analogy of "religion as brand" as the structural metaphor, this article presents the idea that "ISIS and Al-Qaeda are sub-brands of Islam"[10] as its hypothesis. Sub-brands are brands connected to a mother brand[11], parent brand[12], or master-brand[13] and augment or modify the associations of that mother/ parent/ master brand. Masterbrand, parent brand, and mother brand are different interpretations of the same strategic concept in brand management. Sub-brands stretch a primary frame of reference from the mother brand to add an attribute association, application association, a signal of prosperous novelty, and a brand characteristic.[14] Swystun also defines a parent brand as the leading brand in a brand family. It is the master, primary brand, and it takes on an endorsing function for one or more sub-brands. Even though a sub-brand has its name and visual identity, marketers design it to leverage the history and equity of the masterbrand and stretch it into a new category, benefit, or target.[15]

To prove its hypothesis, this review paper takes a comparative approach to religion and brand by referring to both first-hand and second-hand references. The article reviews approximately fifty references as second-hand references to reveal how these two groups utilize Islamic narrative to communicate to their audience and endorse their brands in association with Islam as the master-brand. First-hand materials also include statements by Ayman Al-Zawahiri and Bin Laden from Al-Qaeda and Abu Musab Al-Zarqawi from ISIS and propaganda materials including videos.

---

[4] Sartori, "Concept Misformation in Comparative Politics," 1038.
[5] Black, *Models and Metaphors*.
[6] Gick and Holyoak, *"Analogical Problem Solving."*
[7] Pinder and Bourgeois, "Controlling Tropes in Administrative Science," 649.
[8] Berlin, *Concepts and Categories: Philosophical Essays*, 158.
[9] Rosenthal, "Metaphors, Models, and Analogies," 297.
[10] Extracting concept from structural metaphors is based on Lakoff and Johnson theory on metaphors which will be explained in the next part.
[11] Gopal and Rajagopal, "Architecting Brands."
[12] Kotler et al., *Principles of Marketing*.
[13] Swystun, *The Brand Glossary*.
[14] Gopal and Rajagopal, "Architecting Brands."
[15] Swystun, *The Brand Glossary*, 94–113.

Theoretical Background

Religion and Market

Many scholars have studied the relationship between religion and market and the position of religion in market. These studies encompass three categories, including examination of the interaction between religion and consumer society[16], the competitive nature of religion from an economic viewpoint[17], and the similarity between religions and brands in the context of marketing.[18]

In the field of religious consumerism, Lofton and Modern deliberate about how new religions emerge in a consumer society like America by examining and criticizing the position of religions in consumer society through a variety of cases from celebrities to rituals and corporate culture. They clarify how different social contexts like corporate culture or pop culture create new religious behaviours.[19] Einstein considers religion and marketing as two territories not really at war and demonstrates how religious institutions and different religious movements, cults, or sectarian movements apply branding strategies to compete in a material world and recruit disciples.[20] By integrating and systematizing contributions from economics of religion, marketing, and sociology of religion, Stolz and Usunier provide an interdisciplinary account of the societal causes as well as individual and organizational effects of religious consumer society. In a neutral effort to understand consumerism, Gauthier and Martikainen described the contemporary rising trends and alterations in the world of religions.[21]

Beside studies in Judaism and Christianity, other scholars have concentrated on consumerism in the Islamic world. Concentrating on the concept of Halal in Islamic tradition, Shirazi defines and analyzes Brand Islam (Halal) as a highly successful marketing strategy. Furthermore, she demonstrates a growing trend toward consumer loyalty that is exclusively linked to Islam.[22] Considering the connotations associated with Islamic brand and referring to the principles of Islamic trading and commerce, Temporal

---

16 Einstein, *Brands of Faith, Marketing Religion in a Commercial Age.*
17 Finke and Stark, *Acts of Faith: Explaining the Human Side of Religion.*
18 Atkin, *The Culting of Brands: Turn Your Customers into True Believers.*
19 Lofton and Modern, *Consuming Religion.*
20 Einstein, *Brands of Faith, Marketing Religion in a Commercial Age.*
21 Gauthier and Martikainen, *Religion in Consumer Society.*
22 Shirazi, *Brand Islam: The Marketing and Commodification of Piety.*

investigates the situation of the Islamic brands in the commercial world and examines the necessity of establishing an Islamic economic union.[23]

In the context of religion economy, scholars like Lechner concentrate on the competitive nature of religions[24] in accordance with rational choice theory by Adam Smith.[25] However, Stark and Finke developed a more specific approach in this field. Based on the principle of supply and demand, they construct the theory of meaning market based on humans' desire to live meaningful lives. According to this theory, religion is one of the meaning suppliers which is in competition with other narratives that promise different answers and incentives. Introducing religious capital as a concept in meaning market, Stark and Finke conceptualize the notion of religious brand loyalty.[26] Accordingly, they believe that preserving religious capital is so important for the populace that converting to other religions is costly for them.

In the specific field of branding/marketing science, scholars tend to compare religions and brands in terms of responding to human needs. Sawicki, for example, by following a brief discussion of what the term "rite" means, examines some areas of probable resemblance between brand and rite in order to illustrate a reciprocal and positive synergy between consumerism and religion, since both are in the service of the human person. In a broader sense, Atkin by focusing on universal needs of human beings including meaning making, belonging, and establishing identity discusses that the tools, mechanisms, and techniques which brands utilize to meet these needs are completely homogenous to religions' mechanisms. These techniques were so strong in his eyes that they guaranteed the success of brands and religions as two social constructs throughout history.[27]

Theoretical Framework

Analogy as the Framework

The core argument of this paper is based on the potential of analogy in concept creation and extending theory. Therefore, in this part of the paper I clarify the analogy as a cognitive tool and discuss the model of "religion as brand" as a foundation to demonstrate how Al-Qaeda associates its brand with Islam. Gick and Holyoak define fruitful analogies as a mapping of relations

---

[23] Temporal, *Islamic Branding and Marketing: Creating a Global Islamic Business.*
[24] Lechner, "Rational Choice and Religious Economies."
[25] Smith, *An Inquiry into the Nature and Causes of the Wealth of Nations.*
[26] Finke and Stark, *Acts of Faith: Explaining the Human Side of Religion.*
[27] Atkin, *The Culting of Brands: Turn Your Customers Into True Believers.*

between two very disparate domains.[28] Generally, metaphors are powerful linguistic tools and the primary fundamental of language. Scholars with various approaches from linguistics[29] to cognitive science[30] have studied analogies and metaphors. This essay concentrates on the cognitive aspect of analogy, which results in problem-solving. Therefore, Gentner's theory in examining the cognitive analysis of analogy by the mind is the most suitable framework for this study.

In understanding any analogy the mind considers attributes and relations between two domains. Based on Gentner's model, the mind shapes the mapping between two fields like 2:3 :: 4:6. As an example, the relationship between electron and nucleus in an atom is parallel with the relationship between planet and sun in the solar system.[31] Figure 1 illustrates how she depicts this analogy to show attributes and relationships between them. It is remarkable that although this figure demonstrates a similarity in the field of natural science, as Gentner mentions, this is the structural mental model in decoding any analogy:

---

[28] Gick and Holyoak, "Analogical Problem Solving," 307.
[29] Lakoff and Johnson, *Metaphors We Live By.*
[30] Jaynes, *Origin of Consciousness in the Breakdown of the Bicameral Mind.*
[31] Gentner, "Structural Mapping, a Theoretical Framework for Analogy."

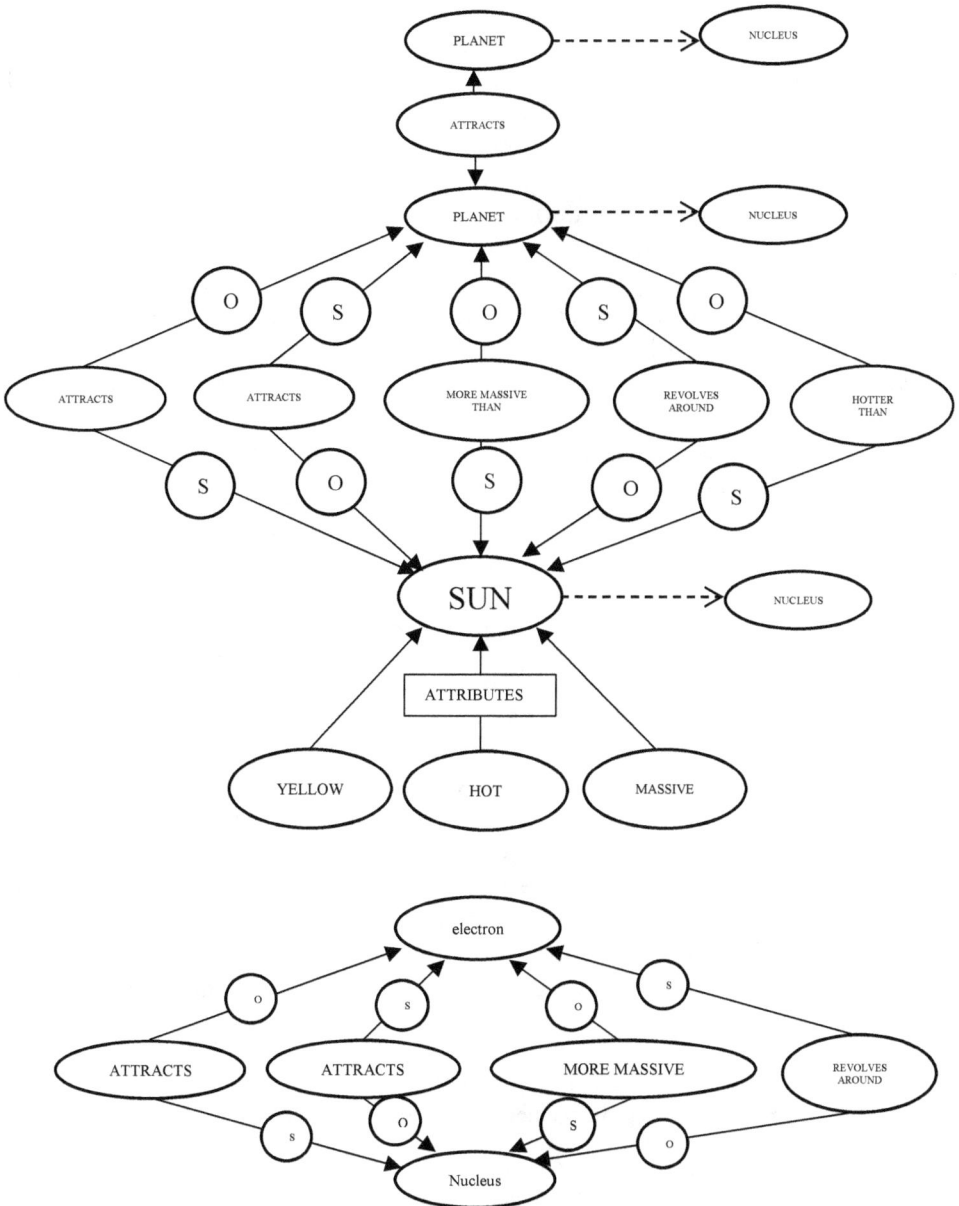

Figure 1: Structural mapping for Rutherford analogy (The atom is like the solar system- S: Subject to – O: object to) (Gentner 1983)

Religion as Brand

Based on Gentner's model, an analogy was defined as "religion: populace :: brands: customer" and based on this analogy, the structural mapping can be defined as it is depicted in figure 2. In this section, the attributes of this analogy will be discussed. Although both concepts, religion and brand, are too complicated to have a single comprehensive definition, reviewing different aspects of the two phenomena can provide the mind with a holistic panorama.

Scholars and theorists define brand from various aspects.[32] The classic definition from the American Marketing Association says that brand is a "name, term, sign, symbol, or design, or a combination of them, intended to identify the goods and services of one seller or group of sellers and to differentiate them from those of competition."[33] Although many researchers strictly adhere to AMA's classic definition[34], others assert that this definition has orientations toward product and manufacturer.[35] Therefore, for creating its analogical model in comparison between religion and brand, this study refers to definitions which address more intangible assets of brands. Accordingly, the common aspects of brands and religions as they are clarified in theory include the following.

Competition

Every brand is the representative for a particular seller, which must be differentiated from its competitors.[36] In semiotic terms brands are made up of discourses and build worlds of meaning. One of the characteristics of these worlds is that they are in competition with each other.[37] Religions are in competition with each other, too.[38] Justifying religious behaviour, organization, and religious change, Adam Smith discusses how people weigh costs and benefits in light of their preferences when choosing to join a church, taking on a religious commitment, or accepting a religious belief.[39] Finke and Stark expand the discussion and argue that any other meaning-making system can be a competitor of religion in the meaning market.[40] Implying that the key to all explanatory story-telling is the meaning-making, Lechner concludes that new

---

[32] de Chernatony and Dall'Olmo Riley, "Defining a 'Brand'."

[33] American Marketing Association, *Marketing Definitions*.

[34] Aaker, *Building Strong Brands*.

[35] Crainer, *The Real Power of Brands*.

[36] Bruce and Barnes, *The Blackwell Encyclopedia of Management. Marketing*.

[37] Semprini, *Le marketing de la marque, approche sémiotique*.

[38] Smith, *An Inquiry Into the Nature and Causes of the Wealth of Nations*.

[39] Smith, *An Inquiry Into the Nature and Causes of the Wealth of Nations*.

[40] Finke and Stark, *Acts of Faith: Explaining the Human Side of Religion*.

suppliers of meaning would alter the very nature of the demand in other competitive markets.[41]

Communication

Experts define brand management as a communication function.[42] According to Eco, a communicative process is the passage of a signal from a source to a destination.[43] Semprini clarifies brand identity as the result of continuous interactions and incessant exchanges amongst three sub-systems called encyclopedia of production (sub-system A), environment (subsystem B), and encyclopedia of reception (sub-system C).[44] Beyer defines the same structure of communication in religious definition. Beyer defines religion as a type of communication based on the immanent/transcendent polarity, which functions to lend meaning to the root indeterminability of all meaningful human communication, and which offers ways of overcoming or at least managing this indeterminability and its consequences. To provide meaning, religion posits the possibility of communication between humans and the transcendent (Fig. 2). [45]

Faith

Many experts believe that the most significant attribute of religion is faith.[46] Faith itself has a wide variety of definitions. The Encyclopedia of Religion defines it as faithfulness, obedience, trust, dependence, experience, and credo.[47] Some parts of these definitions, like trust, experience, and even faithfulness, are in common with brand attributes. In this sense, global brands are akin to religious objects. Atkin asserts that Cult brands are suppliers of modern metaphysics, enriching the universe with meaning.[48]

Myth

Muthos, in its meaning of "myth," describes a story about gods and superhuman beings. A myth functions as a model for human activity, society, wisdom, and knowledge. Mircea Eliade considers cosmogony as fundamental

---

[41] Lechner, "Rational Choice and Religious Economies," 90–91.

[42] Matusitz, *Symbolism in Terrorism,* 241.

[43] Eco, *La production des signs.*

[44] Semprini, *Le marketing de la marque, approche sémiotique*, 40.

[45] Beyer, *Religion and Globalization*, 6.

[46] Geertz, *The Interpretation of Cultures*, 34.

[47] Pelikan, "Faith," 3157.

[48] Atkin, *The Culting of Brands.*

of myth, while for Rolland Barthes, myth is a part of a semiological system of communication, whereby an object is defined.[49] It is a construct that attains significance through culture, and not due to the "nature" of things. Leo Straus analysed its structure, and Joseph Campbell studied its psychological aspects versus metaphysical ones.[50] However myth is defined, what matters is that it will influence individual and collective behaviours.[51] In both fields of religion and branding studies, myth plays a significant role. As a sacred speech, myth relies on one of the three forms of religious expression: sacred speech, acts, and places. As such, it occurs side by side in most traditions with sacred places or objects (symbols) and sacred acts.[52] On the other hand, Holt sees brand myths as a powerful force reflecting cultural content. In his eyes, cultural branding is the most effective means by which to infuse brands with enduring meanings that enable them to become icons.[53]

Narrative

Yamane asserts that the nature of religious experience is narrative. He has argued in the more general context of the study of religious experience that it is important for scholars to recognize that conversion accounts must not be understood as literal descriptions of what has actually happened but as narratives, stories constructed to explain and present one's experience of transition in a meaningful way to one's self and to others.[54] Semprini and his predecessor Floch believe in narrative as the heart of brand communication. Floch analyzes the structure of narrative in advertisements and recognizes a brand master narrative behind the organization of the narrative schema. [55] Semprini believes that at the heart of a brand identity system lies the intermediate level of brand narrative. At this level, the base values are organized in the form of narratives. A narrative grammar allows for the ordering of base values in relations of opposition.[56]

---

[49] Bolle, "Myth," 6356.

[50] Bolle, "Myth," 6359.

[51] Bouchard, *Social Myths and Collective Imaginries.*

[52] Bolle, "Myth," 6363.

[53] Holt, *How Brands Become Icons,* 84.

[54] Yamane, "Narrative and Religious Experience."

[55] Floch, *Semiotics, Marketing and Communication.*

[56] Semprini, *Le marketing de la marque, approche sémiotique.*

Metaphoric Language

Danesi believed in "a poetic logic" in brands' language. Accordingly, "the logical reasoning involved is hardly deductive or rational, it is rather based on a poetic sense of the meaning nuances built into words."[57] The exemplary manifestation of this poetic logic in the core of brands' significance is the metaphorical aspect of brands' language: "Brands are essentially metaphors. As such, they become themselves constructs for further rhetorical processes."[58] In the field of religious studies many scholars argue that religious language is metaphorical.[59] They suggest that conventional manners of comprehending religious discourse are no longer sufficient to encompass religious experience and that religious statements can be relevant only if they are reinterpreted as metaphor.

Emotion

According to Atkin, as much as markets are characterized by services and products with little physical differences, brands have to become more central in satisfying emotional needs. Marketers' only real choice is to become more dependent to emotional ties.[60] Among brand identity models, Aaker and Keller emphasized the importance of emotion in designing brand identity.[61] In the field of religious studies, in contrast with rationalist anthropologists, others argue that the distinctive characteristic of ritual behaviour is that it stems directly from emotions and not from beliefs.[62] For Malinowsky religions are seen as essentially cathartic. They have their roots in emotional stress and tension to which they give release.[63]

Community

Community has been one of the the most widely used concepts in social science, and scholars have examined it for at least the past 200 years. For Warner, a community is essentially a socially functioning whole: "a body of people bound to a common social structure which functions as a specific

---

[57] Danesi, *Brands*, 114.
[58] Danesi, *Brands*, 115.
[59] Tillich, "The Religious Symbol."
[60] Atkin, *The Culting of Brands*.
[61] Aaker, *Building Strong Brands*, 85.
[62] Marett, *The Threshold of Religion*.
[63] Malinowski, *The Foundation of Faith and Morals*, 59–60.

organism, and which is distinguishable from other such organisms."[64] Among all incentives like ethnicity or locality, religion is one of the factors to define the community.[65] Based on observations of Muniz and O'Guinn, adherence to a brand can also result in constructing a community. Accordingly, a brand community is a specialized, non-geographically bound community, based on a structured set of social relations among admirers of a brand.[66] Both religious and brand communities have common characteristics, among which moral and ritual will be discussed here.

Ethics/Moral

Religion and morality are two interwoven, yet conceptually distinct phenomena. Although morality is considered to conduct human affairs and relations between persons, religion is believed to involve the relationship between human beings and a transcendental reality. There has been a controversy among thinkers whether moral (ethical) commitment must be dependent on religion. However, these two concepts still signal two related ideas in the mind of many people.[67] In brand management ethics is revealed in two manners: first, in the framework of corporate social responsibility (CSR)[68] and secondly, through narrative moral slogans like "The United Colour of Benetton" which disseminates a universal ethic.[69] On the other hand, Muniz and O'Guinn believe that a sense of moral responsibility toward community both as a whole and as individual members is the common characteristic of all brand communities.[70]

Ritual

Anthropologists like Clifford Geertz and Victor Turner are interested in the explicit religious meaning of ritual symbolisms and assert that ritual acts endow culturally important cosmological concepts and values with persuasive emotive force, thus unifying individual participants into a genuine community.[71] However, Leach believes that the term ritual should be applied to all "culturally defined sets of behaviour"—that is, to the symbolic dimension of

---

[64] Warner, "Social Anthropology and the Modern Community."
[65] Anderson, *Imagined Communities.*
[66] Muniz and O'Guinn, "Brand Community."
[67] Green, "Morality and Religion."
[68] Brunk, "Towards a Better Understanding of the Ethical Brand and its Management."
[69] L.Borgerson, Magnusson, and Magnusson, "Branding ethics."
[70] Muniz and O'Guinn, "Brand Community."
[71] Zuesse, "Ritual."

human behaviour as such, regardless of its explicit religious, social, or other content.[72] That is how Muniz and O'Guinn observe rituals and traditions as evident in brand communities. They assert that rituals and traditions represent vital social processes by which the meaning of the community is reproduced and transmitted within and beyond the community.[73] For Danesi, modern consumerist cultures have elevated shopping to much more than acquiring the essentials required for daily living; they have bestowed upon it the same kinds of meaning that we associate with ritual.[74] The remarkable fact here is that whether ritual is defined psychologically or anthropologically, meaning and symbolism are its inseparable aspects.[75]

Symbolism

A symbol, as Geertz defines it, may be "any object, act, event, quality, or relation which serves as a vehicle for a conception."[76] The ultimate function of symbols is to mediate, reveal, express, and communicate that which in essence cannot be fully grasped, spoken of, or communicated.[77] For Tillich symbolism plays a positive and indispensable role in religious language.[78] Brands also have a symbolic aspect, or as Semprini describes, "The brand is a semiotic engine which its fuels are such disparate elements as names, colours, sounds, concepts, objects, dreams, desires, etc."[79] Danesi believes that a brand is a sign in the semiotic sense. It stands for something other than itself in some meaningful or meaning-bearing way.[80] In symbolic economy brands transform crass products and their meaningless material benefits into living vessels of meaning.[81]

Meaning

Berger believes that, "Religion is the audacious attempt to conceive the entire universe as humanly significant."[82] Geertz discusses that religion excites believers by formulating concepts of a general order of existence. People need

[72] Leach, "Ritual," 524.
[73] Muniz and O'Guinn, "Brand Community."
[74] Danesi, *Brands*, 52.
[75] Zuesse, "Ritual."
[76] Geertz, *The Interpretation of Cultures*, 91.
[77] Durkheim, *The Elementary Forms of Religion Life*, 47.
[78] Tillich, "The Religious Symbol."
[79] Semprini, *Le marketing de la marque, approche sémiotique*, 27.
[80] Danesi, *Brands*, 25.
[81] Atkin, *The Culting of Brands*, 111.
[82] Berger, *The Social Reality of Religion*, 37.

to see the world as meaningful and ordered. They cannot tolerate the view that it is fundamentally chaotic, governed by chance and without meaning or significance for them.[83] A brand also is defined as a cluster of meanings. Without brand meanings there is no brand. When we craft brand experiences, we are doing so to communicate brand meanings.[84] For Atkin, brands are full-fledged meaning schemes. They are places where a customer (or an employer) can publicly express a collection of beliefs and values.[85] MacCracken believes in four consumption rituals for transferring meaning from culturally constituted world to consumer good and from good to individual. Meaning moves from world to goods through advertisements and from goods to individuals through four rituals, including possession, exchange, grooming, and divestment.

Figure 2 demonstrates the common aspects of religion and brand in accordance with the model of analogy by Gentner:

---

[83] Geertz, *The Interpretation of Cultures.*
[84] Batey, *Brand Meaning*, 6.
[85] Atkin, *The Culting of Brands.*

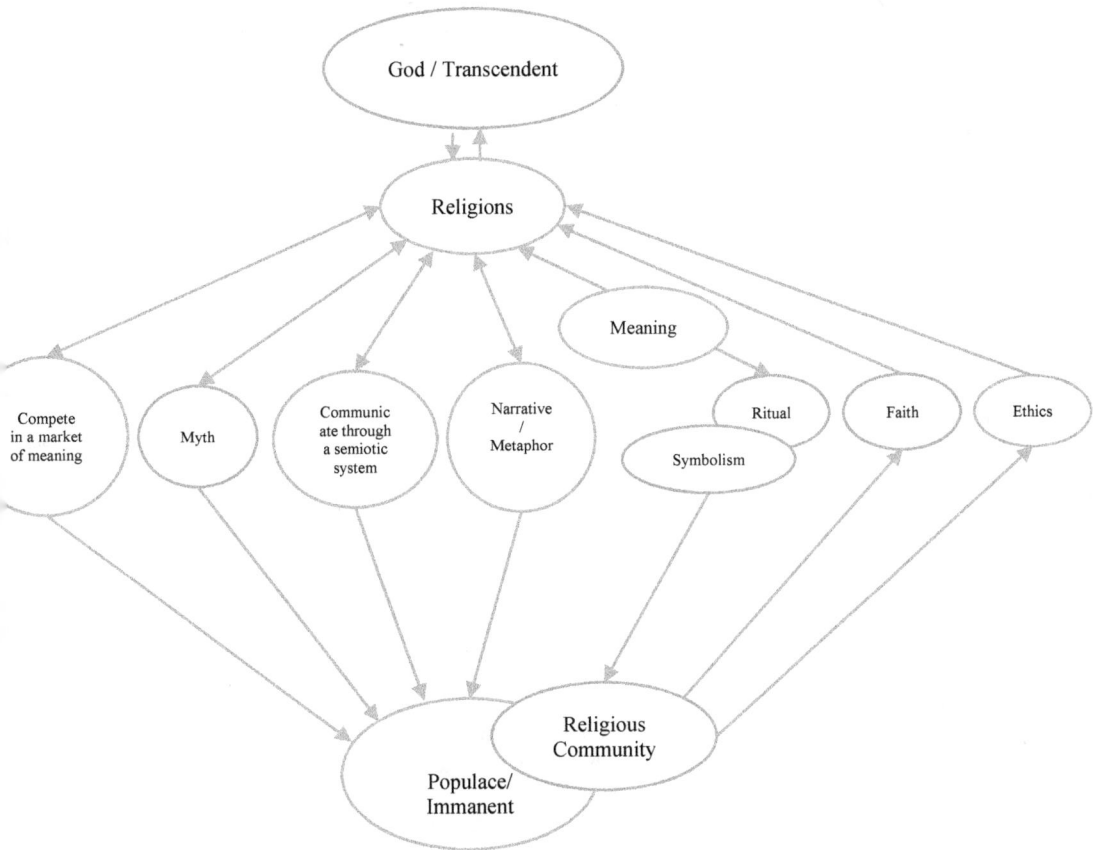

Figure 2.1: The structure mapping for the analogy of religion: populace :: brand: customer based on Gentner model – religion as origin domain (author)

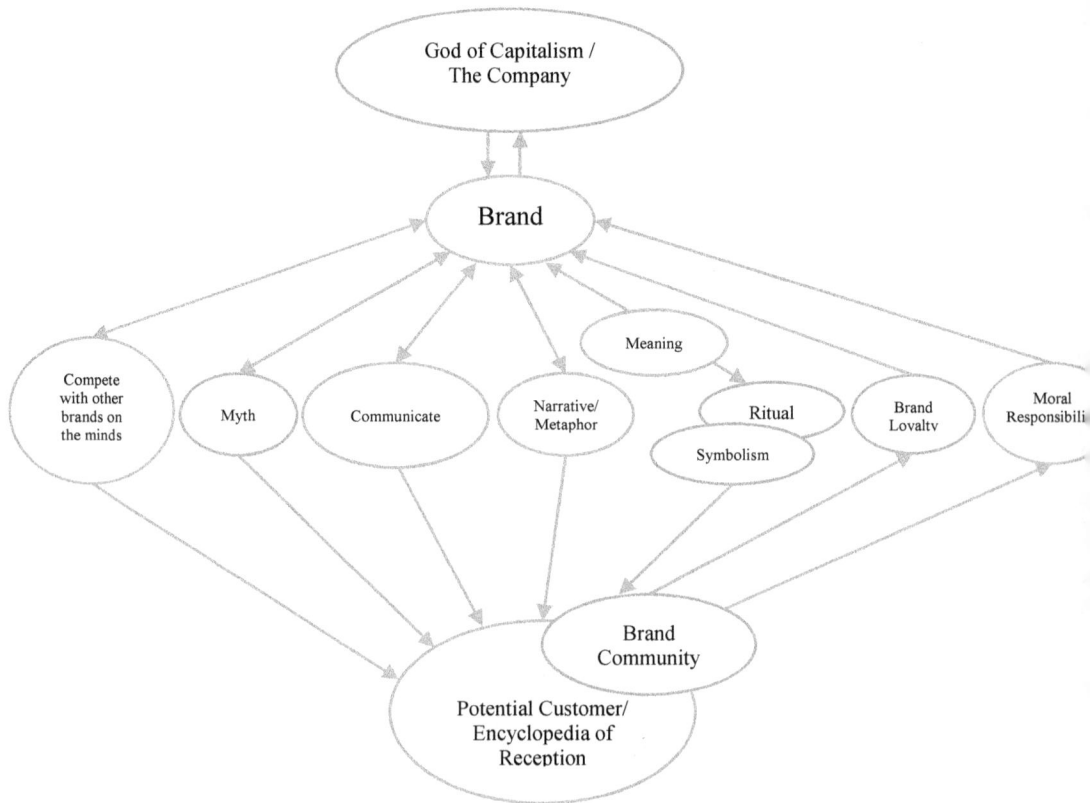

Figure 2.2: The structure mapping for the analogy of religion: populace :: brand: customer based on Gentner model – brand as destination domain (author)

Research Design

The complexity of terrorism as a social phenomenon has resulted in a condition of impossibility for the development of a single theory to describe it. In other words, social scientists perform different heuristic functions encountering this phenomenon.[86] Two terrorist organizations, ISIS and Al-Qaeda, have emerged in the Middle East as a result of a complicated network of social, political, economic, and ideological factors as serious threats for global security.[87] Many papers have studied these two organizations as brands[88] and numerous publications have investigated them from religious and ideologic perspective;[89] however, to best of my knowledge the overlap of these two domains is ignored.

Ideologies play a crucial role in branding process as many brands tend to use ideologies as anchors of identity and attraction for consumers in various manners. ISIS[90] and Al-Qaeda[91] have established their brands based on Islamic thoughts, and scholars believe that the confrontation with these groups should be fundamentally ideological.[92] Therefore, the main objective of this paper is to illuminate ideological aspects of these two terrorist organizations from the lens of branding via the framework of an analogy. More specifically, the paper aims to explore and understand how ISIS and Al-Qaeda utilize religion (Islam) as ideology of their brands.

The paper could achieve its aim by analyzing promotional materials produced by these two groups, but based on a primary search of databases including Taylor and Francis, Science Direct, and Emerald Insight, numerous papers have analyzed the content of magazines and statements of ISIS and Al-Qaeda; therefore, I discerned to fulfill the objectives of the paper through a review on this accumulation of data. The search process for this review was started from databases including Taylor and Francis, Science Direct, and Emerald Insight with broader key words like "Terrorism" and "brand" and "Terrorism communication" and was specified step by step from "ISIS" and "brand" or "AL Qaeda" and "brand" to "ISIS mythology," "Al-Qaeda mythology"), "ISIS communication strategy," "Al-Qaeda communication strategy," "ISIS recruitment," and "Al Qaeda recruitment." Sources were collected in first phase based on relevancy of title and abstract, and in the second

---

[86] Locatelli, "What Is Terrorism? Concepts, Definitions and Classifications."
[87] Gerges, *The Rise and Fall of Al-Qaeda*, and Gerges, *ISIS, a History*.
[88] Simons, "Islamic Extremism and the War for Hearts and Minds."
[89] Perry and Long, "'Why Would Anyone Sell Paradise?'"
[90] Gerges, *ISIS, a History*.
[91] Gerges, *The Rise and Fall of Al-Qaeda*, 31.
[92] Solomon, "The Particular Role of Religion in Islamic State," 8.

phase, other text books, book chapters and essays were mined through the snowball method from the references of the first phase resources. Figure 3 demonstrates the procedure of selecting papers for this review article:

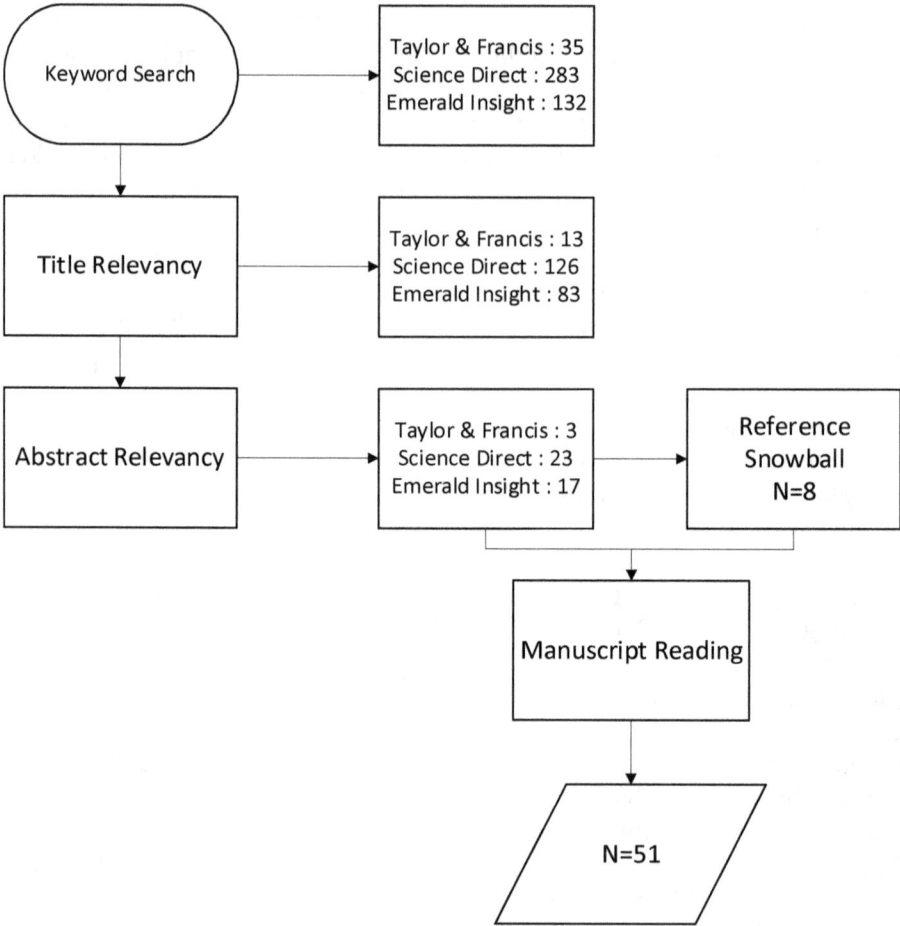

Figure 3 - the procedure of paper selection for the review

These 51 references including papers, book chapters, books, statements, and videos were analyzed in accordance with the analogical framework of the paper i.e., "religion as brand." Five attributes of analogy were identified in 51 papers (table 1). As such, the allocation of the references according to ideologic foundations of ISIS and AQ also provides a solid foundation to identify and highlight relevant research questions as it will be argued in the discussion section:

Attributes	References
Communication	Al-Zawahiri, "Letter From Al-Zawahiri to Al-Zarqawi"; Blanchard, "Al Qaeda: Statements and Evolving Ideology. CRS Report for Congress, Congressional Research Service"; Bloom, "Constructing Expertise: Terrorist Recruitment and 'Talent Spotting' in the PIRA, Al Qaeda, and ISIS," Bockstette, *Jihadist Terrorist Use of Strategic Communication Management Techniques;* Cowen, "Terrorism as Theater: Analysis and Policy Implications"; Harris, *Civilization and Its Enemies: The Next Stage of History;* Hoffman, *Terrorismus—der unerklärte Krieg. Neue Gefahren politischer Gewalt;* Locatelli, "What Is Terrorism? Concepts, Definitions and Classifications"; Maggioni and Magri, "Twitter and Jihad: The Communication Strategy of ISIS"; Matusitz, *Symbolism in Terrorism: Motivation, Communication, and Behavior;* Melki and El-Masri, "The Paris Attacks: Terror and Recruitment, Countering Daesh Propaganda"; Picard, *Media Portrayals of Terrorism: Functions and Meaning of News Coverage;* Seib and Janbek, *Global Terrorism and New Media: The Post-Al-Qaeda Generation;* Simons, "Islamic Extremism and the War for Hearts and Minds"; Venhaus, *Why Youth Join Al-Qaeda May*; Winter, "The Virtual Caliphate: Understanding Islamic State's Propaganda Strategy."
Mythology	Al-Rasheed, Kersten, and Shterin, *Demystifying the Caliphate: Historical Memory and Contemporary Contexts;* Amarsingam and Aymenn, "Is ISIS Islamic and Other 'Foolish' Debates"; Bin Laden, *Messages to the World: The Statements of Osama Bin Laden*; Bouchard, *Social Myths and Collective Imaginaries;* Fromson and Steven, "ISIS: The Dubious Paradise of Apocalypse Now"; Gerges, *The Rise and Fall of Al-Qaeda*; Gerges, *ISIS, a History;* Hafez, "Martyrdom Mythology in Iraq: How Jihadists Frame Suicide Terrorism in Videos and Biographies"; Holt, *How Brands Become Icons: The*

Table 1: **Five attributes of analogy and related references**

		Principles of Cultural Branding; Lynch, "Al Qaeda's Media Strategies"; Rowland and Theye, "The Symbolic DNA of Terrorism"; Toguslu, "Caliphate, Hijrah and Martyrdom as Performative Narrative in ISIS Dabiq Magazine."
Competition		Armstrong, *The Battle for God*; Gerges, *The Rise and Fall of Al-Qaeda*; Jordan´, Torres, and Horsburgh, "The Intelligence Services' Struggle Against Al-Qaeda Propaganda"; Lynch, "Al Qaeda's Media Strategies"; Pollard, Poplack, and Casey, "Understanding the Islamic State's Competitive Advantages: Remaking State and Nationhood in the Middle East and North Africa"; Robinson, "Just Terror: The Islamic State's Use of Strategic 'Framing' to Recruit and Motivate"; Salama and Bergoch, "Al Qaeda's Strategy for Influencing Perceptions in the Muslim World"; Simons, "Brand ISIS: Interactions of the Tangible and Intangible Environments"; Simons, "Islamic Extremism and the War for Hearts and Minds"; Solomon, "The Particular Role of Religion in Islamic State."
Capital	*Social*	Hafez, "Martyrdom Mythology in Iraq: How Jihadists Frame Suicide Terrorism in Videos and Biographies"; Neumann, "Chapter Four: The Message"; Perry and Long, "'Why Would Anyone Sell Paradise?': The Islamic State in Iraq and the Making of a Martyr"; Robinson, "Just Terror: The Islamic State's Use of Strategic 'Framing' to Recruit and Motivate"; Simons, "Brand ISIS: Interactions of the Tangible and Intangible Environments"; Toguslu, "Caliphate, Hijrah and Martyrdom as Performative Narrative in ISIS Dabiq Magazine"; Venhaus, *Why Youth Join Al-Qaeda May*; Winter, "The Virtual Caliphate: Understanding Islamic State's Propaganda Strategy."
	Symbolic	Gerges, *The Rise and Fall of Al-Qaeda*; Gerges, *ISIS, a History*.
promise		"Flames of War"; Gerges, *The Rise and Fall of Al-Qaeda*; Hoffman, *Terrorismus—der unerklärte Krieg. Neue Gefahren politischer Gewalt*; Perry and Long, "'Why Would Anyone Sell Paradise?': The Islamic State in Iraq and the Making of a Martyr"; Richardson, *What Terrorists Want: Understanding the Enemy, Containing the Threat*; Bainbridge and Stark, *The Future of Religion: Secularization, Revival and Cult Formation*; Finke and Stark, *Acts of Faith: Explaining the Human Side of Religion*.

ISIS and Al-Qaeda as Religious Brands

At first sight, ISIS and Al-Qaeda are two fundamentalist groups. "Fundamentalism" implies the contemporary and global nexus of an approach in religion that, under the surveillance of modernization, was supposed to be obsolete and sentenced to death. It represents an obviously probable variant of religious representation in contrast to more liberal and non-exclusive religion, both of which appear to appertain to a globalized society.[93] Experts have interpreted the appeal of fundamentalism as providing a firmer anchor for identity than is generally available under conditions of late modernity.[94]

On the other hand, these two brands are terrorist groups that use violence as an instrument to send their message to the audience and use religion as a factor for the cohesion of their groups.[95] Bockstette explains that the Jihadist terrorists use communication as an asset to compensate for their asymmetry in military might. In his eyes, Jihadists know how to apply strategic communication management techniques, the mass media, and especially the internet. Analyzing their audience carefully, they design their strategies and accord their messages and delivery methods strongly, with adherence to the substantial principles underlying any communication or public relations campaign.[96]

Findings

In this section, according to the analogical model of the study, "religion as brand," five attributes of two brands, ISIS and Al-Qaeda, will be discussed. These five aspects include communication, competition, attracting capital, brand promise, and brand mythology.

Communication

As it was explained in previous section, one of the focal points of the branding process is communication function.[97] According to Bockstette,

Strategic communication management is defined as the systematic planning and realization of information flow, communication, media development,

---

[93] Beyer, *Religion and Globalization*, 102.
[94] Armstrong, *The Battle for God*.
[95] Gerges, *ISIS, a History*, 26.
[96] Bockstette, *Jihadist Terrorist Use of Strategic Communication*, 5.
[97] Matusitz, *Symbolism in Terrorism: Motivation, Communication, and Behavior*.

and image care on a long-term horizon. It conveys the deliberate message(s) through the most suitable media to the designated audience(s) at the appropriate time to contribute and achieve the desired long-term effect.[98]

Two aspects of communication discernible in this definition include communicating through media and designated audience. I am going to discuss these two aspects of the communication strategy of ISIS and Al-Qaeda.

The first aspect of the communication strategy is information flow, communication, or media care on a long-term horizon. ISIS and Al-Qaeda utilize a well-designed visual system including logo, flag, color symbolism, and semiology of pictures to launch their brands. In addition to their visual identity, each group uses other outlets to disseminate their messages. The Islamic State sees itself as engaged in a conflict that is more than merely physical: "It is a psychological war made of texts, images, iconographies that the organization intends for widespread distribution."[99] Al-Qaeda's leader also believes in the war on media: *"We are in a battle, and more than half of this battle is taking place in the battlefield of the media [...]. (W)e are in a media battle for the hearts and minds of our Ummah*.*"[100]* Al-Qaeda believes in itself as a message. In Inspire it has been written that, "Al-Qaeda is a message before being an organization, a message which has spread and reached by the Grace of Allah, and Muslims have embraced it."[101] The message is simple and comprehensible: "O Muslims, if you want to live freely, gloriously and honorably, you have to defend this glory."[102] The difference between the two brands of ISIS and Al-Qaeda is that instead of using Osama bin Laden as a key public personality, ISIS utilizes the symbolic, ideological, and policy attraction as the fundamentals of their brand. This is remarkably different from Al-Qaeda's communication strategy.[103]

Terrorist attacks also work as media for terrorist groups.[104] As Picard explains, terrorism is an organized campaign of violence as communication.[105] The particular characteristic of terrorist attacks in comparison to outlets like Dabiq or YouTube videos is that due to the vast media coverage, these attacks

---

[98] Bockstette, *Jihadist Terrorist Use of Strategic Communication Management Techniques*, 9.

[99] Maggioni and Magri, "Twitter and Jihad: The Communication Strategy of ISIS."

[100] Al-Zawahiri, "Letter From Al-Zawahiri to Al-Zarqawi."

[101] Adh-Dhawāhiry, "Iman Defeats Arrogance."

[102] Adh-Dhawāhiry, "Iman Defeats Arrogance."

[103] Simons, "Islamic Extremism and the War for Hearts and Minds," 9.

[104] Locatelli, "What Is Terrorism? Concepts, Definitions and Classifications."

[105] Picard, *Media Portrayals of Terrorism.*, 41.

send terrorists' messages to the global audience.[106] Seib and Janbek described the media as "terrorism's oxygen."[107] Casting terrorist attacks, news agencies serve the attackers by offering them publicity, identification, and legitimacy. The more horrible the atrocity, the more expansive the media coverage, reaching even a "perverted form of entertainment."[108]

The Paris attack, for instance, was a successful campaign for ISIS to attract Muslims from around the world. The immediate happiness of certain ISIS supporters, as they assert, taps into longstanding resentment toward Western powers, which ISIS has long integrated into its branding strategy to attract Muslim youths around the world.[109] German modernist composer Karlheinz Stockhausen also suggested that the 9/11 attacks were "the greatest artwork of all time."[110] Others interpreted this attack as a piece of performance art for fund-raising or provoking other terrorism actions.[111]

The second aspect of strategic communication is the audience or the question to whom the group is branded. Different studies suggest various typologies of the audience for these two groups. A comparative analysis on Inspire and Dabiq reveals while both magazines are dominated by narratives designed to empower its readers towards action, Inspire (AQ magazine) relies heavily on identity choice appeals while Dabiq (ISIS magazine) tends to balance identity- and rational-choice messaging.[112]

Bockstette recognizes three segments of the audience based on their relationship to Islam: The Ummah Outsiders, The Ummah Insiders, The Adversary Outsiders. They are further dissected into the near enemy (apostates, secular Muslim regimes) and the far enemy (Jews, unbelievers, and Western society). Main communication channels for Ummah Insiders include face-to-face communication, prayers, sermons, and speeches in mosques and Koran schools; the mass media, and increasingly, the internet. For Ummah Outsiders, the internet is the primary communication channel and the second is the mass media. The communication channel preferred for adversary outsider is the global mass media and secondly the internet (Bockstette 2008: 19).[113]

The propaganda of ISIS is also designed based on the segmentation of the market in its own manner. The market of ISIS is divided into two segments:

---

[106] Blanchard, "Al Qaeda: Statements and Evolving Ideology."

[107] Seib and Janbek. *Global Terrorism and New Media.*

[108] Hoffman, *Terrorismus—der unerklärte Krieg,* 272.

[109] Melki and El-Masri, "The Paris Attacks," 29.

[110] Harris, *Civilization and Its Enemies: The Next Stage of History,* 4.

[111] Cowen, "Terrorism as Theater: Analysis and Policy Implications."

[112] Ingram, "An Analysis of Inspire and Dabiq."

[113] Bockstette, *Jihadist Terrorist Use of Strategic Communication Management Techniques,* 19.

individuals seeking excitement and bloodshed who are addressed by graphic Game of Thrones-like propaganda videos. At the same time, there are the softly lit positive message videos that emphasize the benevolent aspects of the "Islamic State" and address people who seek personal meaning.[114] In addition to military forces, some terrorist organizations such as ISIS, which are a state inside the state, need to recruit experts for social services, for instance, nurses, dentists, doctors, and so on. Propaganda that is crafted to appeal to military forces is entirely different from the advertisements aimed at recruiting expert human resources. While the pictures of drastic violence and simulation of emotions attract the "low hanging fruit" for addressing the professional audience, the messages communicate concepts of philanthropy.[115]

Brand Mythology

Marketing theorists define the brand as a historic entity whose root of appreciability is in myths that address the most remarkable social pressures of a nation.[116] According to the sociological perspective, myth is a type of common presentation (sometimes advantageous, sometimes disadvantageous), as a medium of values, beliefs, inspirations, aims, ideals, predispositions, or attitudes.[117] Holt recognizes three basic building blocks for a myth market: national ideology, cultural contradictions, and populist worlds. National ideology is a complex of thoughts that interconnect everyday life—the aspirations of individuals, families, and communities—and those of the nation. These ideologies create models for living, and the distance between that model and everyday life works as a cultural engine, creating demand for myths that manage these differences. These differences are called cultural contradictions. Populist worlds are situations in which people's actions are supposed to be motivated by belief instead of interest. Populism thrives wherever people act according to their own beliefs rather than have their actions shaped by society's institutions.[118] In Holt's eyes, an identity myth is a simple story that resolves cultural contradictions.[119] In this section, these three building blocks and their myths are discussed for the two brands ISIS and Al-Qaeda.

Nation for Al-Qaeda's Strategists is *Islamic Ummah*, as it refers to Islam's history.[120] Therefore, they have defined their national ideology as

---

114 Winter, "The Virtual Caliphate."
115 Bloom, "Constructing Expertise."
116 Holt, *How Brands Become Icons*, 75.
117 Bouchard, *Social Myths and Collective Imaginaries*.
118 Holt, *How Brands Become Icons*, 106–111.
119 Holt, *How Brands Become Icons*, 37.
120 Lynch, "Al Qaeda's Media Strategies."

returning to the golden epoch of Islam: "Our remedy is in the Qur'an and the traditions of the Prophet."[121] However, in their discourse, signs of ignored identity are observable. A description of Islam is at the heart of bin Laden's rhetoric. He describes Islam as under siege from the "Crusader-Jewish alliance," which has "insulted the pride of our ummah and sullied its honor, as well as polluting its holy places."[122] This functions as the cultural contradiction for the brand audience and is exacerbated emotionally by Jihadists in Iraq who create narratives based on themes of contempt, conspiracy, and salvation to demonize their enemies and enhance the possibility of the threat facing Muslims to convince their coreligionists to accept using extraordinary cruelty toward those foes.[123] Theoreticians have created two mythologic spaces for responding to this cultural contradiction. The first myth promotes the idea that this threat could be overcome by returning to the power and heroism present at the origin of Islam.[124] The second myth, which is extracted from Islamic rhetoric and is used by Al-Qaeda, is martyrdom.[125] The populist world for these myths is crusade wars which are associated with Iraq's history. Notably, the conflict in Iraq was also associated with a heroic Islamic past for Bin Laden. He analogized Iraqi people as the "descendants of Salah al-Din" and labeled them the "descendants of the great knights who brought Islam as far east as China."[126]

Nation, in the eyes of ISIS, is *Islamic Ummah.* In Dabiq, ISIS defines apocalypse as its national ideology.[127] Emblematic of ISIS's emotive core was its founder, Abu Musab al-Zarqawi. Zarqawi's formulation of the apocalypse allowed him to inscribe his role as '*sheik*[ii] of the slaughterers' within the "framework [of] conflict as an absolute life or death scenario."[128] His successors in ISIS were even more wedded to the possibilities offered by an apocalyptic worldview. However, the cultural contradiction about this ideology is the long-lasting waiting period (*Intizar*[iii]) for the resurrection of *Mahdi*[iv] so that answering this contradiction ISIS, announced to its supporters: "We are strong; we are winning; *we will wait for nothing and no one in fulfilling the prophecies of old.*" Thus, they have created their myth, *caliphate,* to alleviate this killing *Intizar*. The revival of the prophesied *caliphate* allows ISIS to make grandiose claims of power and is used to justify its extreme violence.[129] There

---

[121] Bin Laden, *Messages to the World: The Statements of Osama Bin Laden,* 92.
[122] Rowland and Theye, "The Symbolic DNA of Terrorism," 74.
[123] Hafez, "Martyrdom Mythology in Iraq," 111.
[124] Rowland and Theye, "The Symbolic DNA of Terrorism," 70.
[125] Hafez, "Martyrdom Mythology in Iraq," 103.
[126] Bin Laden, *Messages to the World: The Statements of Osama Bin Laden,* 208.
[127] Amarsingam and Aymenn, "Is ISIS Islamic and Other "Foolish" Debates."
[128] Fromson and Simon, "ISIS: The Dubious Paradise of Apocalypse Now," 28–32.
[129] Fromson and Simon, "ISIS: The Dubious Paradise of Apocalypse Now," 28–32.

are different interpretations and realizations around this polemical debate on the concept of *caliphate*. Some argue that *the caliphate* is God's representative on earth, and the *caliph* is semi-divine and the chief executive of the *Ummah*.[130] In an analysis of Dabiq, an ISIS online magazine, Toguslu demonstrates that the populist world for creating this myth is also a vast background of Islamic history and culture besides biographies of ISIS fighters who joined ISIS in different times. He also recognizes other signifiers in ISIS discourse that strengthen this myth, including Armageddon, Crusade, State, Martyrdom, *Hijrah*, *Jihad*, Community, Unity (*Ummah*), Morality, Hypocrisy, *Takfir*, and West Islam.[131]

Competition

The other aspect of brand definition, as mentioned before, is competition. Keller believes that for being successful in competition, the marketing manager needs to consider designing the company's offer and image so that it occupies a distinct and valued place in the target customer's minds. In other words, marketers need to know (1) who the target consumer is, (2) who the main competitors are, (3) how the brand is similar to these competitors, and (4) how the brand is different from them. The last two imply two characteristics of brands, as Keller mentions: points-of-parity and points-of-difference. Points-of-parity associations (POPs) are the characteristics of the brand which are not necessarily unique to that brand but may be shared with other brands. Points-of-difference (PODs), however, are formally defined as attributes or benefits that consumers strongly associate with a brand.[132] This section will discuss the four aspects of brand positioning or brand competition in ISIS and Al-Qaeda brands. In the section dedicated to communication, the paper addressed the audience of Jihadists. In this part three other aspects of competition—POP, POD and competitors—will be discussed.

Jihadists compete in a two-layered market. In the first layer, their competition is in the high competitiveness in the terrorism marketplace in which they compete with other terrorist groups,[133] and in the second layer, their competition is with other nation-states in the global marketplace.[134]

---

[130] Al-Rasheed, Kersten, and Shterin, *Demystifying the Caliphate*.

[131] Toguslu, "Caliphate, Hijrah and Martyrdom as Performative Narrative in ISIS Dabiq Magazine," 8–14.

[132] Keller, *Strategic Brand Management*, 83–84.

[133] Simons, "Islamic Extremism and the War for Hearts and Minds," 10.

[134] Pollard, Poplack, and Casey, "Understanding the Islamic State's Competitive Advantages."

The point of parity in the first layer is committing terrorist attacks to declare a message, and the point of difference is establishing a nation-state,[135] which can be exactly the point of parity between Jihadists and their competitors in the second layer. Their competitors in this layer are Western countries, Muslim countries in alliance with apostate states, Shi'i nations, and the Jewish state, Israel.[136] Founding the Islamic state and restoring the Caliphate was the main objective of Al-Qaeda's propaganda. Their final achievement from that objective was to help to dismiss "apostate" governments, to overcome "Crusaders and Jews," to fight the oppression of Islam, and to mobilize the world to adhere to the Jihad, which from Al-Qaeda's perspective is a war "in defense of their religion."[137] A comparative critical analysis of Dabiq and Inspire reveals that both magazines support and further construct an "us versus them" dichotomy that polarizes differences between their Jihadist ideologies and those of Westerners/non-believers.[138]

However, the most critical point of difference between these brands (Jihadists) and their competitors (West, *Shi'is*, Jewish) is the issue of religion. From its very inception, Al-Qaeda's strategy has been to embroil the United States in an all-out confrontation with the world of Islam and to brand itself as the vanguard of the *ummah*, its spearhead of armed resistance.[139] ISIS also divides the world as headed towards a global confrontation between the forces of liberal democracy and those of Islamist extremism[140] or as Simons and Robinson explain based on an analysis on Dabiq, two distinct camps: "Islam and faith" and "*kufr*[v] and hypocrisy."[141]

Designing and communicating the propaganda of a battle of civilizations (*Dar al-Islam*[vi] versus *Dar al-Harb*[vii]), the fundamentalist Islamist groups, particularly Al-Qaeda and its various regional franchises (Islamic Maghreb, Arabian Peninsula, Iraq), seek to attract and employ supporters.[142] Al-Qaeda's final objective is to revitalize the *Islamic Ummah* in confrontation with the West and to lead this mobilized Muslim community in a revolutionary

---

[135] Pollard, Poplack, and Casey, "Understanding the Islamic State's Competitive Advantages."

[136] Pollard, Poplack, and Casey, "Understanding the Islamic State's Competitive Advantages," 15.

[137] Jordan', Torres, and Horsburgh, "The Intelligence Services' Struggle Against Al-Qaeda Propaganda," 34–38.

[138] Lorenzo-Dus, Kinzel, and Walker, "Representing the West and "Non-Believers" in the Online Jihadist magazines Dabiq and Inspire."

[139] Gerges, *The Rise and Fall of Al-Qaeda*, 66.

[140] Solomon, "The Particular Role of Religion in Islamic State," 15.

[141] Robinson, "Just Terror."

[142] Salama and Bergoch, "Al Qaeda's Strategy for Influencing Perceptions in the Muslim World."

change of the new world order.[143] In these references, three facts are remarkable about competition issues. First, Al-Qaeda's goal is to establish a state precisely like its competitors. Hence, this is the point of parity of this group and its competitors, which are defined as *Dar al-Harb*. Second, the *Ummah* is going to be founded in confrontation with the West, which is the main competitor of Al-Qaeda. The third point of difference between Al-Qaeda and its competitor is the belief in Islam as Al-Qaeda's slogan is "inspire the believers."

In ISIS declarations, three main brand competitors are discernible. The first issue is that the Islamic State concerns the West as a probable existential threat. They utilize this threat as a justification for their call for defensive *jihad*; moreover, the Islamic State concentrates on the threat that Apostate political rulers, and more generally by the *kafir*[viii], pose, rulers who claim authority over the *Ummah,* which is living in the borders of existing secular states. They also see themselves threatened by *Shi'i* Islam at different levels. On the military and political level, ISIS strategists consider the '*Shi'i*-crescent' as a linkage between the regimes of Iran, Iraq, and Syria, along with Hezbollah in Lebanon, which can be a potent anti-*Sunni* alliance.[144] On the other hand, ISIS is propagating the view that Western imperialist forces are partnering with *Shi'i* entities (Iranian, Syrian, and Iraqi) and Saudi-led, "apostate" GCC states to suppress the *Sunni* nation—the nation that the *Caliphate* intends to reinvigorate, and empower.[145] The point of difference between this brand and its competitors precisely is what we describe as religious competition.

Capital

Brymer believes that leading brands communicate their promise to the market, encouraging customers to purchase the product or service.[146] In this section, purchasing a product will be discussed as an aspect of branding. Based on Keller's presumption that the product which is offered by a brand can also be an idea,[147] we can conclude that purchasing the product of the brands, ISIS and Al-Qaeda, can be defined as accepting their core idea and joining them. Blanchard asserts that the main objective of Jihadists in using Islamic outreach is to enable their movement better to employ "the [Islamic] nation's potentials, including human and economic resources" by attracting more supporters.[148] In

---

[143] Lynch, "Al Qaeda's Media Strategies," 53.

[144] Robinson, "Just Terror."

[145] Pollard, Poplack, and Casey, "Understanding the Islamic State's Competitive Advantages," 15.

[146] Brymer, "What Makes Brands Great," 69.

[147] Keller, *Strategic Brand Management*, 31.

[148] Blanchard, "Al Qaeda: Statements and Evolving Ideology," 9.

this part of the paper, I discuss how Al-Qaeda and ISIS use Islamic discourse to recruit members as social capital and seize land as symbolic capital.

Attracting Social Capital

Jihadist groups utilize Islamic narratives (*Da'wah*) to invite potential disciples to join the Jihad. The sense of belonging to the Islamic community (*Ummah*) is stronger than the sense of nationhood. Understanding recruits' exclusive and robust identification with the Ummah, Neumann explains how "home-grown" terrorists can bring themselves to launch attacks against their communities.[149] Furthermore, Jihadists borrowed the concept of Hijrah from Islam's history. ISIS defined motivating pious Sunnis to migrate (Hijrah) to the Islamic State as a primary goal of its activities.[150] ISIS slogans to recruit members was "join the caravan of Islamic State knights in the lands of the crusaders."[151] Words like "caravan" and "crusaders" in this phrase reveal the implications of Islamic culture and history in the ISIS promotional project. The term "crusaders" especially associates one of the historical hostilities between Islam and Christianity and therefore represents the issue of competition between two religions (brands).

Two significant factors which attract the youth in the Inspire magazine include overcoming negative emotions under protection of Allah, and defining their identity as vanguards of Islam or the knights of Allah. In this regard, Bin Ladan writes in Inspire: "Trust in Allah, and do not fear, for He shall suffice you, and He is the best of Protectors." And Inspire asserts that: "Know O' noble knight that you are heading for a deed which is among the greatest of virtues, and the most glorified of worships. So, purify your intention, for help comes from Allah commensurate to the purity of intention." [152]

A comparative analysis on Dabiq and Rumiyah demonstrates that Dabiq magazine prioritizes this issue (e.g., through the promotion of hijrah). On the other hand, Rumiyah (the other ISIS online magazine) is much less interested in inciting followers to join its ranks in the Middle East. Instead, it focused on calling *Ummah* to participate in jihad against the infidels, especially in the form of lone-wolf terrorist attacks. This analysis discovers three themes of inciting populace to join ISIS including: direct recruitment employed by both periodicals, with special emphasis put on the significance of hijrah, legitimizing violence against the kuffar (infidels), murtaddin (apostates), and mushrikin

---

[149] Neumann, Peter R. "Chapter Four: The Message," 49.

[150] Robinson, "Just Terror," 10–13.

[151] Simons, "Brand ISIS," 7.

[152] Bin Laden, "Advice for Martyrdom-Seekers in the West," 14–16.

(polytheists), and the calls to violence, such as incitement to "lone-wolf" terrorist attacks.[153]

As I will discuss in the next section, the Islamic promise of Heaven after martyrdom is another factor that encourages people to join the group.[154] The organization's utopian promise is also most alluring to recruits.[155] Brand mythology also plays a significant role in recruiting members for these two brands. For mobilization, the icons and symbols of the martyr, *jihad*, and *caliphate* in Dabiq are vital because they make events sensible and meaningful. [156] The mythology of martyrdom is part of Al-Qaeda's communication strategy in recruiting new members. [157] Furthermore, the vectorless energy of the youth who need to identify themselves leads them to find the answer to their questions in the media environment, which is highly charged by Al-Qaeda.[158] The concept of martyrdom (*Shahada*[ix]) and the glory associated with it in this space play a crucial role in the recruitment of the youth for Al-Qaeda.

Land as a Symbolic Capital

As Karl Marx explains in his masterpiece, *Capital*, one of the three kinds of capital is the land.[159] The crucial fact to consider here is that both groups, ISIS and Al-Qaeda, more than financial resources, regard the land as a property that must be seized. As sacred places are one of the three human religious expressions,[160] the land can be considered as a symbolic capital for these two brands. As was aforementioned, the competitors of these brands are non-Muslim nations, Muslim nations who ally the USA, and *Shi'a* Muslims. Therefore, the war on land is the competition between these brands on capital. Bin Laden vowed to expel US troops from the lands of the two holy places— Mecca and Medina—regardless of how long it would take and how costly it would be.[161] Thus, the sanctity of the land, according to holy text and Islamic

---

[153] Lakomy, "Recruitment and Incitement to Violence in the Islamic State's Online Propaganda."

[154] Perry and Long, ""Why Would Anyone Sell Paradise?": The Islamic State in Iraq and the Making of a Martyr."

[155] Winter, "The Virtual Caliphate."

[156] Toguslu, "Caliphate, Hijrah and Martyrdom as Performative Narrative in ISIS Dabiq Magazine," 9.

[157] Hafez, "Martyrdom Mythology in Iraq."

[158] Venhaus, *Why Youth Join Al-Qaeda May*, 8.

[159] Marx and Engels, *The German Ideology*.

[160] Bolle, "Myth."

[161] Gerges, *The Rise and Fall of Al-Qaeda*, 55.

history, is the definitive criteria for Al-Qaeda to define its enemies (brand competitors) and act against them to seize the land.

For ISIS also the land or territory is accounted as capital more critical than financial resources, at least in propaganda. ISIS belligerence with its brand competitors is even harder than Al-Qaeda so that the idea of cleansing the lands of Islam is entirely ingrained in the mind of fundamentalist religious activists; however, ISIS is the first one which attempted to realize it. Gerges also implies cleansing the land from any signs of atheism:

> as Islamic State militants swept across Syria and Iraq, they destroyed, damaged, or looted numerous cultural sites and sculptures, condemning them as idolatry. Celebrating their cultural cleansing in spectacular propaganda displays, Islamic State fighters show by deeds, not words, their intent to purify the lands and resurrect the caliphate.[162]

Brand Promise

Meeting the expectations of consumers is the real achievement of successful brands; in other words, they advertise a promise which is kept.[163] Batey believes that from the marketer's eyes, a brand is a promise, a vow. For the customer, a brand is the complex of associations, comprehensions, and expectations in his or her mind.[164] In the sociology of religion, scholars also believe in compensators or promises. The premise of Stark and Bainbridge's social psychology is that human beings are unable to obtain the intense rewards that they greatly desire (e.g., immortality) through direct action. Therefore, they tend to accept "compensators" or promises of future rewards. The most potent anticipations, however, are predicated on explicit supernaturalism.[165]

Stark and Finke consider the possibility that the tendency to supernatural remunerations could vary. They also suppose that humans "will attempt to appraise explanations according to outcomes, maintaining those that seem to work most efficiently."[166] To explain why rational actors should want to join more costly groups, Stark and Finke suggest that "despite being costly, they offer a more remarkable value," and they can do so "partly *due to* their cost."[167]

---

[162] Gerges, *ISIS, a History*, 30.
[163] Blackett, "What Is a Brand?" 18.
[164] Batey, *Brand Meaning*, 4.
[165] Bainbridge and Stark, *The Future of Religion*.
[166] Finke and Stark, *Acts of Faith*, 87–88.
[167] Finke and Stark, *Acts of Faith*, 145.

Suicide terrorism is, first and foremost, an instrumental strategy with the goal of publicity at the highest possible price.[168] Thus, according to Stark and Fink, the reward of this form of terrorism must be so high that it must seem rational for terrorists to commit it. Perry and Long explain that first, Jihadist ideology "offers potential adherents the opportunity to enter a narrative (source of meaning) that specifically recapitulates Islamic history and develops a compelling new identity based on that history." Second, the Islamic State "promises the Jihadist that should he be killed, he becomes a martyr, leaving a powerful story that recaptures religious history and inspires others."[169]

As a result, Jihadists have two promises for their audiences: eternal life and meaning, both of which are religious rewards. A comprehensive analysis on Dabiq and Rumiyah shows that creating meaning and heroic stories which glorify Jihadists are remarkable aspects of these magazines' content. [170] Offering rewards in the afterlife and proving legitimacy, religion facilitates recruiting terrorists, for people who are prepared to pay in this life.[171] People who join ISIS "are trying to find a path, to answer a call to something, to right some perceived wrong, to do something truly meaningful with their lives."[172] Al-Qaeda also called his young and old mujahideen for battling a godless enemy, seeking martyrdom, and dreaming of heavenly, not earthly, fruits and rewards.[173] Like in other propaganda material, "Flames of War" portrays ISIS' fight as one of "good versus evil," where the deaths of its fighters are not a setback, but are rather rewarded with eternal paradise as a reward.[174]

Discussion and Conclusion

The relationship between brand and religion has been studied by many scholars in various perspectives (e.g., see Atkin[175] or Finke and Stark[176]). In this regard, Atkin focuses on the similarities between brands and religions in terms of the needs which these two social phenomena meet.[177] In this context, the present study in the first phase designed an analogical model to extend the theory and clarify other aspects of resemblance between religion and brand. In

---

[168] Hoffman, *Terrorismus—der unerklärte Krieg,* 258.
[169] Perry and Long, ""Why Would Anyone Sell Paradise?"
[170] Welch, "Theology, Heroism, Justice, and Fear."
[171] Richardson, *What Terrorists Want.*.
[172] Horgan, "In Why It's So Hard to Stop ISIS."
[173] Gerges, *The Rise and Fall of Al-Qaeda,* 40.
[174] Al Hayat, "Flames of War."
[175] Atkin, *The Culting of Brands: Turn Your Customers Into True Believers.*
[176] Finke and Stark, *Acts of Faith: Explaining the Human Side of Religion.*
[177] Atkin, *The Culting of Brands: Turn Your Customers Into True Believers.*

next phase, this research discussed five attributes of this analogy in accordance with ISIS and Al-Qaeda brands to clarify them as sub-brands of Islam. In other words, I explained how these two brands endorse themselves in association with Islamic ideology. Table 2 demonstrates five dimensions of this analogy in summary:

Table 2: Five aspects of two brands in association with Islam			
		Al-Qaeda	ISIS
Communication	Media	Internet, Inspire magazine, Terrorist Attacks, Speeches for Muslims, prayers, sermons	Iconography, Dabiq magazine, Videos, Terrorist Attacks
	Audience	The Ummah Outsiders, The Ummah Insiders, The Adversary Outsiders	Individuals Seeking Excitement, Military Forces, Experts
Brand Myth	National Ideology	Return to the strength of Islam	Apocalypse
	Cultural Contradiction	Humiliation, Impotence and Collusion	long-lasting waiting period for Savior
	Populist World	Crusaders wars associated historically with Iraq	Islamic history and culture
	Myth	Martyrdom The glory of the origin of Islam	*Caliphate*
Competition	Main Competitors	Western countries, Muslim countries in alliance with apostate states, *Shi'i* nations and Jewish state, Israel	Western countries, *Shi'i states*, Israel
	Point of Parity	Establishing Nation-State	Establishing Nation-State
	Point of Difference	Religion *(Dar al-Islam* versus *Dar al-Harb)*	Religion "Islam and faith" and "kufr (unbeliever) and hypocrisy"

Capital	Social Capital	Utilizing Concept of Martyrdom to recruit members	Implying Islamic History (Crusaders, Hijrah) Promise of heaven Giving meaning to their lives Utopian Islamic offer (apocalypse)
	Symbolic Capital	repel US troops from the two holy places— Mecca and Medina	cleansing the land from any signs of atheism
Brand Promise		eternal life meaning	becoming a martyr heaven after martyrdom

One of the other cases is the communicative part of religion in the Israel-Palestine conflict. In this regard, by investigating the Palestinian encounter with Israel and the productive cultural schemes generated by the encounter, the aesthetics of the performance of Palestinian missions of "suicide bombing," their cultural representations, and the poetics that their performance and representations produce, Abufarha argues that the practice of sacrificing Palestinian bodies and applying violence against the "enemy" in the same act is a media for cultural ideas of uprooting and rootedness, fragmentation and unity, confinement and freedom, domination and independence. [178] This can be a crucial issue for future studies to examine and evidence the role of religion as brand in another context.

The most important limitation of this research was the predominance of the "war on terror" discourse in the majority of publications in this field which could increase the probability of bias in interpretations. The communication aspects of these two groups were mostly interpreted as propaganda rather than a communication strategy of an organization. Despite of the common aspects in propaganda and communication strategy there are nuances between them due to negative implications in propaganda and this interpretation is the result of "war on terror" discourse. However, the messages of a terrorist group can be interpreted as the expression of injustice or infringement in the global arena. Furthermore, the affiliation of authors in this field to different security organizations or intellectual orientations from various countries with different approaches toward terrorism in general and Al Qaeda and ISIS in particular

---

[178] Abufarha, *The Making of a Human Bomb an Ethnography of Palestinian Resistance.*

resulted in dispersed opinions in publications and made it challenging to sum up the discussions and achieve a comprehensive insight. On the other hand, terrorism and its complexities made the analysis more complicated.

In terms of theory and practice, the paper entails a variety of implications. As it was explained, theorists and philosophers believe in the role of analogy in the process of thinking and creating novel concepts in social science. The analogical approach in this paper not only extends the field of study theoretically but paves the way for academicians to extend the theory in this field through other attributes of this analogical model. The Ashura ceremony in Shi'i tradition, for example, can be studied as a reach system of signs and this is merely one of myriad.

BIBLIOGRAPHY

Aaker, David A. *Building Strong Brands*. New York: The Free Press, 1996.
————. *Managing Brand Equity: Capitalizing on the Value of a Brand Name*. New York: The Free Press, 1991.
Abufarha, Nasser. *The Making of a Human Bomb an Ethnography of Palestinian Resistance*. Durham and London: Duke University Press, 2009.
Adh-Dhawāhiry, Aiman. "Iman Defeats Arrogance." *Inspire* 12, March (2014): 10–12.
Al-Rasheed, Madawi, Carool Kersten, and Marat Shterin. *Demystifying the Caliphate: Historical Memory and Contemporary Contexts*. Oxford: Oxford University Press, 2015.
Al-Zawahiri, Ayman. "Letter From Al-Zawahiri to Al-Zarqawi." In *Office of the Director of National Intelligence*. n.d. Accessed 11 October 2005. https://irp.fas.org.
Amarsingam, Amarnath, and Al-Tamimi Aymenn. "Is ISIS Islamic and Other "Foolish" Debates." Jihadology, 4 March 2015.
American Marketing Association. *Marketing Definitions: A Glossary of Marketing Terms*. Chicago: American Marketing Association, 1960.
Ammerman, Nancy T. *Bible Believers: Fundamentalists in the Modern World*. New Brunswick, NJ: Rutgers University Press, 1987.
Anderson, Benedict. *Imagined Communities*. London: Verso, 1983.
Armstrong, Karen. *The Battle for God*. New York: Knopf, 2000.
Atkin, Dauglas. *The Culting of Brands: Turn Your Customers Into True Believers*. New York: Portfolio, 2004.
Bainbridge, William Sims, and Rodney Stark. *The Future of Religion: Secularization, Revival and Cult Formation*. University of California Press, 1985.
Batey, Mark. *Brand Meaning*. New York: Routledge, 2008.
Berlin, Isaiah. *Concepts and Categories*. London: Hogarth Press, 1978.
Beyer, Peter. *Religion and Globalization*. London: Sage, 2000.
Bin Laden, Osama. *Messages to the World: The Statements of Osama Bin Laden*. Translated by J. Howarth and B. Lawrence. London: Verso, 2005.

———. "Advice for Martyrdom-Seekers in the West." *Inspire* 17, May (2017): 14–16.

Black, Max. *Models and Metaphors*. Ithaca: Cornell University Press, 1962.

Blackett, Tom. "What is a brand?" In *In Brand abd Branding*, edited by Rita Clifton and John Simmons, 13–27. London: The Economist, 2003.

Blanchard, Christopher M. "Al Qaeda: Statements and Evolving Ideology. CRS Report for Congress, Congressional Research Service." The Library of Congress, 17 December 2018.

Bloom, Mia. "Constructing Expertise: Terrorist Recruitment and "Talent Spotting" in the PIRA, Al Qaeda, and ISIS." *Studies in Conflict & Terrorism* 40, no. 7 (2017): 603–23.

Bockstette, Carsten. *Jihadist Terrorist Use of Strategic Communication Management Techniques*. Germany: The George C. Marshall European Center for Security Studies, 2008.

Bolle, Kees W. "Myth." In *Encyclopedia of Religion*, edited by Lindsey Jones, 6359–71. New York: MacMillan Reference, 2005.

Bouchard, Gérard. *Social Myths and Collective Imaginries*. Translated by Howard Scott. Toronto: University Of Toronto Press, 2015.

Bruce, Margaret, and Liz Barnes. *The Blackwell Encyclopedia of Management. Marketing*. Edited by Dale Littler. Oxford: Blackwell Publishing, 2005.

Brunk, Katja H. "Towards a Better Understanding of the Ethical Brand and its Management." In *The Routledge Companion to Contemporary Brand Management*, edited by Francesca Dall'Olmo Riley, Jaywant Singh, and Charles Blankson, 280–94. London and NewYork: Routledge, 2016.

Brymer, Chuck. "What Makes Brands Great." In *Brand and Branding*, edited by Rita Clifton and John Simmons, 65–77. London: The Economist, 2003.

Cowen, Tyler. "Terrorism as Theater: Analysis and Policy Implications." *Public Choice* 128, no. 1/2 (2006): 233–44.

Crainer, Stuart. *The Real Power of Brands: Making Brands Work for Competitive Advantage*. London: Pitman Publishing, 1995.

Danesi, Marcel. *Brands*. London and NewYrok: Routledge, 2006.

de Chernatony, Leslie, and Francesca Dall'Olmo Riley. "Defining a "Brand": Beyond the Literature With Experts' Interpretations." *Journal of Marketing Management* 14, no. 5 (1998): 417–43.

Durkheim, Emile. *The Elementary Forms of Religion Life*. Translated by Karen E. Field. NewYork: Free Press, 1995.

Eco, Umberto. *La production des signs*. Paris: Librairie générale française, 2007.

———. *Le signe: Histoire et analyse d'un concept*. Michigan: Labor, 2002.
   Shortened Footnote: Eco, *Le signe: Histoire et analyse d'un concept*.

Einstein, Mara. *Brands of Faith, Marketing Religion in a Commercial Age*. London and NewYork: Routledge, 2008.

Finke, Roger, and Rodney Stark. *Acts of Faith: Explaining the Human Side of Religion*. University of California Press, 2000.

"Flames of War." Al Hayat, 2014. Video.

Floch, Jean-Marie. *Semiotics, Marketing and Communication*. London: Palgrave Macmillan, 2001.

Fromson, James, and Simon Steven. "ISIS: The Dubious Paradise of Apocalypse Now." *Survival* 57, no. 3 (2015): 7–56.

Gauthier, François, and Tuomas Martikainen. *Religion in Consumer Society, Brands, Consumers and Markets.* Burlington: Ashgate, 2013.

Geertz, Cliford. *The Interpretation of Cultures.* London: Hutchinson, 1975.

Gentner, Dedre. "Structural Mapping, a Theoretical Framework for Analogy." *Cognitive Science*, no. 7 (1983): 155–70.

Gerges, Fawaz A. *ISIS, a History.* Princeton: Princeton University Press, 2016.

———. *The Rise and Fall of Al-Qaeda.* Oxford: Oxford University Press, 2011.

Gick, Mary L., and Keith J. Holyoak. "Analogical Problem Solving." *Cognitive Psychology*, no. 12 (1980): 306–55.

Gopal, Raja, and Amritanshu Rajagopal. "Architecting Brands." *Journal of Transnational Management* 12, no. 3 (2007): 25–37.

Green, Ronald M. "Morality and Religion." In *Encyclopedia of Religion*, edited by Lindsay Jones, 6177–89. Detroit: Thomson Gale, 2006.

Hafez, Mohammed M. "Martyrdom Mythology in Iraq: How Jihadists Frame Suicide Terrorism in Videos and Biographies." *Terrorism and Political Violence* 19, no. 1 (2007): 95–115.

Harris, Lee. *Civilization and Its Enemies: The Next Stage of History.* New York: The Free Press, 2004.

Heilbrunn, Benoît. "Cultural Branding Between Utopia and a-Topia." In *Brand Culture*, edited by Jonathan E.Schroeder and Miriam Salzer- Mörling, 92–106. New York: Routledge, 2006.

Hoffman, Bruce. *Terrorismus—der unerklärte Krieg. Neue Gefahren politischer Gewalt.* Bonn, Germany: Bundeszentrale für politische Bildung, 2007.

Holt, Douglas. *How Brands Become Icons: The Principles of Cultural Branding.* Boston: MA: Harvard Business School Press, 2004.

Horgan, John. "In Why It's So Hard to Stop ISIS." The Atlantic, 27 February 2019.

Ingram, Haroro J. "An Analysis of Inspire and Dabiq: Lessons from AQAP and Islamic State's Propaganda War." *Studies in Conflict & Terrorism* 40, no. 5 (July 2016): 357–75. https://doi.org/10.1080/1057610x.2016.1212551.

Jaynes, Julian. *Origin of Consciousness in the Breakdown of the Bicameral Mind.* Houghton Mifflin Harcourt Trade & Reference Publishers, 2000.

Jordan´, Javier, Manuel R. Torres, and Nicola Horsburgh. "The Intelligence Services' Struggle Against Al-Qaeda Propaganda." *International Journal of Intelligence and CounterIntelligence* 18, no. 1 (January 2005): 31–49. https://doi.org/10.1080/08850600590905663.

Keller, Kevin Lane. *Strategic Brand Management: Building, Measuring, and Managing Brand Equity.* 4th ed. Boston: Pearson, 2013.

Kotler, Philip, Gary Armstrong, John Saunders, and Veronica Wong. *Principles of Marketing.* Hemel Hempstead: Prentice Hall Europe, 1996.

Lakoff, George. *Metaphors We Live By.* Chicago: University of Chicago Press, 1980.

Lakomy, Miron. "Recruitment and Incitement to Violence in the Islamic State's Online Propaganda." *Studies in Conflict & Terrorism*, February 2019, 1–16. https://doi.org/10.1080/1057610x.2019.1568008.

L.Borgerson, Janet, Martin Escudero Magnusson, and Frank Magnusson. "Branding ethics: negotiating Benetton's identity and image." In *Brand Culture*, edited by Jonathan E. Schroeder and Miriam Salzer-Mörling, 153–66. London and NewYork: Routledge, 2006.

Leach, Edmund R. "Ritual." In *International Encyclopaedia of the Social Sciences*, edited by David L. Sills. New York: MacMillan Reference USA, 1968.

Lechner, Frank J. "Rational Choice and Religious Economies." In *The SAGE Handbook of the Sociology of Religion*, edited by James A. Beckford and Nicholas Jay Demerath, 81–98. London: Sage Publication, 2007.

Locatelli, Andrea. "What Is Terrorism? Concepts, Definitions and Classifications." *Understanding Terrorism*, 2015, 1–23. https://tinyurl.com/36sur6xc.

Lofton, Kathryn, and Lardas Modern. *Consuming Religion*. Chicago: University of Chicago Press, 2017.

Lorenzo-Dus, Nuria, Anina Kinzel, and Luke Walker. "Representing the West and "Non-Believers" in the Online Jihadist magazines Dabiq and Inspire." *Critical Studies on Terrorism* 11, no. 3 (2018): 521–36. https://tinyurl.com/4ya6wjut.

Lynch, Marc. "Al Qaeda's Media Strategies." *National Interest Summer*, 2006, 50–62.

Maggioni, Monica, and Paolo Magri. "Twitter and Jihad: The Communication Strategy of ISIS." Milan: ISPI, 2015.

Malinowski, Bronislaw. *The Foundation of Faith and Morals*. Oxford: Oxford University Press, 1936.

Marett, Robert Ranulph. *The Threshold of Religion*. London: Methuen, 1914.

Marx, Karl, and Friedrich Engels. *The German Ideology*. 3rd ed. Moscow: Progress Publishers, 1976.

Matusitz, Jonathan. *Symbolism in Terrorism: Motivation, Communication, and Behavior*. Rowman & Littlefield Publishers, 2015.

Melki, Jad, and Azza El-Masri. "The Paris Attacks: Terror and Recruitment, Countering Daesh Propaganda." *Action-Oriented Research for Practical Policy Outcomes*, February (2016): 28–34.

Muniz, Albert M., and Thomas C. O'Guinn. "Brand Community." *Consumer Research* 27, no. 4 (2001): 412–32.

Neumann, Peter R. "The Message." *Adelphi Papers* 48, no. 399 (2008): 43–52.

Pelikan, Jaroslav. "Faith." In *Encyclopedia of Religion*, edited by Lindsay Jones, 2954–59. Detroit: Thomson Gale, 2006.

Perry, Samuel P., and Jerry Mark Long. "'Why Would Anyone Sell Paradise?': The Islamic State in Iraq and the Making of a Martyr." *Southern Communication Journal* 81, no. 1 (2016): 1–17. doi.org/10.1080/1041794x.2015.1083047.

Picard, Robert G. *Media Portrayals of Terrorism: Functions and Meaning of News Coverage*. Ames: Iowa State University Press, 1993.

Pinder, Craig C., and V. Warren Bourgeois. "Controlling Tropes in Administrative Science." *Administrative Science Quarterly*, no. 27 (1982): 641–52.

Pollard, Stacey Erin, David Alexander Poplack, and Kevin Carroll Casey. "Understanding the Islamic State's Competitive Advantages: Remaking State and Nationhood in the Middle East and North Africa." *Terrorism and Political Violence* 29, no. 6 (2015): 1045–65. https://tinyurl.com/z2bj838d.

Richardson, Louise. *What Terrorists Want: Understanding the Enemy, Containing the Threat*. Random House, 2006.

Robinson, Leonard C. "Just Terror: The Islamic State's Use of Strategic "Framing" to Recruit and Motivate." *Orbis* 61, no. 2 (2017): 172–86. https://doi.org/10.1016/j.orbis.2017.02.002.

Rosenthal, Debra C. "Metaphors, Models, and Analogies in Social Science and Public Policy." *Political Behavior* 4, no. 3 (1982): 283–301. https://doi.org/10.1007/bf00990109.

Rowland, Robert C., and Kirsten Theye. "The Symbolic DNA of Terrorism." *Communication Monographs* 75, no. 1 (March 2008): 52–85. https://doi.org/10.1080/03637750701885423.

Salama, Sammy, and Joe-Ryan Bergoch. "Al Qaeda's Strategy for Influencing Perceptions in the Muslim World." In *Influence Warfare: How Terrorists and Governments Fight to Shape Perceptions in a War of Ideas*, edited by Jf Forrest, 291–310. Westport, CT: Praegar Security International, 2009.

Sartori, Giovanni. "Concept Misformation in Comparative Politics." *American Political Science Review* 64, no. 4 (1970): 1033–53. https://doi.org/10.2307/1958356.

———. *Social Science Concepts, a Systematic Analysis*. Beverly Hills: Sage, 1984.

Seib, P., and D. M. Janbek. *Global Terrorism and New Media: The Post-Al-Qaeda Generation*. London and New York: Routledge, 2011.

Semprini, Andréa. *Le marketing de la marque, approche sémiotique*. Paris: Editions Liaisons, 1992.

Shirazi, Faegheh. *Brand Islam: The Marketing and Commodification of Piety*. University of Texas Press, 2016.

Simons, Greg. "Brand ISIS: Interactions of the Tangible and Intangible Environments." *Journal of Political Marketing* 17, no. 4 (September 2018): 322–53. https://doi.org/10.1080/15377857.2018.1501928.

———. "Islamic Extremism and the War for Hearts and Minds." *Global Affairs* 2, no. 1 (January 2016): 91–99. https://doi.org/10.1080/23340460.2016.1152446.

Smith, Adam. *An Inquiry Into the Nature and Causes of the Wealth of Nations*. Oxford: Clarendon Press, n.d.

Solomon, Hussein. "The Particular Role of Religion in Islamic State." *South African Journal of International Affairs* 23, no. 4 (October 2015): 437–56. https://doi.org/10.1080/10220461.2016.1272486.

Speckhard, Anne, Ardian Shajkovci, Claire Wooster, and Neima Izadi. "Mounting a Facebook Brand Awareness and Safety Ad Campaign to Break the ISIS Brand in Iraq." *Perspectives on Terrorism* 12, no. 3 (2018): 50–66.

Struck, Peter T. "Symbol and Symbolism." In *Encyclopedia of Religion*, edited by Lindsay Jones, 8906–15. Detroit: Thomson Gale, 2005.

Swystun, Jeff, ed. *The Brand Glossary*. London: Palgrave Macmillan UK, 2006. https://doi.org/10.1057/9780230626409.

Temporal, Paul. *Islamic Branding and Marketing: Creating a Global Islamic Business*. Wiley & Sons, Incorporated, John, 2011.

Tillich, Paul. "The Religious Symbol." *Daedalus*, no. 87 (1958): 321.

Toguslu, Erkan. "Caliphate, Hijrah and Martyrdom as Performative Narrative in ISIS Dabiq Magazine." *Politics, Religion & Ideology* 20, no. 1 (December 2018): 94–120. https://doi.org/10.1080/21567689.2018.1554480.

Turner, Mark, and Gilles Fauconnier. "Metaphor Metonym and Fusion." In *Metonymy and Metaphor in Grammar (Human Cognitive Processing)*, edited by Antonio Barcelona, 223–44. Amsterdam / Philadelphia: John Benjamins Publishing Company, 2009.

Venhaus, John M. *Why Youth Join Al-Qaeda May*. Washington, DC: United States Institute of Peace, 2010.

Warner, W. Lloyd. "Social Anthropology and the Modern Community." *American Journal of Sociology*, no. 46 (1941): 785–96.

Welch, Tyler. "Theology, Heroism, Justice, and Fear: An Analysis of ISIS Propaganda magazines Dabiq and Rumiyah." *Dynamics of Asymmetric Conflict* 11, no. 3 (September 2018): 186–98. https://doi.org/10.1080/17467586.2018.1517943.

Winter, Charlie. "The Virtual Caliphate: Understanding Islamic State's Propaganda Strategy." Quilliam International, 2015.

Yamane, David. "Narrative and Religious Experience." *Sociology of Religion* 61, no. 2 (2000): 171–89.

Zuesse, Evan M. "Ritual." In *Encyclopedia of Religion*, edited by Lindsay Jones, 7833–48. New York: Thomson Gale, 2015.

ABOUT THE AUTHOR

Razieh Mahdieh Najafabadi: She started her academic life in design studies with a concentration on branding science. However, religion was always a major concern in her mind. In the path of her studies, she came to the point that these two phenomena (brand and religion) follow similar mechanisms in influencing human beings. This was the starting point of her major project called "religion as brand," obtaining an MA in Social Studies with a focus on this project. She is working on a book called, *Religion as Brand: An Analogy to Reconceptualize Religion.*

---

[i] World Islamic Community
[ii] Arabic word meaning old and in expression, we can translate it to the leader
[iii] The concept of waiting for Mahdi in Islamic Culture
[iv] The Savior in Islamic Tradition
[v] Unbeliever
[vi] The house of Islam/Peace
[vii] The house of War
[viii] unbelieved people
[ix] Concept of Martyrdom in Islamic culture

SHERM 5/1 (2023): 161–167

Defending the Hypothesis of Indifference

Tori Helen Cotton,
University of California, Irvine

Abstract: *The problem of evil is the philosophical question regarding how to reconcile the existence of an omnipotent, omnibenevolent, and omniscient God with the pain and suffering in the world. The Hypothesis of Indifference is Paul Draper's proposal considering that question. His claim is that the pain and pleasure we experience in our lifetimes has nothing to do with God or some other supernatural force acting as an agent of good or evil. In this paper, I argue that Draper's Hypothesis of Indifference is a better explanation for why we experience pain and pleasure than theism is and that it survives major contemporary criticisms posed by Peter van Inwagen and William Alston.*

Keywords: Problem of Evil, Theodicy, Suffering, Philosophy of Religion, Atheism

T he Problem of Evil raises several important questions for theodicists— those who attempt to rationalize and argue for the existence of God despite the multifarious needless suffering in the world. Early evidential arguments from evil focused on instances of evil as proof that God is unlikely to exist,[1] and responses to those arguments from the theistic stance focused on analyzing what sort of epistemic access humans can have to the reasons for suffering and evil to begin with.[2] This has led to debates between philosophers about the epistemic access humans may have to know God's moral positions.[3]

In contrast to these traditional positions, Paul Draper's text, "Pain and Pleasure: An Evidential Problem for Theists," introduces a novel perspective— the Hypothesis of Indifference. Drawing from Hume's *Dialogues Concerning Natural Religion*, Draper contends that the pain and pleasure we experience in

---

[1] For further reading with respect to early evidential arguments from evil see Rowe, "The Problem of Evil and Some Varieties of Atheism," 335–41.

[2] For further research into the origins of Draper's theory, see Nozick, "Knowledge and Skepticism," and the refutation of the evidential argument from evil most notably credited to Wykstra, "The Humean Obstacle to Evidential Arguments from Suffering: On Avoiding the Evils of 'Appearance'" 783–793.

[3] For further reading see: Howard-Snyder, "Seeing through CORNEA," 25–49.

Socio-Historical Examination of Religion and Ministry
Volume 5, Issue 1, Summer 2023 shermjournal.org
© Tori Helen Cotton
Permissions: editor@shermjournal.org
ISSN 2637-7519 (print), ISSN 2637-7500 (online)
https://doi.org/10.33929/sherm.2023.vol5.no1.08 (article)

GCRR GLOBAL
CENTER for
RELIGIOUS
RESEARCH
ACADEMIC INSTITUTE

our lifetimes has nothing to do with God or some other supernatural force acting as an agent of good nor evil. Furthermore, even if some God-like being did exist, it would be entirely indifferent to our suffering.[4] His argument is influential because it extends the scope of those earlier evidential arguments from evil.

In this paper, I argue that Draper's case for the superiority of the Hypothesis of Indifference over theism survives existing criticisms from William Alston and Peter van Inwagen. After summarizing these objections, I present two supporting arguments: first, that the Hypothesis of Indifference explains the biological roles of pain and pleasure better than theism, and second, that expecting morally sufficient reasons for suffering in a theistic framework is reasonable. Finally, I address potential counterarguments and incorporate responses from Draper, concluding with some additional considerations on the roles of pain and pleasure and on Draper's position.

Draper argues that his Hypothesis of Indifference better explains the roles of pain and pleasure as biological functions in humans compared to theism. Moreover, he posits that certain aspects of how we experience pain and pleasure provide compelling reasons to reject theism. Pain and pleasure serve various biological purposes. For instance, pleasure serves as a means of encouraging human reproduction, while pain acts as a deterrent to prevent us from damaging our bodies. Humans experience pathological pain or pleasure when their biological system fails to function correctly. Similarly, biologically appropriate pain and pleasure responses occur when they serve some sort of biological function. If pain and pleasure either serve some biological imperative or are the direct result of some dysfunction in pain or pleasure response, then that real-world experience aligns with the Hypothesis of Indifference but would not align with a viewpoint under which pain and pleasure serves some moral goal. This implies that the probability of the Hypothesis of Indifference being true is much higher than the probability of theism.[5]

Draper's text had two major contemporary critics: Peter van Inwagen, and William Alston. For this discussion, I will begin by examining the critiques put forth by Van Inwagen. Van Inwagen claims that if Draper's argument were successful, then the Hypothesis of Indifference would, in fact, be a better explanation for why we experience pain and pleasure than theism is. However, he introduces a critical challenge for Draper's account: every possible world

---

[4] Draper, "Pain and Pleasure: An Evidential Problem for Theists," 338–39.
[5] Ibid., 335.

that contains sentient life should include patterns of suffering morally equivalent to the patterns of suffering in our own world, or else the rules of that world are massively irregular. As such, we should expect to be able to predict similar patterns of pain and suffering in worlds created by an omnibenevolent, omniscient, and omnipotent God. Yet, Van Inwagen argues, our epistemic limitations prevent us from knowing whether such patterns would occur in another divinely-created world.

In other words, if these possible worlds do not abide by the morally aligned patterns existent in our world, then there is a substantial failure in its laws of nature. He contends that good in the world relies on thinking moral beings, and this good outweighs the observed patterns of evil and suffering. Van Inwagen then clarifies that, according to his argument, two patterns of suffering are morally equivalent only when there are no clear moral reasons to prefer one over the other. He then suggests that this gives us reasons to doubt, though not necessarily wholesale discount, Draper's hypothesis.[6]

Building on this, van Inwagen claims that our only rational conclusion within our epistemic reach is to suspend our judgements on the Hypothesis of Indifference, the existence of God, and our observations on it entirely. But if only rational response is to suspend judgment though, then there is no way for us to have epistemic access to knowledge of patterns of pain and suffering like those contained in our world or in a God-created one. Van Inwagen suggests that there may exist a true account of the world incorporating both God's existence and our observations of suffering, but we lack certainty. As such, our epistemic position prevents us from accurately anticipating patterns of pain and suffering in theistic or atheistic worlds.[7]

Draper has a response to this challenge with the following line of reasoning: If the theistic narrative posits that humans cannot have epistemic access to knowledge concerning which claim to accept, then the observations of patterns of pain and pleasure under the theistic framework, as opposed to the Hypothesis of Indifference, are based on an individuated outlook of what is considered to be probable.

Draper then uses Bayesian reasoning to counter van Inwagen's argument.[8] He asserts that theistic narratives do not significantly increase the

---

[6] van Inwagen, "The Problem of Evil," 140–2.

[7] Ibid., 143.

[8] Bayesian reasoning is a vital component in discussions of how hypotheses are confirmed, namely in the philosophy of science and epistemology. For more information about

probability of the theistic account.[9] Moreover, even if we disregard our observations of evil in the world and do not factor in the likelihood of the Hypothesis of Indifference, the Hypothesis of Indifference remains more probable than reconciling those observations of evil with any theistic account. For a theistic position to support the thesis that humans are not in the position to compare these antecedent probabilities, that theistic representation of the world would need to be able to judge any range of value to the representation given that theism were indeed true, ultimately good, and undefeated. Since there is no actual, existent theistic portrayal which accomplishes all three, the skepticism about the probability of Draper's hypothesis does not follow, and Van Inwagen's criticisms fail to undermine Draper's overall argument.

As a second point in support of Draper's argument, if we apply the theistic view of good and evil, we are left with a view of pain and pleasure which does not reflect the state of affairs in the world as we know it. Assuming that pain is inherently bad, and pleasure is inherently good, it would be reasonable to expect that we experience pain for some morally sufficient reason. Consequentially, bad actions would lead to God's punishment by suffering, while good actions would directly result in God rewarding us with pleasure. But this is simply not the case, and there are two significant reasons why. Dreadful things happen to good people all the time; and evil people go unpunished. As an extension of that, non-moral agents such as infants or animals suffer needlessly in the world. Beyond that, even though pain teaches us lessons such as "don't touch the hot kettle on the stove," there is no reason that would extend to the argument that "pain teaches us some moral lesson" or, "we need pain in order to be motivated towards moral actions." (In fact, some ethicists might argue that if you are only motivated to do good things to avoid pain or punishment, that these actions may not really be considered 'good' at all). This points back to Draper's first assertion, that pain and pleasure serve biological functions rather than God-given moral functions.

A potential counterclaim comes from Alston. He begins his reply by citing the fact that the typical evidential argument for evil, Draper's argument included, proceeds in the following manner: if the assertion that the traditional understanding of God would have morally sufficient reasons to allow suffering

---

Bayesian epistemology and confirmation theory, see: Bayes, "An Essay Towards Solving a Problem in the Doctrine of Chances," 337–418.

[9] For some background on conditional epistemic probability and the burden of proof within the context of the problem of evil, consider: Plantinga, "Warrant and Proper Function."

is unlikely, then God's existence would be similarly improbable. Alston attempts to refute this reasoning by stating that if we are not in an epistemic position to make judgements on the likelihood of God's reasons for suffering, then the atheistic claim that God has no morally sufficient reason for suffering must be implausible. If that claim is in fact unfounded, then the atheistic claim that God's existence itself is improbable must also be unfounded. It then follows that if the atheistic claim regarding God's existence being unlikely is unfounded, then all evidential arguments from evil must fail.[10]

Alston's argument takes a different approach. He argues that all epistemic arguments from evil fail due to human limitations in judging the likelihood of an omnipotent and omniscient being's moral reasons for allowing suffering. However, Draper points out that many evidential arguments do not argue for the improbability of God's existence based of God's improbability for having morally sufficient reason for allowing suffering. [11]

Alston gives no reason for assuming the truth of this claim. So, even if we were genuinely unable to make judgments on the likelihood of God's morally sufficient reasons for suffering, some evidential arguments— particularly those not disputing the possibility of God having such reasons— could theoretically be successful. Consequently, Alston's interpretation of Draper's Hypothesis not only mischaracterizes Draper's claim but also falls short in undermining the potential likelihood of the Hypothesis of Indifference over theism.[12]

In order to keep the scope of this paper narrow, I have attempted to focus on Draper's main argument and his direct respondents. However, there is one consideration that, while I have not included it in a substantive manner within this short paper, seems prudent to mention as further support for Draper's argument. That consideration is the possibility that an all-powerful and all-good God could design our biology in such a way that we do not actually need pain or pleasure to orient our goals in the first place. To counter this, a theist might take up a similar position to that of philosopher John Hick and claim that suffering is an inherent part of the process of soul-making, or character-building.[13] Hick's claim is essentially that pain and suffering serves the purpose

---

[10] Alston, "The Inductive Argument from Evil," 60–1.

[11] Ibid., 29–30.

[12] Draper, "The Skeptical Theist," 164.

[13] John Hick's claim regarding pain and suffering is that it serves the purpose of soul-building, and he seems to analogize the relationship between God and mankind to the relationship between a parent and their child. Under his position, we are just as ignorant of God's reasoning

of soul-building, and he analogizes the relationship between God and humankind to the relationship between a parent and child.[14] Under his position, we are just as ignorant of God's reasoning for allowing suffering in the world, as a child is ignorant for their parent's reasons for allowing perceived suffering.[15] Yet this proposition seems objectionable at best.

Even if we were to suspend our disbelief and claim that God purposely designed our biology in such a way that we lack epistemic access to any understanding of his reasons for good and evil, we would have to further posit that our lack of understanding really does serve a divine purpose which leads us to some higher path. In doing this we would still be actively undermining the scale of suffering in the world, and how many people suffer only to die, leaving no possibility for further spiritual growth in life (as in examples of mass genocide); we would need to wholly discount the prevalence of people who go through terrible experiences, and who end up completely spiritually unchanged or even convert to atheism *because of* that terrible experience.

If the aftermath of atrocity and suffering leaves individuals unchanged, or if it results in their immediate demise, precluding any opportunity for spiritual growth or transformation, the potential response to Draper, drawing from Hick, appears inadequate. This shortcoming lies in both the overcomplication of the purpose of suffering and a deliberate neglect of its harsh realities. Draper's argument appears quite modest by comparison. Thus, my personal endorsement of Draper's perspective on this third point stems from its apparent satisfaction of Occam's razor. The simplest explanation is de facto more likely. When compared to its opposing theodicies, The Hypothesis of Indifference offers a simpler explanation for why we experience pain or pleasure. With this further consideration in mind, combined with the successful defense of Draper's position from his critics, it seems clear to me that Draper's case for the superiority of the Hypothesis of Indifference over theism succeeds.

---

for allowing suffering in the world, as a child is ignorant of their parent's reasons for allowing perceived suffering. This can be found in: Hick, "Soul Making and Suffering," 255–261.

[14] Stephen Wykstra makes an adjacent comparison in his theory on conditions of reasonable epistemic access, in Stephen, "The Humean Obstacle to Evidential Arguments from Suffering," 783–93.

[15] Hick, "Soul Making and Suffering," 255–61.

BIBLIOGRAPHY

Alston, William P. "The Inductive Argument from Evil and the Human Cognitive Condition." *Philosophical Perspectives*. Vol. 5 (1991): 29–67.

Bayes, Thomas. "An Essay Towards Solving a Problem in the Doctrine of Chances." *Philosophical Transactions of the Royal Society of London*. Vol. 53 (1763): 370–418. https://doi.org/10.1098/rstl.1763.0053.

Draper, Paul. "Pain and Pleasure: An Evidential Problem for Theists." *Noûs*. Vol. 23, no. 3 (1989): 331–50.

———. "The Skeptical Theist." In *The Evidential Argument from Evil*. Edited by Daniel Howard-Snyder, 175–92. Bloomington, IN: Indiana University Press, 1996.

Hick, John. "Soul Making and Suffering." In *Evil and the God of Love*, 255–61. Tallahassee, FL: Harper and Rowe Publishers, 1996.

Howard-Snyder, Daniel. "Seeing through CORNEA." *International Journal for Philosophy of Religion*. Vol. 32, no. 1 (1992): 25–49.

Hume, David. *Dialogues Concerning Natural Religion*. 1776.

Nozick, Robert. "Knowledge and Skepticism." *Philosophical Explanations*. Cambridge, MA: Harvard University Press, 1981.

Plantinga, Alvin. *Warrant and Proper Function*. Oxford: Oxford University Press, 1993.

Rowe, William. "The Problem of Evil and Some Varieties of Atheism." *American Philosophical Quarterly*. Vol. 6, no. 4 (1979): 335–41.

van Inwagen, Peter. "The Problem of Evil, the Problem of Air, and the Problem of Silence." *Philosophical Perspectives*. Vol. 5 (1991): 135–65.

Wykstra, Stephen. "The Humean Obstacle to Evidential Arguments from Suffering: On Avoiding the Evils of 'Appearance.'" *International Journal for Philosophy of Religion*. Vol. 16, no. 2 (1984): 783–793.

ABOUT THE AUTHOR

Tori Helen Cotton is a Eugene Cota-Robles fellow in the Department of Logic and Philosophy of Science at the University of California, Irvine. She holds a bachelor's degree in Fine Arts from the University of Texas and a Master's in Philosophy from the University of Arkansas, where she served as the Instructor of Record for courses in introductory philosophy, ethics, and logic. Tori's research interests span a broad range, including topics in the philosophy of science, epistemology of belief, and social dynamics.

Book Review:
When Religion Hurts You
By Laura E. Anderson

Marsha Vaughn,
Adler University

Abstract: *Licensed psychotherapist, podcast host, and religious trauma survivor, Dr. Laura Anderson, has contributed a volume drawing from both her own experiences and trauma studies scholarship. Anderson avoids harsh and direct condemnation of high-control religions (HCRs) but, rather, describes the human experiences and biological explanations of lives immersed in fear, shame, and mistrust. Her book,* When Religion Hurts You, *will likely connect most with religious trauma survivors who have already left an HCR (or are on the way out) and with professionals unfamiliar with the specific biological and relational theories of trauma. Anderson provides cautious optimism, noting the time and effort needed to "live in healing bodies."*

Keywords: High Control Religion, Religious Trauma, Trauma, Purity Culture

Trauma Theories, Embodied

The collection of deconstruction literature is growing rapidly, including both first-person narratives from those who have been deeply hurt by religious institutions and theological or social-scientific explanations about why either (1) institutionalized religion has failed, or (2) former believers have deconstructed or deidentified from religion. A third type, written primarily by mental health professionals, focuses on understanding the unique experience of religious trauma and bridges the divide between individual experiences and theoretical explanations. Dr. Laura Anderson's book, *When Religion Hurts You*, falls into this third group.

Anderson, a licensed psychotherapist and podcast host, interweaves her own story of growing up in and leaving a high-control religious group (HCR) while sharing current biological and relational models of trauma. To her credit, she includes the pioneers and current "heavy hitters" in the fields of trauma studies and trauma-informed therapy, including Judith Herman, Bessel van der Kolk, Deb Dana, Bruce Perry, and Peter Levine. By centering on the effects of adverse religious experiences, rather than a pointed argument to leave religion,

Socio-Historical Examination of Religion and Ministry
Volume 5, Issue 1, Summer 2023 shermjournal.org
© Marsha Vaughn
Permissions: editor@shermjournal.org
ISSN 2637-7519 (print), ISSN 2637-7500 (online)
https://doi.org/10.33929/sherm.2023.vol5.no1.09 (article)

GLOBAL
CENTER *for*
RELIGIOUS
RESEARCH
ACADEMIC INSTITUTE
GCRR

Anderson allows readers to reflect on and develop trust in their own trauma responses. She makes no argument for or against leaving religion altogether but only outlines the impact of religious trauma, which is consistent with the ethical codes of the major mental health professions. For example, Anderson logically connects an HCR's use of fear as a motivator with the somatic responses to threats (an activated sympathetic nervous system). Readers are then left with considering the consequences of staying in that fear-saturated environment, which contributes to all sorts of physical and mental symptoms. This is also the approach psychotherapists frequently use with adults experiencing intimate partner violence. Direct appeals to leave as fast as one can rarely work.

Anderson provides accessible explanations from multiple theories related to attachment and nervous system responses, appropriate for survivors and others who do not have clinical mental health training. The last pages of the book contain a solid list of trauma-related resources organized by topic/chapter. Most of these resources are not from peer-reviewed academic journals but, rather, are written for a general audience or professional therapists. While that could be construed as a weakness, it does maintain the accessibility the author seems to desire.

She makes a valid argument early on that (1) religious trauma *is* trauma, and (2) the human brain's response to any kind of trauma is remarkably similar, regardless of the particular triggering event. Therefore, at least in theory, this book can connect with anyone who has a history of religious trauma irrespective of the faith group. Yet I wonder if there is something particular about white evangelical Christianity of the last decade that makes it unlike other religious groups: Is there a parallel term for "ex-vangelical"?

This prompts the question: Who exactly is this book *for*? Because of the generous use of her own story (indeed, every chapter except one begins with a first-person narrative), those who will most closely connect with and benefit from this book are people like the author: white women leaving conservative Christian spaces. (In full disclosure of my positionality and bias, this does include me.) Anderson makes occasional references to the harm HCRs have perpetrated on the LGBTQ+ and BIPOC communities, as well as suggests additional support beyond the scope of her book. But some may consider her discussion on religious trauma in this particular book to be somewhat limited only to those of her background and experience.

For example, the healing themes Anderson outlines are familiar: accepting the goodness of one's sexuality in light of the toxic teachings of purity culture; giving permission to feel the full spectrum of emotions, including anger; and showing self-compassion throughout a life-long journey of healing one's body and mind. These themes dominate discussions of religious trauma among white, heterosexual women, specifically dismantling virginity, submission, and meekness as core identity values. So, the majority of the illustrations seem to be from that demographic. There are a few stories from men, as well as members of the LGBTQ+ community. I appreciate the dilemma in sharing stories from others, even composite stories from clients, while maintaining professional confidentiality, but I wonder if a wider variety of stories would connect with a broader audience. The amount of time spent emphasizing the *embodied* experiences of trauma, the impact of trauma on one's physical and mental functioning, invites more overt recognition of the wide range of bodies that actually exist on our planet.

While reading this book, I had hoped that Anderson would address the rejection of psychotherapy among HCRs more overtly. Often, HCRs teach that all problems are ultimately spiritual problems, so any physical or emotional symptoms should be addressed in only spiritual ways. Indeed, seeking therapy, receiving a diagnosis, or taking psychotropic medication frequently invokes shame even after one has left an HCR. So, while she discusses trauma, post-traumatic stress, PTSD, and a few other diagnoses, she assumes the reader is familiar enough with (1) what diagnoses of trauma-related mental illness are and (2) the process of receiving them, including finding a competent and compassionate therapist. Maybe this is beyond the purpose of her book, which Anderson does not state until the conclusion. In the author's words, the book is to "point out healing themes and help you learn what it looks like to move from the version of yourself that was altered because of an HCR to a whole and healing version of yourself." It is not a self-help book nor a memoir, but it has shades of both. It would have helped either to align more clearly with one of those genres or to state the purpose and tone of the book in the introduction.

In conclusion, it would be unfair to ask a single book on recovering from religious trauma to be all things to all people. Other authors (for academic and general audiences) have provided evidence for the lasting damage of evangelical purity culture[1] and the similarities between HCRs and intimate partner violence.[2] Those three sources provide a different lens besides trauma theory and also capture the relational dynamics of HCRs more succinctly. Trauma theories, in general, are more individual/biologically based. As such, Anderson shines at providing clear explanations of trauma responses without oversimplifying them. However, some readers unfamiliar with trauma theories

---

[1] Gregoire, Lindenbach, and Sawatsky, *She Deserves Better.*
[2] Keller, "Development of a Spiritual Abuse Questionnaire"; Norton, "Narrative Inquiry."

may need to revisit some chapters multiple times. Readers who do not resonate with the specifics of Anderson's stories may benefit from also reading or listening to stories from survivors who are more similar to them. Professionals new to trauma studies, and religious trauma in particular, will also benefit from reading this book and recommending it as they see fit.

BIBLIOGRAPHY

Gregoire, Sheila Wray, Rebecca Gregoire Lindenbach, and Joanna Sawatsky. *She Deserves Better: Raising Girls to Resist Toxic Teachings on Sex, Self, and Speaking Up*. Baker Books, 2023.

Keller, Kathryn H. "Development of a Spiritual Abuse Questionnaire." Doctoral diss., Texas Woman's University, 2016.

Norton, Naomi R. "Narrative Inquiry: White Fundamental Evangelical Construction of a Mental Illness Paradigm." Doctoral diss., Northcentral University, 2022.

ABOUT THE AUTHOR

Dr. Marsha Vaughn, LMFT, is Professor and Core Faculty at Adler University (Chicago, IL). She is an AAMFT-Approved Supervisor and teaches in both master's and PhD programs in Couple and Family Therapy. She has presented both empirical and theoretical work on spiritual abuse and religious trauma at regional and national conferences. She also is part of a group private practice in the Chicago suburbs.

www.ingramcontent.com/pod-product-compliance
Lightning Source LLC
Chambersburg PA
CBHW060228030426
42335CB00014B/1373